Feminine Agency and Transgression
in Post-Franco Spain

Juan de la Cuesta
Hispanic Monographs

FOUNDING EDITOR
Tom Lathrop
University of Delaware

EDITOR
Alexander R. Selimov
University of Delaware

EDITORIAL BOARD
Samuel G. Armistead
University of California, Davis

Annette G. Cash
Georgia State University

Alan Deyermond
Queen Mary, University of London

Daniel Eisenberg
Cervantes Society of America

John E. Keller
University of Kentucky

Steven D. Kirby
Eastern Michigan University

Joel Rini
University of Virginia

Donna M. Rogers
Middlebury College

Russell P. Sebold
*University of Pennsylvania, Emeritus
Corresponding Member, Real Academia Española*

Noël Valis
Yale University

Amy Williamsen
University of Arizona

Feminine Agency and Transgression in Post-Franco Spain:

Generational Becoming in the Narratives of Carme Riera, Cristina Fernández Cubas and Mercedes Abad

by

MARIA DIFRANCESCO

Ithaca College

Juan de la Cuesta
Newark, Delaware

Copyright © 2008 by Juan de la Cuesta-Hispanic Monographs
An imprint of LinguaText, Ltd.
270 Indian Road
Newark, Delaware 19711-5204 USA

(302) 453-8695
Fax: (302) 453-8601

www.JuandelaCuesta.com

MANUFACTURED IN THE UNITED STATES OF AMERICA

ISBN:978-1-58871-130-4

Table of Contents

1. Introduction 7

2. Carme Riera's Fiction:
   Traces of Sapphic Love and the Case of
   the (Missing?) Erotic Mother 17

3. Cristina Fernández Cubas:
   Girls, Women, and the Games they Play 73

4. Erotica or Monstrous Subtexts in
   Mercedes Abad's *Ligeros libertinajes
   sabáticos* and *Sangre* 161

   Conclusion 205

   Bibliography 211

I

Introduction:
Feminine Agency and Transgression in Post-Franco Spain:
Generational Becoming in the Narratives of Carme Riera, Cristina Fernández Cubas and Mercedes Abad

CARME RIERA (PALMA DE Mallorca, 1948), Cristina Fernández Cubas (Arenys de Mar, 1945) and Mercedes Abad (Barcelona, 1961) have gained unparalleled acclaim as writers who have raised vital questions regarding feminine cultural agency and transgression in Spain following the dictatorship of Generalíssimo Francisco Franco (1892-1975). Riera, Fernández Cubas and Abad first won the attention of the general public as short story writers. Riera published her first two collections of short fiction, *Te dejo, amor, en prenda el mar* and *Y pongo por testigo a las gaviotas* in 1975 and 1976, respectively.[1] Fernández Cubas followed suit shortly thereafter, publishing *Mi hermana Elba* in 1980 and *Los altillos de Brumal* in 1983. Abad, the youngest of the three, began her career in 1986 by winning the *Sonrisa Vertical*, Spain's national literary prize for erotic literature, with *Ligeros libertinajes sabáticos*. Each has maintained her stature in the literary world through

---

1 These works were originally published as *Te deix, amor, la mar com a penyora* (Barcelona: Editorial Laia, 1975) and *Jo pos per testimoni les gavines* (Barcelona: Editorial Laia, 1977).

the cultivation of other genres, particularly novels and plays.[2]

Nonetheless, little scholarship examining a common underlying theme among their narratives—feminine agency and transgression as expressed in generational terms—has been published. This study attempts to fill this gap by exploring the ways in which female protagonists portrayed in works by Riera, Fernández Cubas and Abad do not simply invert patriarchal paradigms of power but rather interrogate and destabilize isomorphic gendered categories that women have traditionally occupied. I dedicate one chapter to each author, specifically analyzing the ways in which each re-writes the categories of "mother," "daughter" and "sister" through her narratives.

The title I have chosen to frame this study, *Feminine Agency and Transgression in Post-Franco Spain: Generational Becoming in Carme Riera, Cristina Fernández Cubas and Mercedes Abad,* calls to mind popular Western beliefs that portray women as either passive sexual objects manipulated by male authorities; or as *femme fatales* and *agent provocateurs*, women who stererotypically incite harm by using their aberrant sexuality to ensnare hapless men.

But is transgressive activity gendered, and what—if any—relationship exists between gender and agency? Theoretically speaking, transgression itself is not gendered. However, in as much as Western norms have defined males as active participants and females as passive undergoers of taboo, sexual activity, theories of transgression have mimicked and perpetuated like models of male and female behavior. Historically speaking, this pattern of expectations regarding male and female sexual behavior traditionally represented males as independent agents,

---

2 Riera is the author of the novels *Una primavera para Domenico Guarini* (1981), *Cuestión de amor propio* (1987), *En el último azul* (1995), *Por el cielo y más allá* (2001) and *La mitad del alma* (2003). Fernández Cubas is the author of the novels *El columpio* (1995) and *El año de gracia* (1987) as well as the play *Hermanas de sangre* (1998). Abad, for her part, has authored the novel *Sangre* and has several screenplays to her name.

both of self-defined interests and of the social hierarchy as a whole. For their part, women typically served as submissive counterparts to male agents; they patiently waited to gain permission to act within patriarchal social systems and were called to surrender to "maternal natures," instinctively caring for children and extended family members. According to this model, women were ultimately defined as powerless to operate as individuals and branded as self-interested if they acted autonomously. Whereas males appeared to embody agency, implicitly combining sexual potency with self-assuredness in economic, political and social realms, for women, agency was rendered null or dispersed. For instance, female agency might be relatively acceptable if it were allied with maternal functions, such as child-rearing. But one could not accept female agency if doing so meant permitting the female subject to openly express sexual desire. A unique exception to this paradigm in Iberian culture might be found in Renaissance mystics such as Santa Teresa de Jesús, who transcended the secular world while satisfying the requirements of womanliness by being an agent of the Divine.

During the early years of the Franco regime, Spaniards were intensely indoctrinated in accordance with these familiar Western models of gendered agency. According to the nationalist tenets of francoism, a Spanish woman's place was in the home, and that home should be filled with children.[3] A good wife unquestioningly took care of her husband and children, making sure that their needs were seen to before she saw to her own. What's more, while a wife might appear to have some control of the home since she cared for it as well as its inhabitants, legally she had no right to property, nor could she make any decision with regards to the distribution of property within the marriage. If this were not enough to make most women cringe,

---

3 Helen Graham's article, "Gender in the State: Women in the 1940s" is particularly illuminating. The article can be found in *Spanish Cultural Studies: An Introduction*, eds. Helen Graham and Jo Labanyi (Oxford: Oxford University Press, 1995), 182-195.

a wife could not travel, open a bank account or obtain employment outside the home without first gaining her husbands permission. Due to a close relationship between church and state, divorce, a common way out for women searching for independence, was likewise prohibited under Franco. Even legal separation did not guarantee autonomy since, in a legal battle, a wife could lose the only home she had known since leaving her parents.

Male agency and power was also taken as a given within the *Sección Femenina*, the women's division of the National Movement. Founded in 1934 by Pilar Primo de Rivera, the sister of José Antonio Primo de Rivera, the *Sección Femenina* not only sought to endorse the political platforms of the *falangist* organization, but further sought to instill these beliefs in girls by instructing them with regards to proper female behavior. Above all, a good member of the *Sección Femenina* would have children, love God and believe in the *Falange's* way of life. According to this point of view, a woman's primary aim in life should be to become a mother and a housewife. If she were to assume any agency at all, that agency would be totally and utterly contained within the tenets of the party. She should aim to do no more than take a husband, have his children, and support their adherence to the rules of the *Falange* and the Church.

Despite its conservative values, the *Sección Femenina* ultimately inspired groundbreaking changes in legislation that significantly improved the legal position of women in Spain. Nonetheless, the legal changes adopted did not suggest any real transformation in the way women were viewed as Spanish citizens. Rather, legislative changes reflected the inability of the social hierarchy to remain stable without the practical support of women acting outside the home. For example, although *Los Derechos Políticos, Profesionales y de Trabajo de la Mujer* (1961), gave women the right to seek employment outside the home, it still required women to gain her husband's approval to do so. The inception of such laws signaled a bittersweet change for women who previously had been wholly prohibited from pursuing such economic and social opportunities.

In the 1970s, continued economic growth and loosening enforcement of state mandated censorship came to align female agency with sexual and reproductive matters. The *desmadre sexual* is probably best described as a rebellious response to limits imposed by both church and state forces during the Franco dictatorship. The political and social changes that have occurred since the 1970s have aroused a general explosion in the proliferation of sexually charged media in Spain for both men and women. After the elimination of government-mandated censorship in 1977, topics that had been deemed taboo within print and visual media became explicitly permitted. If the censorship of the Franco years served a largely political purpose, having stifled press, radio, television, and film to promote and inspire belief in the politics of the dictatorship, the general liberation of discourse that came with the *desmadre sexual* served a more socio-cultural objective. Namely, it permitted individuals to express themselves in ways that had not been possible previously.

For male authors, this liberation initially manifested itself as an "accelerated continuity rather than as sudden emergence, not least because Francoism had always half-tolerated those sexual differences it could safely label or caricature (transvestism, harmless effeminacy in men, comic manliness of women)."[4] More recently, small, alternative presses specializing in the publication of print media related to homosexuality and military service, HIV, and AIDS have promoted an exchange of controversial ideas which, in turn, demonstrate the existence of a progressive environment allowing open discussion of sex and gender as they are related to politics.

For female writers, the liberation of discourse has meant increased

---

4 Chris Perriam, "Gay and Lesbian Culture," eds. Helen Graham and Jo Labanyi (*Spanish Cultural Studies: An Introduction: The Struggle for Modernity*. Oxford UP, 1995, 393-95), 393.

access to forward-looking media outlets that facilitated and supported their writing about themselves and their experiences as women. In the magazine industry, this has fostered growth in the popularity of magazines chronicling women's liberation and, most notably, has created space for the discussion of lesbian specific issues, such as same-sex marriage and adoption.[5] Magazines such as *Nosotras*, a publication of the Madrid Colectivo de Feministas Lesbianas, have been particularly concerned with the re-presentation of lesbians in Western, and particularly Spanish, culture. By giving voice to this historically silenced population, *Nosotras's* publishers not only hope to de-construct myths about lesbians and their lifestyles, but also to expose interested readers to theoretical writings by and about women's issues. Likewise, the government sponsored *Sol* "offers space—from a center-left and middle-class position—to non-lesbian but anti-heterosexist discourses from throughout Spain."[6]

Yet women have likely found the greatest degree of freedom with regards to sexual expression in fiction. Making their mark in a wide range of literary genres, from the fantastic (Ana María Matute, Carmen Martin Gaite, Cristina Fernández Cubas) and the historical novel (Lourdes Oritiz's *Urraca*) at one extreme, to the erotic (Esther Tusquets, Carme Riera, Ana Rossetti) and pornographic (Mercedes Abad and Almudena Grandes) at the other extreme. The proliferation of women writing in so-called "non-feminine" genres further supports the notion that the elimination of politically motivated censorship and economic globalization has led Spanish female authors to write in styles previously considered forbidden.

Nonetheless, what is most provocative with regards to Riera, Fernández Cubas and Mercedes Abad as a group having emerged from

---

5 The Spanish government finally legalized gay and lesbian marriage in 2005. Under the terms of the law, gay and lesbian adoption of children is also permitted.

6 Perriam, "Gay and Lesbian Culture," 393-94.

the post-dictatorship is that these women's narratives not only speak to women's increased agency within the male/female binary of sexual relationships, but to women's multiple experiences of gendered categories with each other. As women informed by and writing within this cultural framework, a time when popular socio-political discourse has been officially liberated and the influence of increasing globalization and technologies have successfully penetrated Spanish culture, these authors explore how women of different ages and generations relate to each other in contemporary Spain.

Freed of the strictures of the state-mandated censorship that had stifled creative writers for decades, I propose that Riera, Fernández Cubas and Abad each represent successive generations of women who have challenged the very fiber of Spanish culture by relentlessly depicting controversial female agents in their narratives: from Sapphic lovers to monstrous mothers. Each of these generations offers unique insight into portrayals of feminine agency by looking at the cultural construction of motherhood and the mother-daughter bond and examining ways in which women control how their images are marketed in the mainstream media and in the underworld of the erotic. Through my examinations fo their works, I propose that Riera, Fernández Cubas and Abad have gone beyond their initial revolutionary status as literary outsiders to exhibit staying power, achieving not only the popular approval of a general reading public, but also canonical standing within their own lifetimes. The very canonization of these writers' works suggests that mainstream presses have favorably reacted to once "transgressive" agency among women by encompassing such activity and accommodating new limits.

In my chaper on Riera, "Carme Riera's Fiction: Traces of Sapphic Love and the Case of the (Missing?) Erotic Mother," I rely on psychoanalytic notions regarding the male "gaze" as posited by Ann Kaplan and Laura Mulvey to argue that Riera's fiction extensively points to a history of missing figures in literature: the figure of the woman as mother-agent. In as much as this statement is true, Riera's narratives serve both to disrupt the popular male-female rhetoric of complementarity and to assert the need to re-invent the mother's body in erotic ways within narrative discourse. A trajectory of presence and absence related to the eroticization of the maternal figure finds its culmination in the novel *Una primavera para Domenico Guarini* (1980) and the diary *Tiempo de espera* (1998). I assert that Riera's writings offer a re-conceptualization of women in Spanish culture wherein female protagonists come to displace strong paternal figures. In turn, traditional families, which had been dependent upon central male figures as sources of power and authority, submit to a radical reconstruction wherein maternal figures, and the pregnant body itself, come to exceed paternal right. Riera's re-writing of the maternal figure does not simply challenge the customs of a largely heterosexual, patriarchal Spanish culture, but completely undoes these, recasting maternal agency as a locus of ideological resistance and social transformation.

Cast in the light of Riera's eroticization and restoration of the maternal body as a site of cultural transformation, the chapter entitled, "Cristina Fernández Cubas: Girls, Women, and the Games They Play," engages theoretical readings as diverse as Johan Huizinga's *Homo Ludens* (1938) and Georges Bataille's *Literature of Evil* (1957) to Susan Rubin Suleiman's *Subversive Intent* (1990) and Astrid Henry's *Not My Mother's Sister* to argue that the author's narratives question and critique a ubiquitous phenomenon: women writers of all ages, self-described feminists and non- feminists alike, describing relationships between women in familial terms. Fernández Cubas uses family metaphors to discuss the state of feminine agency in contemporary Spain. Conflicting dialogues between women in her works posit feminine experience as not only multiple in form, but also as generational and familial, as passed on from mother to daughter, and experienced between sisters. Female family members in key stories from *Mi hermana Elba* and *Los altillos de Brumal* as well as the novel *El columpio* and the hybrid narrative-drama *Hermanas de sangre* use childhood play, games, fantasy, and sleuthful detective work to both destabilize socio-culturally informed conceptions of male agency and female passivity and to underscore the conflict that occurs between generations of women, all wishing to validate their experiences as women. For Fernández Cubas, play between family members ultimately denotes not only an acknowledgement of experiences shared between women, but also a violent dis-identification with these experiences that allows her protagonists to bring themselves into being by performing personal forms of feminism.

For Abad, feminine agency is defined through an exploration of sexuality and, specifically, the grotesque, monstrous body understood as a site of socio-sexual transformation. Her narratives, and all the erotic, pornographic images associated with them, show a preoccupation with the degradation of the human body. If the female body has been often viewed as an aesthetic object, gazed upon and admired for its beauty, Abad's narratives often depict the female body through what Bakhtin calls "grotesque realism." This is not to say that female agency remains stuck in abject negativity. Rather, for Bakhtin, degradation of the body is as much aligned with lower biological activities (defecation, copulation, and pregnancy for example) as it is with re-generation. Yet degrading the body does not involve simply casting it into an empty abyss, a complete obliteration; rather, degrading the body involves casting it down to a fertile lower stratum, the locus of conception where birth takes place. Indeed, if as Bakhtin suggests, the grotesque body "is always conceiving," the female agents that Abad depicts are consummate examples of this production and re-production. In my chaper, "Erotica, or Monstrous Subtexts in Mercedes Abad's *Ligeros libertinajes sabáticos* and *Sangre*," I propose that "generational" agency not only has to do with the relationships women have with other women within the dynamics of the family, but has to do with the way in which women disrupt mythologized constructions of femininity in order to remove themselves from socially constraining scripts.

Finally, in the concluding chapter, I ostensibly argue that Riera, Fernández Cubas and Abad have written a formidable body of literature that foregrounds female becoming as constantly negotiated. I conclude that, for each writer, feminine agency seems to have little to do with the successes or failures of feminist political agendas or movements and much more to do with an acknowledgment that categories which have defined women—"mother," "daughter," and "sister"—simply mark becomings that point to multi-dimensional forms of gender categorization. Riera, Fernández Cubas and Abad thus maintain their popular status because they resist making categorical political statements about what is liberatory and what is oppressive while uniquely shedding light on the ways women write their own stories, create their own mythos, and with it, their own locus of power.

2

Carme Riera's Fiction: Traces of Sapphic Love and the Case of the (Missing?) Erotic Mother

According to Carme Riera, born to a Mallorcan father and Catalonian mother in Palma de Mallorca in 1948, literature is inherently transgressive in that it owes its very existence to the innate human desire to defy and transcend physical limitations. Like Bataille's idealized agent of transgression who challenges the laws of mortality and nature by attempting to become a "discontinuous subject," one who takes part in prohibited activity in an attempt at opposing death, Riera proposes becoming such a subject through the written word:

> Para mí, que soy agnóstica, la conciencia de la derrota que conduce a la claudicación final—al fin y al cabo la vida es una batalla perdida de antemano—ha llegado a ser tan alucinante, a partir de los cuarenta, que sólo por higiene mental hago el esfuerzo de minimizarla. La literatura ayuda a eso pues es uno de los fármacos más eficaces que conozco para transgredir las leyes que nos conducen a la caducidad porque convierte en duraderas las palabras destinadas a ser solo efímeras y nos permite, como a Scherezade, hacernos la ilusión de que continuamos aplazando la muerte.[1]

---

[1] Riera in "Una ambición sin límites," in *Moveable Margins: The Narrative Art of Carme Riera*, eds. Kathleen M. Glenn, Mirella Servodidio, and Mary S. Vásquez

For Riera, spoken language is not enough. The act of picking up a pen to write, filling a blank page, demonstrates the undeniable desire to communicate with others and, perhaps more significant, to leave behind a message to those who will be born and live long after she passes. Literature, thus becomes closely aligned to transgression in that it is a consummate remainder, a tangible escape by which the writer avoids death, leaving her words as a testament to other times and ideas.

Given that Bataille views writing as an act capable of freeing the writer from death—a so-called discontinuity of subjectivity—Bataille also seems to imply a fundamental symbiotic relationship between the writer and the reader. Namely, the literature that remains as a testament of the writer's existence must serve to seduce its consumer, the reader, or else run the risk of not being read. Riera echoes this belief, "I believe that a writer's first mission is to seduce, because the world is full of books, and if you don't seduce the reader in the first few lines, your book will surely not be read and, in that case, why publish it? Therefore, seduction is an absolute necessity."[2] This is not to say that Riera condones writing simply to quell the desires of an audience, to seduce without considering the repercussions of seduction. As such, for Riera, literature is just as intimately related to a certain degree of social responsibility as it is to the immortality of the author. She recognizes a simple truth: that to write is to take sure action, to become an instrument of change.

While one can only imagine what kinds of transformation might occur as a result of literary seduction, Riera's works point to a clear reproduction and repositioning of women as story tellers. Riera maintains that her childhood writings, like her early short stories and the literature she continues to produce, reflect the lives of women who

---

(Lewisburg: Bucknell UP, 1999. 21-29), 28.

2 Riera in "Conversation with Carme Riera" in *Moveable Margins: The Narrative Art of Carme Riera*, eds. Kathleen M. Glenn, Mirella Servodidio, and Mary S. Vásquez. (Lewisburg: Bucknell UP, 1999. 39-57), 40.

narrate because to do so is not only to defy mortality but to take up a unique subject position within culture:

> [los cuentos] no pretendieron ser otra cosa que un homenaje a una serie de mujeres que conocí, para dejar constancia de unas vidas que, como las de la inmensa mayoría de personas, son insignificantes y a las que sólo la literatura puede ofrecer una cierta tracendencia. Ellas, como otros personajes de mis cuentos, tomaban entidad mediante el recurso de la primera persona, eso es mediante la propia palabra.³

Thus her tales not only serve to reproduce these women storytellers, but to reposition them in textual and cultural history. She imparts authority to those women who might have been otherwise thought of as "insignificant" by preserving their memories in writing and granting them agency within that writing. As characters in her fiction, these women speak through Riera in the first person narrative subject "I." No longer voiceless objects of discourse, these women become its subjects. For Riera, the discursive switch from object to subject position becomes indicative of a general re-conceptualization of women in culture. Specifically, in this chapter, I suggest that Riera ultimately restores agency to the maternal.

❧

Riera's "Te dejo, amor, en prenda el mar" begins with the epigraph:

("Escogeré para siempre jamás tu ausencia, doncella, porque lo que de verdad amo no es tu cuerpo, ni el recuerdo de tu cuerpo tan

---

3 Riera, "Una ambición sin límites," 27.

bello bajo la luna; lo que de verdad amo es la huella que has dejado sobre la arena").[4]

The line that follows this epigraph reads, "fragmento, jamás escrito, de Safo." The epigraph coupled with its denied attribution to Sappho should capture the reader's attention. Why allude to a set of fragmented verses? Why refer to Sappho if she never wrote them? Yet in my first reading of "Te dejo, amor, en prenda el mar" I did not apprehend the significance of this (pre)text. I ignored that what must always catch the reader's attention is precisely that which is not readily displayed. In the words of Joan Copjec, I did not pause to ask, "[W]hat in the graphic space does not show, does not stop not writing itself?"[5] For it is that which appears lacking or invisible to which the reader must most resolutely attend.

In the case of Riera's story, the fragmented verses and Sappho's negated textual (author)ity indicate sexual transgression. Specifically, the epigraph hints at the existence of a lesbian relationship that is not immediately evident to the reader. Sappho's negated textual authority, referred to at the beginning of the text, not only suggests a repression of lesbian identity in Spanish fiction and erotica as a whole, but more emphatically suggests a repression of feminine, and especially maternal, agency in Western culture. An examination of the short stories "Te dejo, amor, en prenda el mar" and "Y pongo por testigo a las gaviotas" furthers my argument as they extensively point to a history of missing figures in literature: the figure of the woman as mother-agent. In as much as this statement is true, Riera's narratives serve both to disrupt the popular male-female rhetoric of complementarity and to assert the need to re-invent the mother's body in erotic ways within narrative

---

4 Carme Riera, "Te dejo, amor, en prenda el mar" in *Te dejo el mar* (Trans. Luis Cotoner, Madrid: Espasa Calpe, 1991. 52-68), 53.

5 Joan Copjec, *Read My Desire: Lacan Against the Historicists* (Boston: MIT P, 1995), 34.

discourse. A trajectory of presence and absence related to the eroticization of the maternal figure finds its culmination in two key later narratives by Riera, the novel *Una primavera para Domenico Guarini* (1980) and the diary *Tiempo de espera* (1998). Writing outside the margins of patriarchal society, Riera replaces dominant cultural ideologies with hierarchies that do not duplicate traditional modes of awareness. Her discourse produces multiple bases for constructing female agency. By crossing the discursive borders of a largely heterosexual culture that ignores the mother as an agent of cultural transformation, Riera calls into question the greatest of all female-female relationships: the one that exists between mother and daughter.

The plot of "Te dejo, amor, en prenda el mar," set in Mallorca and Barcelona, feigns simplicity. In this epistolary text, the narrator addresses her former lover from whom she has been separated some eight years. Recounting the history of their affair, the narrator confesses details that appear to have made the relationship inappropriate. The age of the narrator and her partner's relationship to her, she is her teacher, initially appear to be causes of the affair's labeled impropriety. At the affair's onset, the narrator is fifteen years old, a mere adolescent on the verge of womanhood. In contrast, her lover is an instructor at the protagonist's high school. As knowledge of the affair spreads through the community, the teacher receives anonymous notes filled with insults. They say she corrupts youth and insinuate she lacks moral foundation. The adolescent similarly experiences distress. Constantly teased by school companions, she finds herself to be the topic of their gossip. Yet these troubling events do not hinder the affair's stability. Indeed, only when the narrator's father brazenly confronts his daughter with knowledge of the relationship does he declare it perverse and insist that it end. He sends his daughter away at the conclusion of the school term, hoping that distance will help weaken the lovers' bond. Still, in the textual present of the letter, the narrator admits her motivation for writing to her lover years after these events. Married, pregnant and unsure that she will withstand the birth of her child, she expresses the immutable nature of her love for this individual. The narrator is certain the child she will bear is female, and she confesses the desire to name the child after her lover: María.

The lover's name shocks the reader trained to read within the traditional male/female binary of a dominant heterosexual culture. The reader does not initially consider the possibility that the narrator writes to another woman since certain textual details conspire to encourage and re-assert a heterosexual reading of the tale. Two primary ways through which this textual subversion occurs are through the use of the epistolary mode and the narrator's focus on her lover's work as an academic.

The epistolary mode lends itself as a particularly appropriate literary form to conceal the existence of a sexual relationship between women. As Emilie Bergmann, "[P]ersonal letters and diaries occupy an equivocal generic space as marginalized forms regarded as particularly apt for writing the feminine."[6] The inherent parameters of epistolary rhetoric allow Riera's interlocutor to address her estranged lover from afar. By removing the latter's physical presence, using no adjectives or other gender-specific markers that might expose her game of concealment, the narrator encourages the reader to respond not so much to the physical presence of the addressee as to her absence.[7] The epistolary genre literally turns the reader's gaze away from a physical

---

6 Emilie Bergmann, "Letters and Diaries as Narrative Strategies in Contemporary Catalan Women's Writing" in *Critical Essays On the Literature of Spain and Spanish America*, eds. Luis T. González-Del-Valle and Julio Baena (Boulder: Publications of the Society of Spanish and Spanish American Studies, 1991. 19-28) 19.

7 In "Virtual Sexuality: Lesbianism, Loss, and Deliverance in Carme Riera's 'Te deix, amor, la mar com a penyora,'" Brad Epps eloquently discusses the problematics of the epistolary form. I would add only this to his exceptional work: the reader's responsibility is not only to question the contents and affects of the "virtual" text but also to question how his/her own cultural formation affects reading(s) of the text. Epps' article is included in, *¿Entiendes?: Queer Readings, Hispanic Writings*, eds., L. Bergmann and Paul Julian Smith (Durham: Duke UP, 1995). 317-45.

description, foregrounding the distance that exists between the writer and her lover, the intended reader of the love letter.

The lover's profession further obscures the reader's ability to note the existence of a lesbian relationship. At the on-set of the affair, the narrator reveals that her lover teaches high school while working to obtain a Ph.D. in mathematics. The narrator details that her lover is an active participant in international conferences and that she is so highly esteemed for her research that a Nobel Prize candidate has expressed his desire to work with her. Such factors inform the reader and compel her to reproduce a non-physical image of the lover that aligns itself with the masculine sex.[8] For while Western contemporary culture has certainly progressed to include images of women in many professional roles, one not too common is that of mathematics professor.

Moreover, the narrator inserts these details within an otherwise heterosexual context. After all, she confesses to having had a number of boyfriends after breaking up with her lover, of marrying, and of becoming pregnant, the latter being the impetus for writing the letter. Thus, the use of gender-neutral language coupled with the isomorphic system that conditions the reader compels one to imagine the lover and narrator within a male-female binary.

Nonetheless, an understanding of standard object relations helps to deconstruct the perceived heterosexual harmonies described thus far. Conventional patriarchal ideology generally posits the female as the object of the male gaze. Ann Kaplan and Laura Mulvey have observed that in dominance-submissive structured relationships between men and women, women often see themselves as passive objects of male desire or as passive observers of passive female objects of male desire.[9] As

---

8 "Sex" and "gender" are not synonymous. I use the term "sex" to mark biological difference. "Gender" more pointedly describes "masculine" and "feminine" roles as designated and developed by societies.

9 See especially Ann Kaplan's "Is the Gaze Male?" in *Powers of Desire: The Politics of Sexuality*, eds. Ann Snitow, Christine Stansell, and Sharon Thompson (New

an object of male desire, the subjectivity assigned to a woman is bound up with the structure of the look and the localization of the male eye of authority. Within such a system, women typically censor their words and actions to safeguard transgressing accepted social-sexual laws of behavior. Still, Mulvey and Kaplan note the existence of a feminine gaze that challenges and critiques the privileging of male vision and functions to undermine the authority of male-dominant systems.

For her part, Riera not only recognizes that an alternative to the male gendered gaze exists but goes so far as to cite the ancient Greek poet Sappho as its source. In an interview with Geraldine Nichols, Riera explains:

> [...] me empecé a interesar por Safo de Lesbos como poeta, lo cual me llevó a observar [...] que la gran aportación de Safo era precisamente elevar a la categoría de objeto del deseo a otra mujer por una mujer; que la mujer fuera a la vez sujeto y objeto del deseo en relación a su propio sexo.[10]

My reading of Sappho's poetry supplements and develops Riera's observation. Sappho's poetic voice expresses active female erotic desire and claims an authentic female subject position. Speaking from outside the margins of the principally male structured society, the Sapphic "I" asserts the existence of an alternative to the male gaze.[11] Within this

---

York: Monthly Review P, 1983. 309-27) and Laura Mulvey's, "Visual Pleasure and Narrative Cinema" in *Art After Modernism: Rethinking Representation*, eds. Ann Snitow, Christine Stansell, and Sharon Thompson. New York: New Museum of Contemporary Art, 1984. 361-73).

10 Geraldine Nichols, *Escribir, espacio propio: Laforet, Matute, Moix, Tusquets, Riera y Roig por sí mismas*. (Minneapolis: Institute for the Study of Ideologies and Literature, 1989. 187-227), 209.

11 Sappho lived on the Greek island of Lesbos over two thousand ago. For the record, her sexual preference has never been determined. It has been suggested that as a member of a Greek thiasos (i.e., a "troop" or coven), Sappho could freely express active female desire and construct images of women in subject positions. Thus, in

other system, the female writer does not construct the individual she desires—another woman—as an object, but as another subject. These complementary subjects are conspicuously non-phallic.[12] They do not privilege the corporeality of biological sex; nor do they exploit vision as an authoritative sensory device. The subjects of Sappho's poems are similar to Riera's narrator: they are "huellas en la arena," individuals lacking physical presence but who leave great impressions on the proverbial sands of the writer's memory.[13]

Several segments of Riera's narrative underscore that her narrator utilizes this uniquely feminine gaze to speak from outside the traditional dominant-submissive, subject-object order of relations outlined. The narrative "yo" of "Te dejo, amor, en prenda el mar" transgresses the visual paradigm and distances itself from patriarchal ideology. In one telling statement that demonstrates this overstepping of boundaries,

---

using the term "Sapphic," I chiefly refer to the ability of women to communicate the existence of an alternative, erotic discourse that challenges traditional patriarchal rhetoric.

12   I would like to suggest that the same-sex relationship described by Riera's character at this moment of the story embodies an almost unattainable level of equilibrium between the two characters. Perhaps this is why the physical imprint of the lovers' bodies and their gazes must dissolve as a trace in the narrator's memory. In the end, the sexual orientation of the couple is secondary to the dynamic found within it. María Pilar Rodríguez has written a particularly enlightening chapter on this issue, "La seducción de la carta: El amor como principio de desarrollo en dos relatos de Carme Riera," in *Vidas Im/Propias: Transformaciones del sujeto femenino en la narrativa española contemporánea* (West Lafayette: Purdue UP, 2000). 110-142.

13   Carlos Feal has called my attention to similar images in the poetry of Pedro Salinas. In *La voz a ti debida*, the poetic "yo" addresses his lover in the following way, "Estar ya siempre pensando/ en los labios, en la voz,/ en el cuerpo,/ que yo mismo te arranqué/ para poder, ya sin ellos, quererte./ Yo, que los quería tanto!/ Y estrechar sin fin, sin pena/ —mientras se va inasidera,/ con mi gran amor detrás,/ la carne por su camino— / tu solo cuerpo posible:/ tu dulce cuerpo pensado" (147). Salinas' "yo," like Riera's, eludes questions of sex and gender. Each speaker sings not to a contemplated object of desire per se, but to the intangible, and sexless abstraction that seems to germinate from the lover's thoughts and simultaneously transcends them. Other writers who create similar images are Paul Valéry in his poetry and Maurice Marleau-Ponty in *The Visible and the Invisible*.

the narrator asserts, "Mis ojos, que eran los tuyos, porque yo contemplaba el mundo a través de tu mirada, captaron matices, colores, formas, detalles, que a ti te parecían nuevos y sorprendentes."[14] The writer intimates that her relationship with the addressee is based not on the complementarity of a subject-object relationship, but on a mutual recognition that emerges out of a subject-subject relationship. In this statement, the narrator's gaze surrenders itself to its object of desire. The narrator's eyes symbolically become those of her lover. Sharing a unique visual perspective, they come to share equally valid subject positions.

The object-subject system of complementarity described gains significance as it recurs:

> Un lugar fuera del tiempo y del espacio (un mediodía, un barco) hecho a nuestra medida, donde íbamos a caer sin posibilidad de salvación. Sin salvación porque aquélla era la única manera de salvarnos, porque allí, en las profundidades, en el reino de lo absoluto, de lo inefable, nos esperaba la belleza confundiéndose con mi/tu imagen mientras me miraba en el espejo de tu cuerpo.[15]

Here, the narrator discusses her first lovemaking experience with the lover. Situating this event at sea, the narrator segregates it from the symbolic order of male authority—the mainland, Spain. The body of water serves as a displaced region, a womb-like environment where the power of the feminine gaze neatly evidences itself. The narrator seems to consume her lover; she internalizes her object of desire. Yet rather than demonstrate an objectification of the lover, this consumption is oddly reflexive. At the very moment at which the narrator visually localizes her lover, that image becomes her own in mutual specu-

---

14   Carme Riera, "Te dejo," 55.
15   Ibid., 59.

larity. While one might propose that the subject-subject recognition described is reminiscent of narcissism, a psychological abnormality based in the inability of the child to successfully split from the mother, this cannot be the case.[16]

Obscuring the lesbian nature of the affair does not stop at the employment of the Sapphic gaze. Of Sappho's body of work, approximately two hundred fragments remain today; and only one poem survives in its entirety—a hymn to Aphrodite.[17] Given this knowledge, the intertextual epigraph alluded to at the beginning of this chapter gains import. Namely, it leads the reader to associate the largely fragmentary quality of Sappho's verses with the fragmentary quality of Riera's epistolary text. The narrator accentuates the story's fragmentary nature not only by leaving proverbial gaps in the text but also by referring to the physical loss of past letters: letters she failed to write or tore to shreds before mailing. Early in this examination of the text, I discuss how the physical absence of the addressee sustains the reader's ability to interpret the affair as heterosexual. Yet a re-reading of the text demonstrates that additional narrative fissures serve to prolong the reader's incognizance of the lesbian relationship.

---

16 According to various models of psychoanalysis, narcissism results when a child is unable to successfully split from the mother. In many cases, a mother is blamed for this inability to split as she may, for example, ensure the continued emotional reliance of a child of either sex by playing the role of eternal victim, or dedicating her life to a child, thereby implying that the child should reciprocate by dedicating his/her life to her. In whatever case, narcissism often results in black and white thinking. The adult narcissist often sees the love object as all good or all bad; and while he will displace or otherwise externalize the object's negative characteristics, he will internalize its positive characteristics in order to maintain his own fantasies and understanding of himself. Ultimately, the true narcissist is self-aggrandizing, lacks empathy, and sees his love object as allowing him to achieve his own ends. Thus while María and her lover/professor may certainly be described as ideally viewing each other at this moment, neither may be characterized as appropriately fitting the narcissistic category.

17 Jane McIntosh-Snyder, *Lesbian Desire in the Lyrics of Sappho* (New York: Columbia UP, 1997), 4.

One telling but obscure gap might be the narrator's description of the confrontation she has with her father regarding the impropriety of the affair:

> Tengo aún muy presente el rictus de su rostro crispado, el tono agrio de su voz, pero he olvidado sus palabras. Recuerdo solamente dos frases que me han acompañado a menudo: "Éste es el camino de la depravación. Te mandaré a Barcelona, si esto dura un día más.[18]

One might attribute the father's incensed response to his concern regarding the lovers' age difference and teacher/student relationship. However, a re-reading of the narrative questions the reliability associated with such an interpretation. Earlier in the letter, the narrator emphasizes that she created her own calendar to keep track of the years, months, and days she spent with her lover. She elaborately details their first sexual encounter at sea and remembers the streets the two habitually walked, "Y todavía hoy [...] soy capaz de entusiasmarme recorriendo desde aquí con los ojos cerrados, el barrio marinero del Carme [...].[19] The enumeration of such fine points hints at the possibility that—at this point in the narrative –the narrator simply denies the reader access to her father's words. This critical lapse in memory allows the narrator to accomplish two things. First, it allows the narrator to prolong the reader's incognizance of the lesbian affair. Second, it allows the narrator to render her father's textual presence meaningless. She weakens his narrative influence and undermines the power of the cultural paradigm he represents.

Additional fragmentary qualities spring from a close reading of the lovers' first sexual experience. The reader will find that biological

---

18 Riera, "Te dejo," 57.
19 Ibid., 55.

language—reference to the body—shapes her interpretation of the text. The lover's perfect body seduces and satiates the reader while providing a virtual mask to dissimulate a heterosexual code of order:

> Tu cuerpo siempre me había parecido espléndido y, en aquellos momentos, sentía curiosidad, ganas de saciar mis ojos mirándolo tanto tiempo como quisiera. Por eso te destapé. Y apareció tan perfecto como una estatua de la que me sentí creadora, ya que eran mis ojos los que lo acababan de cincelar. Luego, como en un rito, mis dedos se deslizaron danzando sobre tu piel y volvieron a dibujar tus labios y una por una todas las formas de tu cuerpo.[20]

The erotic quality of the narrator's language might render the reader incapable of perceiving the game of containment at work within the tale. One might perceive the narrator's emphasis on the lover's body as yet another example of the typical ways in which subject-object relations function. Nonetheless, a closer reading of the text serves to demonstrate that what does not write itself in this graphic space is precisely that which it emphasizes: the body. Though the narrator articulates the centrality of her lover's body and goes so far as to characterize herself as its creator, it is—in large part—absent. Avoiding explicit visual representation, the narrator mimics Sappho's non-phallic fragmentary verse. She refers to her lover's body in sensual terms but does not visually render that body to the reader. The absence of explicit, biologically sexual imagery entices the reader and allows her to fantasize. The reader gets "caught up" in the affair and is rendered temporarily unaware of the subversion at hand.

Finally revealing the name of the lover, Riera's narrator explicitly breaks with the patriarchal structure that informs the reader. She

---

20 Ibid., 58.

makes that which is ambiguous conspicuous.[21] In so doing, the narrator forces the reader to admit the extent to which he or she associates certain characteristics with male or female gendered identity. In this sense, the entire narrative serves as a kind of (pre)text that undermines cultural tendencies that classify, constrain and mark relationships within heterosexual limits. On one level, the text incites the reader to find the tell-tale gaps where disruptions in the perceived heterosexual order take place. On another level, the narrative compels the reader to grapple with and question the gender of her own interpretive gaze. For while one might suggest that Riera simply super-imposes a heterosexual model of romantic relationships within a lesbian reality, I argue that the reader informed by a patriarchal code falls prey to textual conventions and complacencies. Re-reading traces of Sapphic love in "Te dejo, amor, en prenda el mar," the reader comes to recognize not only the very real presence of a heterosexual cultural history that has denied openly discussing lesbian and gay love, but that has also denied the maternal body as a powerful locus of sexual and cultural transformation. The apocryphal fragmented verses that precede Riera's narrative thus become dually symbolic of the lesbian relationship subversively covered over in the story and the "original matricide" on which some critics would suggest contemporary culture is founded. In the words of Luce Irigaray, "When Freud, notably in *Totem and Taboo*, describes and theorizes about the murder of the father as the founding act for the primal horde, he is forgetting an even more ancient murder, that of the woman-mother, which was necessary to the foundation of a spe-

---

21 Riera's original Catalan version of the text leaves the question of gender somewhat more ambiguous. The Catalan pronoun "nosaltres" replaces the Spanish pronoun "nosotros." Unlike the gender biased "nosotros" and "nosotras," the Catalan pronoun "nosaltres" may refer to a group of men, women, or a group comprised of both sexes. In an interview with Geraldine Nichols, Riera admits exploiting the pronoun "nosaltres" in the original text. The inclusive yet ambiguous "nosaltres" lends a sense of mystery that is not easily reproducible in the more gender sensitive Spanish.

cific city."²² On recognizing the absence of this lost figure, the reader realizes that Riera not only refers to the taboo of the lesbian relationship in her text but also to the unspoken absence of this lost mother.

Roland Barthes seems to speak of this absented mother in *A Lover's Discourse: Fragments*, "(The one who would accept the injustices of communication, the one who would continue speaking lightly, tenderly, without being answered, would acquire a great mastery: the mastery of the Mother.)"²³ The mother to whom Barthes refers, a mother, symbolically trapped—and notably de-emphasized through the use of parenthetical marks—often goes undetected in narratives not her own. Indeed, if traditional Western patriarchy covers up the debt that culture owes to this mother, what act might make her presence more apparent? Could the act of transcribing names, of creating a genealogical history of mothers and for women do this? In "Y pongo por testigo a las gaviotas," Riera responds to these questions.

Reading "Te dejo, amor, en prenda el mar" and "Y pongo por testigo a las gaviotas" together, the reader immediately recognizes the latter—written two years later—as a complementary text that dialogues with and responds to the preceding narrative. While one of the aims of the earlier text is to expose a lesbian relationship to the reader, an aim of "Y pongo por testigo a las gaviotas," is to re-position the figure of the older lover within the confines of repressive, heterosexual discourse. In so doing Riera confronts her readers with another aspect of the erotic feminine figure: the patriarchal mother who becomes an alienated victim of patriarchy, rather than one of its self-righteous accomplices.

This might lead one to wonder why Riera would so seductively transgress the limits of heterosexual discourse in one tale only to re-instate these limits in another. The apparent destabilization and re-in-

---

22 Luce Irigaray, "Body Against Body: In Relation to the Mother" in *Sexes and Genealogies* (Trans. Gillian C. Gill. New York: Columbia UP, 1993. 9-21), 11.

23 Roland Barthes, *A Lover's Discourse: Fragments*. (*Fragments d'un discours amoureux*) (Trans. Richard Howard. London: Johnathan Cape, 1979), 59.

scription of heterosexual limits points not to the author's submission to the codes of the dominant sexual culture but to something else. The exceeding of margins by itself leads the agent of a transgressive act nowhere. The power of transgression is found not in the performance of prohibited activity but in the conscious weakening of the limits that separate that which is socially acceptable from that which is unacceptable. The weakening of limits ultimately leads the agent of transgression to transcendence inside, not beyond, the limits transgressed. Thus, by introducing the character of Marina, a figure likened to that of María in "Te dejo, amor, en prenda el mar," in "Y pongo por testigo a las gaviotas," Riera subversively alludes to the symbiotic relationship absent from the first story: the relationship between mother and daughter. This subversive movement ultimately allows Riera's reader to see a pattern in the author's writings that foregrounds what Luce Irigaray and Elizabeth Grosz call the debt to the mother.[24]

Various critics have noted and examined the link between the two narratives. Kathleen Glenn has observed that while "Te dejo, amor, en prenda el mar" tells the "other side" of the conventional, heterosexual romance story line, "Y pongo por testigo a las gaviotas" tells the other side of "Te dejo, amor, en prenda el mar."[25] Glenn suggests the content of these narratives cannot be easily reconciled. Part of the problem one has interpreting these stories side by side has to do with their physical writing and re-writing. The Catalan versions of the texts, published in 1975 and 1976 respectively, each function as the title stories of the volumes within which they appear. The two stories were not anthologized together within a single collection of stories until the publica-

---

[24] Luce Irigaray, *An Ethics of Sexual Difference* (Trans. Carolyn Burke and Gillian C. Gill. Ithaca: Cornell UP, 1984) and Elizabeth Grosz, *Sexual Subversion: Three French Feminists*. Sydney: Allen & Unwin, 1989), 120-121.

[25] Kathleen Glenn, "Reading and Writing The Other Side Of The Story in Two Narratives By Carme Riera," *Catalan Review: International Journal of Catalan Culture* 7.1 (1993) 51-62: 56.

tion of *Palabra de mujer* (1980). Originally published in Catalan and translated into Spanish by the author in this volume, these stories appeared for the first time in sequential order, making the intertextual relationship between the two undeniable.[26]

Mirella Servodidio expresses that in her telling of the story, the older lover of "Y pongo por testigo a las gaviotas" shows herself to be the product of a patriarchal culture that represses lesbian identity. To be sure, one cannot disagree with this statement. Servodidio goes on to state the following:

> Is it altruism or cowardice, then, that moves her [i.e., the narrator of the story] to reinstate linearity and force separation? The second story will reveal that by "doing good and feeling bad" (in Jean Baker Miller's words) she becomes the agent of a double victimization, her own and that of her lover, with ineradicable consequences for both: the loss of sanity for the one (the teacher is institutionalized) and the loss of life for the other (appearing to yield to cultural indoctrination, the younger woman marries, gives birth and eventually drowns herself at sea, thereby returning to the originating site of their unorthodox idyll).[27]

My analysis departs from Servodidio's in that I view the curious absence of the mother figure in the tales as indicative of a lost genealogy of transgressive maternal agents within Western literature, art and thought. As previously mentioned, a lost genealogy begins with the elimination of the primordial mother in myth.

---

26 The translation I use in this examination of the text is that found in *Te dejo amor*. This translation follows the original Catalan.

27 Mirella Servodidio, "Doing Good and Feeling Bad: The Interplay of Desire and Discourse in Two Stories by Carme Riera" in *Moveable Margins: The Narrative Art of Carme Riera*, eds. Kathleen Glenn, Mirella Servodidio, Mary S. Vásquez (Lewisburg: Bucknell UP, 1999. 65-82), 69.

Before further linking this absent genealogy to "Te dejo, amor, en prenda el mar" and "Y pongo por testigo a las gaviotas," I must first discuss the function of the epistolary form in the latter story and the importance of the term "testimonio." Like the implied author of "Te dejo, amor, en prenda el mar," the implied author of "Y pongo por testigo a las gaviotas" writes the later as an epistolary text. Unlike the former tale, however, the latter contains two letters. In the first of these letters, the writer formally addresses Sr. D. Alfonso Carlos Comín, who was, in real life, the director of Laia, Riera's publishing company in 1977. She tells Comín to give another, enclosed letter to Riera. In the letter that follows, the narrator directly addresses Riera, asking her to forgive her for writing. After all, she does not know the author personally and cannot guess how she will react to the letter. The narrator acknowledges that she had to write to Riera through her publisher since she prefers not knowing the author's address. She states that by not knowing this informnation, she actively circumvents the temptation to visit Riera. This comment, in turn, suggests a possible compulsion on the part of the letter writer to meet the author, a statement that smacks of fanatical obsession. She finally concedes the source of her preoccupation with Riera. According to her, a real life affair she had with a young, female lover eerily mirrors the relationship of the teacher and the student in "Te dejo, amor, en prenda el mar." The narrator contemplates this uncanny similarity saying, "Pienso que fue por ventura el azar quien hizo que usted imaginara una historia tan parecida a la mía. Literatura y vida, lo sé muy bien, coinciden a veces, y no porque una copie a la otra, la imite, sino porque las dos son frutos del ser humano."[28]

Given the form of the story, a reader might initially consider the epistolary texts of "Y pongo por testigo a las gaviotas" to be genuine

---

28 Carme Riera, "Y pongo por testigo a las gaviotas" in *Te dejo el mar* (Trans. Luis Cotoner, Madrid: Espasa Calpe, 1991. 130-139), 130.

artifacts. Since, in the first letter, the narrator admits knowledge of Riera's fiction, the second epistolary text—the letter addressed to Riera—seems to genuinely frame a real, personal experience. With these letters, fiction becomes confused with historical reality. Moreover, Riera encourages the conflation of fiction with reality through the title, "Y pongo por testimonio a las gaviotas." By definition, a "testimonio" (testimony) is given by a "testigo," an individual who bears witness to events and gives voice to history. Thus, while Western culture may be largely structured by a dominant paternal society that has downplayed the activity of women in written history, the narrator of "Y pongo por testimonio a las gaviotas" seems to insist on the re-construction of that history through this very voice.

The narrator develops this thematic allusion to the recovery of a women's history in the opening phrase of the letter addressed to Riera: "¿Le importaría que comenzara mi historia tomándole prestadas unas palabras?"[29] She alludes to the relationship between what she presents as her real life (historical) experience and Riera's tale, underscoring the double meaning of "historia." Using the verb "prestar" in her question, the narrator further emphasizes that borrowed words quite literally link her epistolary tale to "Te dejo, amor, en prenda el mar." She points to *Te dejo amor*, the collection of stories of which "Te dejo, amor, en prenda el mar" is the first; and to the final words of a vignette, entitled "Final," that punctuates and comes at the end of this collection:

> Cerrar los ojos con el sueño suficiente como para soñarte tan solo una vez más y entregarte después como ofrenda—no prenda, no mar—al necesario olvido, donde, tan a menudo, te he esperado.
>
> Y sin embargo, dime ¿qué hacer con la ternura, indomable y nítida, que se derrama desde el fondo del espejo?
>
> Empiezo a inventarte....

---

29 Ibid., 131.

(Continuará.)³⁰

The narrator of the vignette echoes "Te dejo, amor, prenda el mar." The tangible relationship between the texts manifests itself even more clearly in the form of intertextual allusions in "Y pongo por testigo a las gaviotas," where the narrator directly quotes the vignette's narrator:

"Cerrar los ojos con el sueño suficiente como para soñarte tan solo una vez más y entregarte después como ofrenda—no prenda, no mar—al necesario olvido, donde, tan a menudo, te he esperado." Pronunciar con estos labios, tristes, que se abrasan todavía al deletrear un nombre, una última palabra; para que nunca más nadie escriba ningún otro comentario, ni diga que me conoció a mí o que la conoció a ella.³¹

With the doubling of the phrase "cerrar los ojos" the narrator of "Y pongo por testigo a las gaviotas" literally borrows words from the narrator of the vignette and echoes "Te dejo, amor, en prenda el mar." The intertextual doubling, moreover, constructs a metaphor acutely linking images of feminine bodily absence to unrecognized agency in textual history.

Allusions to the absence of the feminine body in Riera's writings are not in themselves unique to this tale. In "Te dejo, amor, en prenda el mar," the epistolary form creates distance between writer and addressee and physical descriptions of the women's bodies. The reader will further recall that the specular theory of complementary gazes introduced in an earlier section of this chapter does not inevitably result in corporal descriptions of the lovers. Accordingly in "Y pongo por

---

30   Carme Riera, "Final" in *Te dejo el mar*. (Trans. Luis Cotoner, Madrid: Espasa Calpe, 1991. 123), 123.
31   Carme Riera, "Y pongo," 131.

testigo a las gaviotas," the narrator suggests a distance between bodily presence and memory. With the passage of time, mental images become obscured and limit one's ability not only to remember the way one looked, but also what one's relationship with another was like. Images captured in the sands of memory are, in the end, lost to forgetfulness, "olvido."[32]

The association that links the absence of bodily images in memory and the breakdown of relationships may be thematically linked in Riera's work to women's tenuous relationship to language and, ultimately, to a lost genealogy of women in textual and cultural history. As contemporary psychoanalytic theory would have it, language is intimately associated with the symbolic order and the notion that a female child must (to some extent, at least) give up her most basic, necessarily homoerotic connection to the mother in order to enter the symbolic paternal order. According to Lacan, through the Oedipus complex, both sexes must accept the mother's symbolic castration. They must at once surrender the fantasy of the mother as all-powerful and accept her as "positioned in relation to a signifier, the phallus," an event which places her in the position of being rather than having the phallus.[33] Yet in sacrificing the belief that the mother is all-powerful, the child's primary love object up to this time, the child gains access to a position within culture, his/her compensation for having conformed to the law. This position is associated with the father, "It is the name-of-the-father that we must recognize as the support of the symbolic function, which, from the dawn of history has identified his person with the figure of the law."[34] The cultural position that aligns the child with the law simultaneously implicates him in a symbolic debt, gives him a name, and an authorized speaking position within history.

---

32 Ibid., 123.
33 Elizabeth Grosz, *Subversions*, 71.
34 Jacques Lacan, *Écrits. A Selection*. (Trans. Alan Sheridan. London: Tavistock Publications, 1977), 67.

While Lacan underscores the very symbolic nature of the situation posited—the phallus itself is only a signifier, albeit the signifier of all signifiers—Grosz points out that it cannot be viewed as only symbolic since it is the formula used to describe how subjects, through the construction of the unconscious, become able to speak of themselves through the pronoun "I." She argues that because females are positioned within that order as castrated, passive objects of male desire rather than as subjects who desire, the female's position within language is ambiguous and ultimately, tenuous, "when she speaks as an 'I' it is never clear that she speaks (of or as) herself. She speaks in a mode of masquerades, in imitation of the masculine, phallic subject."[35] Having had to break the connection to the mother in order to enter the symbolic, the child—male or female—becomes initiated into a culture that covers over both the very real physical and symbolic debt owed to the mother.

In Riera's story, "Y pongo por testigo a las gaviotas," the narrator not only performs the tenuous relationship women have to language through her narration, but also demonstrates how this tenuous position is further problematized by the covering over of the cultural debt to the mother. The narrator's words exemplify the feminine position within language following Grosz since they seem to show her to be a product of the dominant discourse and power structure. At one point she declares, "No sabré, no he sabido hacerlo nunca, explicarle las cosas de una manera lineal, clara y objetiva; a pesar de ello, voy a intentar poner en orden, en su honor, recuerdos y sentimientos."[36] She later adds:

> Mis palabras, a pesar del afán con el que las escribo, traducen con mucha dificultad la añoranza, la rabia, la impotencia que me at-

---

35 Elizabeth Grosz, *Subversions*, 72.
36 Carme Riera, "Y pongo," 130.

enazan, el esfuerzo que tengo que hacer para continuar viviendo sin otra meta que la de prolongar una angustia enraizada en un pasado que ni siquiera fue del todo mío.[37]

She states that her attempt to translate feelings into language is insufficient and unproductive. These feelings may be attributable to her discursive position as a woman expressing herself in a language and culture already symbolically labeled as paternal.

Regardless of the narrator's confessed frustrations towards language, she evidences a desire to speak with other women as mutual subjects. This desire may be further linked to the disavowed relationship between mother and child, a relationship sacrificed by girls and boys alike at their entrance into the symbolic order. The denied relationship is most consummately confirmed in the final paragraphs of the story. Here, the narrator of "Y pongo por testigo a las gaviotas" deviates from story told by the young lover and narrator of "Te dejo, amor, en prenda el mar" in that the former confesses to Riera as narratee that her lover, whose real name was "Marina," not María as in Riera's tale, committed suicide before giving birth to her child. While the narrator of "Y pongo por testigo a las gaviotas" admits that Riera might doubt this, she maintains that her life has imitated Riera's art:

Creerá usted que todo esto es imposible, inverosímil. El cadáver de los que mueren ahogados flota o, a veces, es arrastrado por la corriente hacia aguas lejanas, pero yo sé, estoy segura, de que el cuerpo de Marina, que jamás fue encontrado, yace en el lugar exacto donde las olas, adentrándose por el cristal de ojo de buey, espiaron por primera vez su cuerpo desnudo, perfecto, y se quedaron embelesadas.[38]

---

37 Ibid., 135-136.
38 Ibid., 138-39.

The eerie verosimilitude linking the narrator's personal experience to Riera's literature seems implausible. According to the account given, Marina's body has never been found. Rather than float or be transported by the sea's current like most drowned bodies, waves, to which the narrator gives agency, embrace a disappeared body. In this lyrically captivating passage, the narrator expresses how waves now guard Marina's invisible body by the porthole where, ironically, the lovers first gazed on each other.

The implicit covering over of maternal genealogy becomes increasingly apparent on considering the floral symbolism also present in the text. Roses inexplicably appear and bloom where Marina's body is said to rest. Flowers, and specifically roses, have often been used as representative of the idealized feminine figures of love poetry. Likewise, the use of roses in funerary memorials is not uncommon.

Perhaps most significant, however, is the symbolism of roses in Catholic typology. Various references linked the Virgin Mary to roses in medieval times, and for authors such as Tertullian and Ambrosius, the root of the rosebud doubled as a reference to Davidic genealogy.[39] The young sprout (the Latin, "virga," or bush) of the flower referred to Mary, and the flower itself was said to represent the Son of Mary, Jesus.[40]

While it is not my intention to render a religious interpretation of "Y pongo por testigo a las gaviotas," the roses to which the narrator refers do invoke the forgotten genealogy of women within the predominantly Catholic culture of Spain. The narrator states, "Estoy segura de que [Marina] descansa allí, porque en aquel remanso he visto florecer rosas. *Rosas encendidas, como un milagro* [emphasis mine], sobre el mar azulísimo, y nadie las ha cortado todavía. Las he visto, lo juro, y pongo

---

[39] Elizabeth Rees, *Christian Symbols and Ancient Roots* (Philadelphia: Jessica Kingsley, 1992), 91-92.

[40] Ibid., 98-100.

por testigo a las gaviotas."⁴¹ Roses grow and burn over a blue sea. She contends that no one has cut these flowers; no one has touched them. They appear and remain miraculously uncontaminated and pure, like the Virgin Mother of Catholic belief. The link between Marina and the Virgin Mother is further informed by the image of the sea, which in turn, may be likened to the female body as a primordial symbol of origin and source of life.

This analysis of "Y pongo por testigo a las gaviotas" suggests an irrefutable bond linking Mary's forgotten genealogy to the more generalized lost genealogy of women in Western cultural and written history. Luce Irigaray points to this specific genealogy in "Body Against Body: In Relation to the Mother:"

> And yet, when the minister of that one and only God, that God-Father, pronounces the words of the Eucharist: "This is my body, this is my blood," according to the rite that celebrates the sharing of food and that has been ours for centuries, perhaps we might remind him that he would not be there if our body and our blood had not given him life, love, spirit. And that he is also serving us up, we women-mothers, on his communion plate. But this is something that must not be known. That is why women cannot celebrate the Eucharist [...]. If they were to do so, something of the truth that is hidden in the communion rite would be brutally unmasked.⁴²

With this statement Irigaray does not so much criticize religious belief as she criticizes the Church and its clergy for banning the Mother from the Trinity. According to Catholic belief, Mary, born free from natural sin, escapes the shadow cast on humankind at the Fall

---

41 Carme Riera, "Y pongo," 139.
42 Luce Irigaray, "Body Against Body," 21.

from Grace. She opposes Eve, the temptation of Adam, the expulsion from Eden and the mortality of humankind. And yet, though Mary is the chosen Mother of the Christ/God, her son serves as the model on which the Mother's figure is based. In the Trinity, He is at once Father and Son. He is Her (male) Mother; and She is His (divine) Mother and (carnal) Daughter. As Grosz points out, in her multiple roles, Mary serves both as a "respected and unrecognized figure, both sexless and fully eroticised."[43]

Again, my intention is not to conclude with a religious interpretation of the narratives, but to substantiate the claim that an underlying reading of "Y pongo por testigo a las gaviotas"—informed and shaped by "Te dejo, amor, en prenda el mar" and the vignette, "Final"—emphasizes a lost history, a genealogy of women covered over by Western patriarchal traditions and culture.[44] Only on reclaiming this genealogy, the lost relationship with this disappeared mother, can women learn to speak and relate to each other as mutual subjects. It is for this reason that Grosz, following Irigaray, suggests the mother must give the daughter more than food to nourish her daughter. A mother must give her daughter words to hear and speak.[45]

The relationship between Irigary's theory and Riera's narratives

---

[43] Elizabeth Grosz, *Subversions*, 83.

[44] The cult of the Virgin in all Spanish-speaking cultures serves as evidence that Mary is a primary figure within the religion. However, in that Mary is often "covered up" within Western culture, she may dually be viewed as of secondary import. For example, on Mother's Day of 2000, the Cable Broadcasting System (CBS) premiered a television miniseries, "Jesus." While the program's premier on Mother's Day could simply be attributed to coincidence, it is plausible to posit that the figure of Jesus, associated with Mary, "covered up" Mary on a day set aside to remember mothers. At another extreme, the link between Catholic symbology and Riera's story may seem far fetched in that the number of devout followers has dwindled and continues to diminish in Spain. However, Riera's biblical allusions in *Tiempo de espera* and incessant references to myth in other narratives convince me that more than casual coincidence underlies the symbology.

[45] Elizabeth Grosz, *Subversions*, 124-25.

emerges to substantiate this claim. Addressing Riera as narratee, the narrator of "Y pongo por testigo a las gaviotas" initially claims that what sparks her desire to write to the author is a certain debt she feels compelled to repay.[46] The "deuda" to which the narrator refers is precisely the gift of life that Western patriarchal culture covers over in giving precedence to the name of the father. Riera suggests that her fictional narrator not only symbolically acknowledges this debt to the primordial mother, but also re-produces her own (textual) offspring, without looking for repayment. "Te dejo, amor, en prenda el mar," "Final" and "Y pongo por testigo a las gaviotas," thus echo and dialogue with each other. As complementary narratives that call attention to a prevalence of disappeared maternal bodies, they subversively give voice to the power of the maternal function. By relentlessly foregrounding an absent feminine genealogy, Riera undermines the culture within which she writers while simultaneously calling on fellow insurgents to join with her to protest the authority of a largely paternal system.

I have thus far tried to show that there is a repression of the figure of the eroticized mother in two of Riera's short stories. These narratives demonstrate a common disregard for the maternal figures implied in them. In "Te dejo, amor, en prenda el mar," María foregrounds her father's agency and presence in her life by describing the way in which he puts a stop to her love affair. She never mentions her mother as having influence in her personal identity, and perhaps most significant, she denies she can ever become a mother.

Indeed, he narrator of "Te dejo, amor, en prenda el mar" disavows the maternal function as something over which she has control:

Me siento demasiado débil y las fuerzas me fallan. Creo que po-

---

46 In an especially illuminating passage, the narrador states, "Esa casualidad hace que, en cierta medida, me sienta en *deuda* [my emphasis] con usted y me induce, no sabe con qué fuerza, a hablarle de mi historia, consciente, como soy, de que no sabré escoger con precisión las palabras [...]", 131.

> siblemente no conoceré a la niña, porque será una niña, estoy segura—y no podré decidir su nombre, si no lo hago ahora. Quiero que le pongan el tuyo, María, y quiero también que echen mi cuerpo al mar, que no lo entierren. Te suplico que esparzas mis cenizas, en aquel remanso donde las aguas espiaron nuestro amor, para que las acoja la inmensidad ilimitada. Te añoro, añoro el mar, el nuestro, y te lo dejo, amor, en prenda.[47]

The statement alludes not only to the narrator's anxiety regarding what she perceives to be her own imminent death, but also regarding the process of giving birth.[48] One might go so far as to say that beyond literal, physical death, she views giving birth as aligned with the loss of self.

Pregnancy has been intimately linked to a process of identity abandonment, re-shaping and adoption that cannot be uniquely attributed to the narrator of "Te dejo, amor, en prenda el mar." A rather long literary history speaks to this process. Simone de Beauvoir refers to the changes that accompany pregnancy in *The Second Sex*. For Beauvoir, the pregnant woman exists both in immanence and transcendence. Her immanent body, physically and experientially limited, "turns upon itself in nausea and discomfort; it has ceased to exist for itself and thereupon becomes more sizeable than ever before"[49] There is no escape from the reality of the changes implied in the pregnant body. At the same time, the pregnant body signifies transcendence because "in the mother-to-be the antithesis of subject and object ceases to exist; she and the child with which she is swollen make up together

---

[47] Carme Riera, "Te dejo," 68.

[48] One recently published example of this process is Carole Maso's *The Room Lit by Roses: A Journal of Pregnancy and Birth* (2000). She ambiguously treats pregnancy, aligning it with the sublime at times, and at others questioning whether she has subverted her own feminist project by "giving into" maternity.

[49] Simone de Beauvoir, *The Second Sex* (New York: Vintage, 1989), 495.

an equivocal pair overwhelmed by life."⁵⁰ It is precisely this transgressive indeterminacy between immanence and transcendence, subject and object to which the narrator of "Te dejo, amor, en prenda el mar" refers. In not speaking of her in the narrative (literally absenting her mother from the narrative), revealing the weakness of her body, and then surrendering herself as well as her child to the sea, María literally makes the maternal body disappear from the narrative. She most distinctively disavows the authority of the maternal body by refusing to come to terms with her own maternal body if doing so precludes her from her prior identities. Instead, she returns to the sea, a symbolic return to the womb.

In "Y pongo por testigo a las gaviotas," the narrator alludes to the debt owed to a lost genealogy of women. Intentioned or not, the symbols associated with Marina link this character to a primordial mother, the mother sacrificed at the hands of patriarchal mythologies and culture.

One distinctive characteristic differentiates Isabel Clara Alabern, the central character of *Una primavera para Domenico Guarini*, from the narrators and repressed maternal figures previously discussed: Clara is a professional journalist by trade. Thus, unlike the narrator of "Te dejo, amor, en prenda el mar," a writer who remains nameless and identifies herself with Sappho, a poet denied (author)ity within history, and the narrator of "Y pongo por testigo a las gaviotas," who begs Riera to use the utmost discretion in transcribing her name, maintaining her anonymity in the published text, Clara signs each newspaper article included in the novel. Moreover, unlike the narrators I have studied who consciously or unconsciously deny maternity, Clara chooses to become a mother. Actively choosing to bear a child outside of marriage, she rejects sexual and social passivity and transgresses the codes of proper female behavior within traditional Western patriar-

---

50 Ibid.

chal culture. Clara leaves her mark on the world in a very visible way, not only through her pregnant body and the child she will bear, but also in the graphic space of the text. Clara's preoccupation with filling gaps, the empty page and the blank canvas which she reinterprets within the novel, represent her desire to signify and to occupy a space in written history.

It is useful to give a brief summary of the events and structure of the novel before discussing the way in which Clara signifies in the text. As Akiko Tsuchiya points out, the novel contains two essential plot lines, "each serving to dramatize the search for truths and veiled meanings."[51] Likewise, these plots may be related to the internal and external events of the story. By external, I refer to the event that brings Clara to Florence, Italy where the novel takes place. She goes there to report on an act of violence that Domenico Guarini carries out against Boticelli's painting, *La Primavera* (*Allegory of Spring*):

> Aparentemente, Guarini actuó solo y sin tomar precauciones. Llevó a cabo su agresión el año pasado, coincidiendo con el inicio de *La Primavera*, el 21 de marzo, a las doce y media de la mañana, en la Sala X-XIV del Museo de los Uffizi y ante más de cincuenta personas. Utilizando un "spray" embadurnó el cuadro con pintura roja, opuso alguna resistencia a los guardianes e hirió con una navaja a uno de ellos, pero no intentó huir. Y, como si esperara la llegada inevitable de la policía, se quedó junto a su obra. Luego se dejó conducir esposado, manso como un cordero, a la comisaría donde negó pronunciar palabra.[52]

---

[51] Akiko Tsuchiya, "Seduction and Simulation in Carme Riera's *Una primavera per a Domenico Guarini*" in *Moveable Margins The Narrative Art of Carme Riera*, eds. Kathleen Glenn, Mirella Servodidio, Mary S. Vásquez. (Lewisburg: Bucknell UP, 1999. 83-103), 85.

[52] Carme Riera, *Una primavera para Domenico Guarini* (Trans. Luisa Cotoner. Barcelona: Montesinos, 1981), 42.

The senselessness of the crime surprises the reader of the narrative, who doubles as Clara's Barcelona newspaper audience. The irrational nature of the crime, one without motive, serves as the focal point that drives the novel's external plot. Clara's duty as a journalist is to uncover the reason for which Guarini committed this act.

The external narrative soon becomes entangled with the novel's internal plot: Clara's search for self and decision to become a mother. Various critics have associated the external and internal plots delineated with the compositional complexity of Riera's novel. *Una primavera para Domenico Guarini* is comprised of three distinct parts and an epilogue. In the first section of the novel, Clara, speaking in the second person singular pronoun, begins weaving the tale, describing her train trip from Barcelona to Florence. The second section of the novel is comprised of two sets of texts, respectively numbered or lettered, that alternate and dialogue with each other. In the numbered narratives, Clara, always speaking in the second person singular "tú" form, steps outside of herself to describe her private life while in Florence. She discusses her past relationship with Alberto, a journalist and past lover; her affair and break-up with Enrique, a more recent lover and the father of her unborn child; the hesitant emotions she has regarding pregnancy, and her own obsession with Botticelli's painting. In contrast to the private numbered sections, the lettered sections represent Clara's journalistic writings on Guarini and *La Primavera*. The reader assumes these to be the articles Clara regularly sends to her editor in Barcelona. The third section of the novel presents a professor's explanation of the painting. Printed in italics, and intermixed with Clara's stream of conscious narrative regarding her experiences from childhood to adulthood, the professor's authoritative exegesis of the painting echoes conventional neoplatonic interpretations of the painting in harmony with patriarchy. *Una primavera para Domenico Guarini* culminates in an epilogue that stylistically and thematically mimics the novel's beginning. While Clara initially depicts her journey from

Barcelona to Florence as a trip within a dark train tunnel, a description that emblematically captures a spiritual regression to the womb, the place of the pre-symbolic, at the end of the novel she emerges from this tunnel, figuratively pointing to a rebirth and regeneration of the maternal function outside the limits within which it was previously conceived.

Clara's narrative voice, which systematically distances itself from established discursive structures, further complicates a reading of the novel. Constantly making intertextual allusions to myriad literary genres, characters and periods as well as to popular media, such as film and print journalism, Riera's narrator performs as a critic of traditional discourses. Elizabeth Ordóñez in "Writing 'Her/story': Reinscriptions of Tradition in Texts by Riera, Gomez Ojea, and Ortiz," makes reference to the disparate media informing Clara's telling of the story, "a lawyer calls the case a horror story fit for the 19th century 'folletín' or the neorealistic cinema, leftists criticize it as a 'western,' the Italian public is fascinated by its melodramatic sensationalistic aspects."[53] By cataloguing the various genres invoked by Clara, Ordóñez suggests the postmodern implications that underlie such allusions. While such references may appear unrelated to Clara's external and internal plots—forming a veritable meaningless pastiche—another reading shows that they symbolically disclose Clara's desire to transgress the traditional rules of narrative signification. With its allusions to various literary genres, characters and periods, *Una primavera para Domenico Guarini*, becomes an exemplary model of postmodernism which foregrounds for the reader the historical moment at which the novel was produced. Journalistic chronicles, which starkly contrast and dialogue with other intertextual references, allow Clara to make a public name for herself as a writer. Moreover, it is through the articles she authors that Clara

---

53 Elizabeth Ordóñez, "Writing 'Her/story': Reinscriptions of Tradition in Texts by Riera, Gomez Ojea, and Ortiz" in *Voices of Their Own: Contemporary Spanish Narrative by Women* (Lewisburg: Bucknell UP, 1991. 127-48) 130.

gains access to the cultural agency so intrinsically aligned with the maternal function.

The word "crónica" appears numerous times in Riera's novel. By definition, a chronicle gives its readers a historically accurate, chronological account of the events described therein. A chronicle should exclude analysis and interpretation of events, allowing only for the objective statement of fact. Yet from the novel's onset, several factors complicate the reader's understanding and interpretation of this narrative form. Clara demonstrates personal interest in Guarini's crime, an interest that definitively precludes her from writing an objective description of events. The editor of the newspaper for which Clara works, Canals, fuels her personal interest in Guarini's act of violence, "Si la objetividad resulta demasiado fría, toma partido, Isabel Clara. Al público hay que darle marcha de vez en cuando, sobre todo ahora que está medio aplatanado, esperando las vacaciones [...]."[54] Acknowledging Clara's talent for making what might otherwise be a rather mundane newspaper article attractive, his statements call attention to the intimate relationship between personal and public: the personal often becomes political, and Guarini's case will become historically significant she makes it so. Moreover, Canal's has faith that Clara's has the ability to do this. Indeed, though her career began as an outgrowth of an affair she had with Enrique, a fellow writer and political activist involved with the Progressive Party, it was Clara who edited and polished his political essays, articles and speeches for publication in the newspaper. Enrique compelled her to support him in the movement, "Sé tú mi lazarillo," implying his blind reliance on her ability to lead him.[55] Entreaties such as these moved Clara to become independently active in the Party such that she began writing her own anonymous political articles on behalf of the movement. Though the newspapers'

---

54 Carme Riera, *Primavera*, 36.
55 Ibid., 171

readers have continued to attribute these articles to Enrique, Canals now emphatically encourages Clara to accept the credit she deserves, "Eres bastante buena periodista, empiezan a conocerte—y no lo digo por aquel embrollo en el que te viste envuelta, no—, firma las crónicas. Escribes bien. Estamos pasando una crisis, mandarte a Italia es carísimo [...] El periódico no se vende, el negocio se tambalea [...]."[56] His confidence in Clara's ability to attract a wide readership and solidify the newspaper's status in the media market, demonstrates Canal's belief in Clara's agency as a writer. By indicating that she sign her articles, he encourages her to break with Enrique's labels of her as his "compañera," "amante" and "amiguita."[57] Canal's recognizes her authority as a journalist with the power to reach and influence a mass audience.

On another level, signing her name to these chronicles, Clara takes a position of agency not associated with the other narrators I have thus far examined. In doing so, she appropriates a traditionally masculine discourse, the journalistic modality, distinct from the epistolary form employed by Riera's other narrators.[58] Moreover, the chronicles allow her to establish a unique voice that dialogues with and transgresses the limits of aesthetic planes, verbal and pictorial. This action, in turn, seems intrinsically associated with Clara's desire to make a name for herself in print and thus take up a place within written history.

Nowhere does the chronicle more uniquely explode the limits between personal and political than in the sixth chapter the second part

---

56 Ibid., 36-37.
57 Ibid., 131.
58 Though I classify newspaper writing as traditionally "masculine" because of its basis in hard fact and objective reality—as opposed to the most "feminine" modality, poetry—a recent report from the U.S. Department of State suggests this may no longer be the case. The report stated that twice as many women are unemployed as men (30 percent for women as opposed to about 15 percent for men), and women presently constitute about 43 percent of the total work force. However, in some areas, including journalism, health care, and the legal field—women outnumber and often outrank male counterparts.

of the novel. Here, newspaper articles anticipate and trigger ruptures in the conventional modes of signification. Nonetheless, one key aspect of the novel addressing Guarini's act of violence and obsession has been largely, if not completely, ignored. Namely, the structure of chapter six and seven of Part II breaks with the form followed in the rest of Part II. Part II of the novel alternates between personal, numbered accounts of Clara's time in Florence and what the reader assumes to be the chronicles she sends back to Barcelona for publication in the newspaper. Yet there is dramatic break from this pattern in Chapter 6 of this section. Adopting and rewriting Guarini's story, Clara crosses the discursive limit between the chronicle mode and narrative fiction. While one expects an article to appear between chapters six and seven, none does. Moreover, given that Alberto—Clara's former lover and the man with whom she stays while in Florence—states that he has read Clara's account of the Guarini story, one might suggest that chapter six straddles the limit between fiction and non-fiction, "Ya lo he leído, Clara, y no estoy de acuerdo con tu versión de Guarini."[59] Alberto's response to Clara's writing and his use of the word "version" further call attention to the crossing of limits between objective and subjective reporting, between the personal and public.

In Clara's retelling of Guararini's story, she appropriates a provocative subject position, at once becoming a first and third person narrator, both the agent of the crimes committed and a witness to them. This position allows her to disrupt the conventions through which male-female relationships and, in particular, instances of rape have been previously interpreted. Specifically, the sixth chapter in Part II upsets an understanding of Guarini's obsession with Laura that depends on the codes of courtly love. Unlike Petrarch and other bards who kept their idealized objects of desire safely distanced from the male subject of the enunciation, Guarini acts out violently, both towards his object

---

59   Carme Riera, *Primavera*, 104.

of desire—Laura—and the painting that reminds him of that desire. While imagining what thoughts might have occurred to Guarini as he attacked the painting, Clara creates images that liken Laura's death at Guarini's hands to rape. Speaking as Guarini, Clara places a stylus in his hand to stab her in the chest. The stylus clearly doubles as a phallic symbol, a symbol of sexual penetration. The professor who discusses *La Primavera* in the third section of the novel substantiates this interpretation of the instrument in as much as he states that Guarini attacked the painting in much the same way as he attacked Laura. Compare Clara's rendering of Guarini's attack on Laura, "El estilete penetró justo en el centro del pecho," to the Professor's statement regarding the status of the repaired painting, "las manchas de pintura roja han desaparecido, lo mismo que las cuchilladas y destrozos perpetrados en la figura de Flora."[60]

Disruptions of the codes of courtly love are not unique to this chapter of the novel. Framing herself as Guarini in another section, Clara states, "ella [Laura] no conseguirá entender que mis dedos, indecisos y torpes, están enfermos de amor." According to Clara's rendering of the situation, Guarini thinks that Laura could never acknowledge or comprehend that her very existence and image drive his obsession. For while it is he that spends hours gazing at women, it is her gaze that possesses him and on which he becomes fixated, "Mi vida seguirá dependiendo para siempre de una mirada violeta, de un iris teñido con lilas, de unos ojos color de glicinias moradas. Me importa poco que no puedan volver a mirarme nunca. De todos modos jamás podrían volver a hacerlo como entonces."[61]

Nonetheless, the provocative discursive position that allows Clara to gaze on Laura and the painting as Guarini would gaze does not render the same vision, the same interpretation, of the images at hand. As

---

60   Ibid., 129.
61   Ibid., 89, 87, respectively.

we have already seen, the novel's chronicles draw attention to the unraveling of otherwise fixed symbols within the patriarchal socio-symbolic system of signification. If art celebrates the heterogeneity of drives and possesses the power to influence and disrupt the social cohesion it engenders, Riera's novel functions as a quintessential performance of this heterogeneity.[62] From Clara's agency in her journalistic writings to her appropriation of sexual authority in account of Guarini's crime, Riera produces a cacophony of narrative voices that disturb the reader's familiarity with cultural codes associated with femininity and especially maternity. Nowhere is this disruption more evident than in Clara's reinterpretation of Botticelli's *La Primavera*. Just as Clara rejects the typical ways in which Guarini's case has been interpreted by the people and media of Florence, she also rejects the ways in which the mythic figures of Botticelli's painting have been understood. In Clara's reading of these allegorical figures, she rejects the interpretive norms within which they have been previously understood and demonstrates how she would re-classify and re-construct feminine agency within her culture.

The scene created by Botticelli includes a rather eclectic arrangement of mythological figures not traditionally united in any one Greek or Roman myth. Though all of the characters depicted within the painting—Mercury, the Three Graces, Cupid, Venus, Flora, Chloris and Zephyrus—relate to Clara's desire to signify, three prominent figures must be examined at length: Chloris, Flora and Venus. These figures affect Clara, re-positioning her within the novel's story as a woman.

According to Greek legend, Flora, the goddess of spring, owes her existence to a so-called "happy" metamorphosis. Ovid describes this event in his *Fasti*, a work in verse describing the months of the Roman calendar. Ovid explains that one spring day Chloris was wandering in

---

62 Elizabeth Grosz, *Subversions*, 54.

the forest when Zephyrus gazed on her and fell in love. Seeing the wind god and fearing him, Chloris ran away. Zephyrus, far more powerful than the nymph, overcame and raped her, transforming Chloris into Flora. Botticelli recreates this myth in his painting, where we see the winged and ominous, gray figure, Zephyrus breathing into Chloris. She, in turn, exhales flowers, miraculously demonstrating the talents bestowed on her once changed by Zephyrus.

The professor who interprets this scene in Riera's novel reiterates and expands this version of the myth, "la boca de Cloris exhala rosas: Céfiro ha obrado el milagro y la ninfa se ha convertido en Flora. El amante hace germinar el alma de la amada y, como la primavera hace con la tierra, la cubre de flores."[63] According to the professor, Flora should be understood as a product of love born of divine desire, "El amor es una fuerza comparable a las demás fuerzas de la naturaleza que rigen el universo, decía Ficino, el filósofo neoplatónico que tanta influencia ejerció sobre Florencia. El amante comienza una nueva vida, irrumpe en un dominio nuevo en el momento en que aparece la amada."[64]

Zephyrus who comes upon Chloris breathes in her, literally and figuratively engendering her ability to give life in spring. Zephyrus thus becomes Chloris's father, her creator, as well as her husband and lover. Myth explains that although the wind god initially took Chloris by force ("rapina," in the *Fasti*), he rightly compensated for this act of violence through his conduct in marriage.[65] Flora could not complain about their union because Zephyrus was a wonderful husband and lover.

To Flora's right, Botticelli places Venus, recognized as the goddess of beauty and love; and, as the narrator of *Una primavera para Do-*

---

63 Carme Riera, *Primavera*, 138.
64 Ibid., *Primavera*, 137.
65 Frank Zöllner, *Botticelli: Images of Love and Spring* (Trans. Fiona Elliott. New York: Prestel, 1998), 44.

menico Guarini explains, she represents the institution of marriage:

> [...] según todo lo que acabamos de decir, los dos cuadros de Botticelli están íntimamente relacionados por el tema. Uno, el *Nacimiento de Venus*, representa a la Venus Caelestis; el otro, el reino de la Venus Humanitas. Hay que observar además que la Venus de *La Primavera* se parece, tanto en la postura como en el gesto y atuendo, a la Anunciación. La Virgen María asimila muchas de las características de la diosa Venus y, durante el Renacimiento, con el sometimiento de la mitología a las interpretaciones teológicas, ambas figuras se complementan. Ficino, en la carta al joven Lorenzo de la que ya hemos hablado, hace referencia a su horóscopo bajo el signo de Venus y Mercurio para alabar a Venus como "ninfa de origen celestial, amada por Dios más que ninguna otra" y se la recomienda como esposa.[66]

Botticelli surrounds Venus with myrtle twigs, "traditionally associated with weddings and childbirth but also with sexual desire."[67] *La Primavera*'s Venus thus communicates the neoplatonic ideal that one could act on sexual impulse and desire, but only fully in marriage. Moreover, the marriage to which the professor refers expresses the union between Christian theological and secular beliefs, a stance not atypical during the Quattrocento, since Catholicism had adopted and benefited from allegorizing classical Greco-Roman myths.

Indeed, the coming together of Christianity and Greco-Roman myth culminates in the neoplatonic basis of the third section of the novel. According to the philosophical and religious ideas of Florentine philosopher Marsilio Ficino, the principal promoter of neoplatonic intellectualism in Botticelli's Florence, the human soul was considered

---

66 Carme Riera, *Primavera*, 147.
67 Frank Zöllner, *Botticelli*, 48.

to be the center of the universe. An individual's goal was to transcend the material confines of the body to reach union with God. Cheney explains this neoplatonic belief by citing Ficino's verses, "Everything is in God/ God loves himself/ Therefore/ Everything loves God."[68] The syllogism of these verses suggests that pure love, which is God and begins in God, brings about spiritual love. As this love travels down from the heavens to earth, it denatures. Reaching the corporeal sphere, the sphere of humanity, such love becomes sensual, erotic. Yet, Chaney explains, "The individual or human soul can control or choose between the spiritual love and erotic love, the intelligible world and the corporeal world, since he/she has the will and power to choose freely his/her actions and immortality."[69] Thus, the abstract reference to marriage between God and Venus suggests the possible transcendence of the material world and body. It gives the individual hope that he might transcend the need for erotic, human pleasures (associated with Greek myth) in possible union with God (Truth).

Though these interpretations of the painting might seem tangential to Clara's repositioning within the novel, an examination of her own understanding of the three figures demonstrates this is not the case. Clara's re-visioning of *La Primavera*, like her re-visioning of Guarini's crime in Chapter 6 of Part II, disrupts narrative conventions. In Chloris/Flora, we see that oftentimes a woman had little or no say with regards to the selection of the man she would marry. What's more, pursued and sexually assaulted, Chloris/Flora reminds Clara of herself. As she listens to the professor's exegesis of the scene, Clara vividly recalls being chased by a sexual predator as a child in a movie theatre. Almost unable to dodge the sexual advances of her assaulter, a Zephyrus of sorts, Clara runs from her seat in the cinema to the women's bathroom, the only place she thinks he cannot enter,

---

68 Liana Cheney, *Quattrocento Neoplatonism and Medici Humanism in Botticelli's Mythological Paintings* (New York: UP of America, 1985), 22.

69 Ibid., 22.

saying, "No me atrevo a salir, tengo miedo de que él me esté esperando fuera [...]. Sisí ha descendido de la pantalla, ha atravesado la sala de las butacas y, sin que nadie la vea, se ha acercado a consolarme dulcemente [...]."[70] Clara's recollection of being stalked leads not to spiritual fulfillment and marriage as in the neoplatonic explanation given by the professor, but to horrific shame. Clara's companion at the theatre, Sisí, does not offer Clara comfort but rather insinuates that she has spent the time masturbating, "Isabel Clara, ¿qué estás haciendo aquí tanto rato? Ven conmigo inmediatamente. Ya verás a tu madre. Te tendrás que confesar."[71] Sisí continues to mortify her by telling Clara she will have to confess this sin to a priest.

Later, we find that the priest to whom Clara confesses having masturbated is more perversely interested in the details of her sin than in the granting of absolution:

>—Dime cuándo lo haces.
>—¿Por las noches?
>—¿En la cama?
>—¿Es verdad que no sabes si lo has soñado?
>—Dame más detalles [...].[72]

Like the man who attempts to assault her in the movie theatre, the priest takes advantage of Clara. He insists she give him details regarding the attack. He demonstrates interest in finding out the particulars of the molestation through short, pointed questions that suggest his own growing excitement. He ends the inquiry by asking her name, eliminating the anonymity of her confession. The priest's actions ultimately serve to underscore the inadequacy of the myths to which the text alludes time and again. For Clara, the trauma suggested in male

---

70 Carme Riera, *Primavera*, 134.
71 Ibid.
72 Ibid., 137.

figures of sexual violence—Guarini, Zephyrus, the stalker who follows her to the bathroom, the priest—does not lead to the happiness or transcendence that has been read in Botticelli's painting, but time and again to shame and punishment.

Just as there is an underlying subtext invoking a need to expose and recuperate the agency of an absented maternal figure in the epistolary tales of *Te dejo, amor, en prenda el mar*, so to the implied author of *Una primavera para Domenico Guarini* invokes this need. Clara's distinctive response to the image of Venus, rather than recapitulate traditional interpretations of the mythic Roman figure, illustrates this need. The professor who lectures on Botticelli's Venus explains that she should be identified as Venus Humanitas, the Venus associated with materiality, corporeality. Linking this Venus to motherhood, the professor continues, "Pensad que las dos palabras 'mater' y 'materia' tienen la misma raíz."[73] Yet, as the reader will recall, the "superior" Venus to whom the professor later refers is the Venus Caelestis, "Venus celestial engendra el amor divino porque procede solamente de Urano. No tiene madre. Nació en el mar, milagrosamente, cuando los genitales de Urano fueron arrojados a él. Habita sólo en nuestra mente, rechaza la materia por el hecho de no tener madre."[74] Like the professor's earlier statements, which spur Clara to remember being sexually assaulted, these statements cause her to regress to childhood memories regarding the Virgin Mother. She recalls the words her own mother once spoke to her on finding Clara masturbando. "Cuéntaselo todo a la Virgen, porque es la madre del Amor Hermoso y del temor y de la sabiduría y de la santa esperanza. En ella está la gracia para andar el camino hacia la verdad, toda la esperanza de vida y de virtud. Los que se dejen guiar por ella no pecarán [...]."[75]

Not surprisingly, neither image of the Virgin Mother seems par-

---

73 Ibid., 145.
74 Ibid.
75 Ibid., 147.

ticularly imitable. What is surprising, however, is the very real way in which discussion of these images causes Clara to remember her own mother. While Clara oftentimes remembers her mother as having exemplified feminine passivity and as having imposed such conformity on Clara, as the wife of an unfaithful husband, she goes to extreme lengths to publicly acknowledge his affairs in a way that defies such feminine constructs:

> Atención, amigos míos, escuchadme un minuto. Todos sabéis con quién me engaña Perico, ahora os enseñaré con quién le engaño yo.
>
> Con un gesto rapidísimo te arremangaste la falda, deslizaste hacia abajo las bragas de encaje y empezaste a acariciarte el sexo.[76]

Graphically demonstrating her fury, the masturbatory act exposes the mother's ability to please herself and to obtain certain satisfaction and autonomy. In stark opposition to Chloris/Flora and the images of the Virgin Mother, Clara's mother refuses to remain dependent on any male figure to secure her happiness.

So too Clara's stream of conscious response to the painting, culminating in this representation of her own mother's impassioned and angry transgression of cultural and social norms, dramatizes an urgent need to speak, to rupture passive or marginalized representations of women in Western myth and culture. The novel's last section and epilogue, which, like the first section of the novel, systematically uses imagery associated with birth, underscores this point. The symbolic birth Clara describes in the final section of the novel communicates both pleasure and pain in the agency of motherhood, "Después, los espasmos de un dolor desgarrador, como si en tu vientre se librara una lucha de escorpiones y la quemadura áspera de su veneno te royera las

---

76 Ibid., 144.

entrañas; como si las olas te llenaran de tempestades a puñetazos."[77] Tsuchiya notes that these contradictory sentiments suggest the novel remains open-ended, "The protagonist's train may have emerged from the tunnel this time, yet there will be other tunnels through which she must travel in order to rewrite and continually re-envision the narrative of her life."[78]

I would suggest that Riera's open-ended novel defamiliarizes the maternal function. By creating bold female figures, like that of Clara and Clara's mother, who act defiantly and in stark contrast to their maternal literary predecessors, Riera fills in the lacunas of femininity as it has been defined. Presenting her protagonists as driven subjects who desire to actively re-interpret the female figures who came before them, she necessarily defines these women as politically motivated agents whose pursuits and interests cannot be limited to the space of the written page. As a writer of chronicles, Riera's Clara is only too cognizant of this detail; and, unlike Chloris/Flora who is, we are told, unable to escape from Zephyrus, Clara has the author(ity) to choose a narrative vantage point that uncovers the gaps of histories that have often limited the significance of female figures. As a writer she responds to Botticelli's painting, distances herself from its mythic basis, and disrupts the values of its symbols, obliging her readers to re-evaluate the relationship between the seemingly limited figures of the painting and the (necessarily) limitlessness of the gaps that separate these figures and which should keep readers questioning the conventions that shape our cultural belief systems. In a sense, then, the pleasurable pain Clara experiences in the third section of the text and in the epilogue is bound up with the realization that birth can only be a consequence of destrucción, "Sólo destruyéndose, el ser se transforma en un ser nuevo, sólo la transformación de la materia y el espíritu que pasa de un mundo

---

77 Ibid., 195.
78 Akiko Tsuchiya, "Seduction and Simulation," 97.

a uno superior, de lo transitorio a lo permanente, nos puede llevar por el camino de las tinieblas hacia la luz."[79] Transformations in the modes of signification suggested in Clara's own reading of myth underscore a transgressive will to re-write the genealogy of women in history.

Beyond the epistolary narratives of *Te dejo, amor, en prenda el mar* and the serialized chronicles of *Una primavera para Domenico Guarini*, in the diary *Tiempo de espera*, Riera palpably offers herself up as an example of the cultural agency with which she wants to endow the maternal function. In Riera's preface to *Tiempo de espera*, the author tells how the publication of this diary came about. She explains that though she wrote the diary during her pregnancy, in September of 1986 through May of 1987, she had not considered publishing it until 1996. That summer Riera participated in a colloquium on literature, autobiography, and memory at Boston University. It was during the colloquium that Riera first publicly mentioned the diary and discussed the reasons for which she had written it, analyzing, at the same time, the underlying relationship between writing and pregnancy. Her initial evaluation of the writings captured the attention of the Hispanists in attendance, mostly women, who begged Riera to publish it. They assured her that such a work would be truly appreciated by a wide audience, since diaries of pregnant women have not been commonly published. Riera refused to present the diary as a manuscript until the daughter with whom she had been pregnant was able to read it, suggesting that she would ultimately decide whether its publication would be acceptable, "Necesitaba saber si estaba de acuerdo en compartir con otras personas las palabras que sólo a ella iban destinadas, convirtiendo a los demás en cómplices de nuestra historia privada."[80]

It is interesting to underscore Riera's use of the word "historia" in initially discussing the diary. The word "diary" may be etymologically

---

79 Carme Riera, *Primavera*, 187.
80 Carme Riera, *Tiempo de espera* (Barcelona: Lumens, 1998), 10.

traced to the Latin term, "diarum," associated with the word, "dies," days. The author of a diary, an autobiographical modality, primarily writes for his or her own personal use and reflection. Since the diary's content reflects the writer's daily life, with all its complications, choices and feelings, its reader may generally perceive the form as monotonous. Captured within the text, daily life takes on a fragmentary and repetitive emotional quality. Yet it is precisely the tedious nature of everyday experience that compels a diary's author to structure her narrative in a way that might seem more memorable. This genre thus provides its author with a challenge: to confront the limitations of the memories that immediately inform and structure her writings in order to make memorable—as much for herself as for other potential readers—what might otherwise seem mundane. Linda Hutcheon, explaining the importance of "life-writing" in *The Politics of Postmodernism,* recapitulates this notion, saying that although there are problems associated with the self-conscious, self-reflexivity of historical narratives, there is value in representing personal experience. She notes that life-writing must continue and that no matter how arduous the constraints or how "falsifying" the process of writing might seem to the writer, these "constraints must be faced and not used as an excuse for not making the attempt."[81] Riera's diary rises to the challenge to which Hutcheon alludes by obliging readers to consider how pregnancy and maternity have been and are popularly perceived and marketed. She encourages a re-evaluation of the boundaries that separate the private from the public, the experiences of the masses from that of the individual, and the acceptable from the unacceptable. Riera's account of pregnancy and thoughts on maternity thus oppose a culture that would have the "dark cultural space" of the womb remain a thing of mystery charged with a general significance that functions only to repeat conventions

---

81   Linda Hutcheon, *The Politics of Postmodernism* (New York: Routledge, 1989), 167.

that limit women as agents within history.

Riera deals with the bodily changes she undergoes in pregnancy at the same time that she deals with notions of what it means to be a feminist in today's globalized world. In developing this position she alludes to differences between feminism as she understands it and the platform she upholds:

> El feminismo, con el que estoy de acuerdo, se ha planteado reivindicar nuestra capacidad creadora. Sin embargo, es absolutamente necesario reivindicar también la recreadora o reproductora. Es necesario buscar fórmulas para que nuestra condición de dadoras de vida llegue a ser un estímulo, un aliciente. Es necesario que el sufrimiento y la carga sean superados por el gozo y el placer de la maternidad. Llevamos demasiados siglos pariendo con dolor. Ha llegado la hora de trasgredir ese dolor y transformarlo, de pasar de la casi inconsciente gestación a la experiencia de una maternidad consciente, asumida desde la inteligencia.[82]

Riera suggests that while feminism has been generally aligned with creativity—women's roles as agents who plan, build on, and influence their communities—women's equally valid and necessary roles as (physically) re-creators and reproducers have often been downplayed. She strongly implies that the feminist movement, itself limited by conventions regarding what "feminist" women should want, has created an image of the "liberated," agent-ful woman as dissociated from the maternal function.[83] Yet as Riera keenly notes, women's agency

---

[82] Carme Riera, *Tiempo*, 61-62.

[83] Riera's observation points to further irony within the feminist movement: the feminist appropriation of Freud's famous question, "What do women want?" Re-writing the question "What do we [women] want?" feminists have often done themselves a disservice of assuming that a feminist platform should precisely oppose those characteristics conventionally viewed as inherently "feminine." For such femi-

in culture can never be separate from women's agency in maternity. She challenges the audience to consider a feminist position inherently aligned with maternity, a unique proposition, given that the condition of pregnancy has not often been viewed within feminist theory as an "act of will or the decision of an agent" and the pregnant woman has been frequently represented as—like the womb itself—a "cipher, a filter."[84] If women have been limited in culture, often posited as the passive objects of male agents who influence their construction and representation, Riera reminds her reader that women have dually limited themselves by limiting pleasure in maternity—shrouding it in negativity, bodily pain, and suffering—and promoting maternity as undoing the good of the feminist movement. Riera concretely points to this negativity when she alludes to a conversation she has with a friend who calls to tell her that he's found out about her pregnancy, "Le digo que no es fruto de ningún descuido ni de ningún error, sino absolutamente buscado, y se queda perplejo. Después se despide hasta dentro de nueve meses. Le pregunto si se va de viaje y me dice que no, que soy yo la que estaré ausente."[85]

While the starkness of this friend's statement clearly demonstrates how pregnancy may be viewed as an "absence," the author discusses how she personally experiences this absence as duplicated in literature. She notes that while hundreds of guidebooks and magazine articles tell women what they can anticipate during pregnancy, these address their readers in disparaging tones that question women's positions as agents-in-maternity. And while she presumes that reading domestic diaries might provide her with extensive access through which to examine the culture of pregnancy, Riera affirms that few women refer to their experiences. Hester Lynch Thrale's diary—a well-known example

---

nists, maternity itself becomes an anti-feminist act, an act irreconcilable with the politics of an all-encompassing "women's liberation."

84 Elizabeth Grosz, *Subversions*, 47.
85 Carme Riera, *Tiempo*, 36.

of this modality and one to which Riera refers—is more an inventory of pregnancy than a full and personal account.[86] These assessments not only agree with the notions previously introduced regarding life-writing, but also with Riera's implicit view that maternity has been veiled in a negativity that has undermined its very real subversive appeal. On the one hand, the banality of pregnancy as itself an everyday experience undermines one's ability to perceive it as transgressive. It is, in fact, seen as in opposition to transgressivity in that a pregnant woman is often viewed as fulfilling a cultural duty inherently assigned to her sex. On the other hand, mass-produced pregnancy journals—diaries inscribed with thoughts on the stages of pregnancy and questions to help inspire the woman to write—confound one's ability to look on the expectant mother as an agent. For while the paucity of published diaries suggests that pregnancy need not be written about, the existence of the latter products not only implies that women need to be guided and inspired in their writings about their experiences, but also that there are appropriate and fixed ways that a woman must react through the various stages of pregnancy. Even fiction seems to fail Riera, "Le he pedido a B., mi librero de confianza, alguna novela interesante que trate de la maternidad, pero sólo recordaba obras sobre abortos."[87] In the end, the literature that does exist on pregnancy seems to generalize the experience and constructs maternity as a product created through the popular myths that have been associated with it. If comments like those of Riera's friends seem unfortunate, they are nonetheless indicative of the fact that culture "sells" commercially acceptable ways of experiencing maternity and motherhood to women while at the same time it seems to suppress and ultimately "absent" individual agency.

As a close reader and critic of the negative classifications surrounding pregnancy, Riera constructs a "transgressive" viewpoint that

---

86 Hester Lynch Piozzi, *Thraliana: the diary of Mrs. Hester Lynch Thrale (later Mrs. Piozzi)*, ed. Katharine C. Balderston (Oxford: Clarendon Press, 1942), 14.

87 Carme Riera, *Tiempo*, 23.

skillfully re-interprets women as agents in maternity. Her allusions to Greco-Roman and early Christian myths and their codes of signification dialogue with the readings I have thus far made and clarify her position on the greatest female-female relationship, that between mother and daughter.

In one such significant highlighting of the affect of myth on contemporary culture and literature, Riera speaks of the mythic meeting of Zeus, Hera, and Tiresias, where Zeus asks Tiresias which of the two genders enjoys sexual relations more. Legend has it that Tiresias could answer this question from experience because, while once watching two snakes copulate, he lashed out and injured the female. For this, Tiresias was turned into a human female. On witnessing a similar scene seven years later, he injured the male snake and was transformed into a human male. All together, Tiresias is said to have lived as a woman for seven years and as a man for one. So when Zeus and Hera disputed whether man or woman enjoyed sex more, they referred to Tiresias for his knowledge, since he had experienced sexual intercourse as both a woman and man. According to Riera, Tiresias answered Zeus by saying that man enjoyed one-ninth of the love shared between man and woman, while woman enjoyed the rest with her soul. Riera recalls Hera's reaction to this statement:

> Hera se molestó mucho y castigó a Tiresias, dejándole ciego. No le gustó eso de gozar con el alma. Zeus, por el contrario, le otorgó poderes adivinatorios y larga vida. Lacan, comentando el pasaje, advierte que, aparte del placer fálico masculino, existe otro goce femenino diferente mucho más complejo y relaciona estas nueve décimas partes con los nueve meses durante los cuales llevamos dentro una criatura.[88]

---

[88] Ibid., 35.

Through this account, Riera vividly demonstrates her knowledge as a professor of Spanish literature, literary critic, and contemporary writer while subversively commenting on her own pregnant state. I say this primarily for two reasons. First, beyond noting that Hera did not like Tiresias's statement—that women loved with their souls more than with their bodies—Riera neglects commenting on Hera's punishment of Tiresias. Second, Riera seems to link the mythic story of Hera and Zeus to authority in erotic pleasure and female agency in pregnancy.

"Hera se molestó mucho y castigó a Tiresias, dejándole ciego. No le gustó eso de gozar con el alma."[89] The importance of this sentence within the diary and in reference to Riera's writings resides in the literal and figurative significance of Hera's defiant action: she renders Tiresias blind. Leaving out her own interpretation of this action, it seems Riera begs the reader to question, why should it be an appropriate punishment? Yet given what I have already stated regarding Riera's narratives, perhaps one might make the case that the deed should be linked to the authoritative power traditionally associated with the male gaze. Riera's curt statement foregrounds Hera's rebellious attempt to disarm Tiresias, to eliminate his potential influence over Zeus's sexual fantasies; for in granting that women enjoyed sexual relations more than men, Tiresias would be simultaneously acknowledging Zeus's fantasies of Hera. To accept Tiresias's appraisal of woman's experience would be to allow Zeus to maintain whatever essentially uninhibited erotic image of Hera he liked. It would be, furthermore, permitting Zeus to have power over that mental image. By rendering Tiresias blind, Hera acts against Tiresias to preserve and defend her own self-representation. Her deed challenges possible objectification. Riera gives details that further substantiate my interpretation of this passage, "Zeus, por el

---

89 Ibid.

contrario, le otorgó poderes adivinatorios y larga vida."[90] Citing that Zeus reacted to Tiresias's response by giving him prophetic powers, she suggests Zeus's desire to reward Tiresias, in part, with (authoritative) visionary powers. It is no coincidence that this allusion draws attention to Tiresias's eye since the power of the gaze is of familiar import in Riera's fictional work. It is of course Tiresias's fatalistic visionary capacity that leads Oedipus's father, Laius, to abandon his son for dead, but also Oedipus to discover that he has already killed his father and slept with his mother—familiar myths linked with taboo and transgression.

This final point leads me to re-examine Riera's description of Hera's jouissance, an experience the goddess seems reluctant to share. According to Riera, Lacan refers to the incident between Zeus, Hera, and Tiresias in a discussion of the excessive and complex sexual pleasure of jouissance.[91] Lacan implies that Western Christian culture created a God who assigned positive worth to the ecstatic, spiritual soul and assigned negative worth to the mundane, physical body. He admits that it is a culture that ascribes real value to physical orgasm and to the phallic function while at the same time it idealizes spiritual pleasure and fulfillment in God. It is a culture that requires one to assume either a masculine or feminine position at the entrance into the Symbolic Order and to "line up" on either side of the symbolic phallus. One must assume that one has the phallus (generally, the position of the man) or assume that one is the phallus (generally, the position of the woman). And while Lacan believes most men are situated on the side of the phallic function because—narcissistically seeing themselves in the image of this God—they idealize ecstatic love and disparage physical love, he remarks that there are cases in which women

---

90 Ibid.

91 Though Riera cites Lacan with regards to the relationship between feminine pleasure and jouissance, in my correspondence with her, she has not been able to tell me the source she cites where Lacan refers to the incident between Hera and Zeus.

have lined up on the side of the phallus. Examples of two such phallic women are the mystics Beguine Hadewijch d'Anvers and St Teresa of Ávila. Of the latter, he explains, "you only have to go and look at Bernini's statue in Rome to understand immediately that she's coming, there is no doubt about it. And what is her jouissance, her coming from? It is clear that the essential testimony of the mystics is that they are experiencing it but know nothing about it."[92] The statement implies a visceral component to the mystic's bodily response. He links this ecstasy to the jouissance beyond the phallus, beyond the capacity of written language, and suggests that the mystic could never verbalize this jouissance because to do so would logically require the use of the same language stabilized by a universal masculine subject. At first glance this explanation of mystic jouissance seems peripheral to Riera's allusions to Greco-Roman myth. Nonetheless, Hera's subversion of Tiresias's optic powers and her own desire to keep private her experience of sexual pleasure are directly related to Riera's re-visioning of pregnancy as a uniquely agent-ful and erotic female experience.

Namely, though Riera invokes Lacan's explanation of feminine jouissance in her description of Hera's sexual satisfaction, the goddess's pleasure is dually linked to authority—in that she usurps Tiresias's optic powers—and to a lost genealogy of women. Hera, after all, is not only known as having given birth to many of Zeus's children, but also as having conceived one child—Hephaestus—alone, and as being the mother of the goddess of childbirth, Eileithya. In this sense, Hera's mythic figure exemplifies that women are not reducible to passivity and the preservation and care of others in motherhood, but always assert their authority and particularity through their thoughts and deeds.

Thus, in much the same way that Lacan revisits the legend of Hera

---

92 Jacques Lacan, "God and the Jouissance of The Woman" in *Femine Sexuality: Jacques Lacan and the école freudienne* (New York: Norton & Company, 1985), 147.

to underscore the similarity between her jouissance and that of the mystic St Teresa of Ávila, I suggest that Riera revisits the myth to inspire her own re-writing of erotic female agency and genealogy in pregnancy. The following telling statement, made on learning of her baby's sex, demonstrates this, "A partir de ahora no sólo escribo a la búsqueda de una destinataria implicada en los acontecimientos de modo directo, sino también de una cómplice que comparte conmigo el género y la historia."[93] In other passages she affirms, "Gestación: interlocución sin palabras. Tacto sin voz. Amor en plenitud. Diálogo entre mi yo y el de mis antepasados en cuyo código genético ha quedado grabada en la memoria de su historia remota y lejana;" and, "Mi hija, pero también mi madre, mi hermana, mi amiga, mi incestuosa amante."[94] These words represent a personal reclaiming of feminine culture in history. Inscribing these words on paper for her daughter to read, the author makes this history palpable, possible for her daughter to readily perceive. By remembering these women in the space of the diary in much the same way as she remembers Hera, she rescues them not only from the obscurity of memory and myth, but reinserts them (literally) into history through the written word.

In the end, it is no coincidence that the term "íntimo" derives from the Latin word "timor" fear.[95] While the confessional modality appears to provide a perfect narrative space within which to freely dialogue with her unborn child, traces of past political, sexual, and social censorship still underlie her words, "Diario: espacio de libertad. Sin ataduras, sin límite, sin estilo, sin censura. Y no obstante, en el es-

---

    93   Carme Riera, *Tiempo*, 84.
    94   Ibid., see pages 111 and 103, respectively.
    95   "timor," *Oxford English Dictionary*. Ed. J.A. Simpson and E.S.C. Weiner. 2nd ed. Oxford: Clarendon Press, 1989. OED Online Oxford University Press. 24 August, 2006. <http://dictionary.oed.com/cgi/entry/50252945?query_type=word&queryword=timor&first=1&max_to_show=10&sort_type=alpha&result_place=1&search_id=IQqT-wSCzpR-6809&hilite=50252945>

pejo de la nada, del sin, del papel en blanco, necesitamos también una imagen gratificante. Nos auto censuramos sin querer."[96] Written laws that once enforced that women be passive and disavow inherently rebellious roles may have been abolished, but Riera's statement demonstrates that amendments meant to liberate women from the repressive notions associated with female gender construction have not exhausted their power. Even in this private testimony of love, Riera alludes to a fear that induces self-censorship. She feels she must sometimes leave in writing only traces of herself, a narrative parallel that once again creates verosimilitude between the author's short stories and reality.

Riera points to a possible solution to the problem of the textual trace, the self-censorship in which women often participate in order to be heard by a wider audience. She implies that what interests her most is not the space outside her body but the space within: "Lo que me interesa ahora es lo que sucede dentro de mí. Lo que pasa ahí donde no hay ni espejo ni reflejos."[97] Without mirrors to reflect images to which women should aspire, Riera cites the safety of the womb as the point of origin beyond convention, beyond the archetypal traces we have been able to examine. This revelation lays bare the most controversial of all of Riera's implicit suggestions. First, women must look within themselves to find their greatest censors; and second, women must not only actively revise staid cultural myths of feminine agency to recuperate a lost genealogy of women, but must also disavow those images—popularized through the media—that betray women's ability to see themselves as feminists and full agents in maternity.

---

96 Carme Riera, *Tiempo*, 23.
97 Ibid., 25.

3
Cristina Fernández Cubas:
Girls, Women, and the Games They Play

BORN IN ARENYS DE Mar, Cataluña in 1945 and having published her first works of fiction after 1975, the year of Franco's death, Cristina Fernández Cubas may be categorized as a writer of the "transición," the period marking the end of dictatorship and the movement towards democratization and reconciliation of political ideologies that had been previously at odds. According to José Ortega, writers of the transition are difficult to characterize as part of a unified group.[1] Yet in attempting to find some common ground among these writers, one might point to Gonzalo Sobejano's article, "La novela poemática y sus alrededores," on the literature of the period. Sobejano observes a self-conscious preoccupation with fiction as fiction in Spanish novels written between 1980 and 1985, "Tiene [la novela] conciencia de querer ser primariamente 'ficción' y suele comunicar a sus lectores la conciencia de esta voluntad."[2] Ortega thus links the writers of the transición, and especially Fernández Cubas's oeuvre, to an interest in self-conscious, reflexive fiction.[3]

Noting a preoccupation with fiction in Fernández Cubas's nar-

---

1 José Ortega, "La dimensión fantástica en los cuentos de Fernández Cubas," *Monographic Review/Revista Monográfica* 8 (1992): 157-63), 157.

2 Sobejano in Ortega, "La dimension,"157.

3 Since publishing her first collection of short stories in 1980, *Mi hermana Elba*, Fernández Cubas has authored two other collections of short stories, *Los altillos de Brumal* (1983)—which inspired a film, directed by Spanish director, Cristina Andreu—and *El ángulo del horror* (1990), as well as two novels, *El año de Gracia*

ratives, Ortega simultaneously calls attention to the modality of the fantastic, "Este predominio de lo ficticio no supone en los relatos de Fernández Cubas que vamos a considerar, una renuncia a la realidad, sino un tratamiento de ésta en virtud del cual se genera lo fantástico, pues lo fantástico depende de la realidad para su existencia."[4] And while Ortega may not be alone in his characterization of Fernández Cubas's fiction as largely pertaining to the fantastic, the innumerable references to games, play and fantasy in her works merit serious analysis beyond that which might be performed using popular theories of the fantastic.[5] Her tales owe a uniquely transgressive quality to these elements. Games, play and fantasy not only become methods by which characters attempt to escape psychological trauma, but also by which they manifest agency. Moreover, the protagonists in Fernández Cubas writings use the language of games, play and fantasy to create discursive positions from which to destabilize social categories often occupied by women, especially the familial roles of "mother," "daughter" and "sister."

In an interview with Kathleen Glenn, Fernández Cubas makes a telling statement by declaring the significance of play in literature, "La literatura es, entre otras muchas cosas, un juego. Un Gran Juego.

(1987) and *El columpio* (1995). The hybrid narrative-drama *Hermanas de sangre* (1998) is one of her most recent works.

    4 "La dimensión," 157. Two notable critics who have written on the fantastic in Cristina Fernández Cubas's narratives are Phyllis Zatlin, Lynn Talbot, and Jessica FOlkart.

    5 In *The Fantastic: A Structural Approach to a Literary Genre*, Tzvetan Todorov defines this modality as obligating the reader "to consider the world of the characters as a world of living persons and to hesitate between a natural and a supernatural explanation of the events described." The hesitation created and experienced by one or more characters is also "entrusted" to the narrative's audience. A reader of this modality must adopt a certain attitude with regard to the fantastic events about which he reads (33).

Pues, por favor, seamos serios y juguemos a fondo."[6] Fernández Cubas's revealing declaration, one that juxtaposes seriousness with play, foregrounds a significant paradox that lies at the heart of any discussion of linguistic play. Susan Rubin Suleiman speaks to this paradox in *Subversive Intent: Gender, Politics, and the Avant-Garde*:

> Does all playing involve a game? Are all games playful? What's the difference between playing with and playing against? Playing at and playing on? Playing up and playing down, playing to and playing around? And what about "just playing"? Do all games have players? Does all play have players? Does the game stop if there is no one around to see it or to play it?[7]

Referring to its physical, emotional and psychological manifestations, Suleiman invokes a definition closely aligned to the function of language and literature. Occupying no fewer than eighteen pages in the *Oxford English Dictionary* the definition of play calls to mind a range of activities, from childhood play, competitions, games, jokes, tricks and dreamlike fantasies, to the intricate, and sometimes convoluted, dynamics implicated in forbidden relationships.[8] Clearly, the language we use to describe play, the way we characterize and define it, creates limits. Those not privy to the language of play, who do not have knowledge of it, remain outside it, at the margins of play, in restricted areas where the language employed to discuss it cannot be fully understood.

---

6 Kathleen Glenn, "Conversación con Cristina Fernández Cubas," *Anales de la literatura española contemporánea* 18.2 (1993): 355-63, 361.

7 Susan Rubin Suleiman, *Subversive Intent: Gender, Politics, and the Avant-Garde* (Cambridge: Harvard UP, 1990), 1.

8 "play," *Oxford English Dictionary*. Ed. J.A. Simpson and E.S.C. Weiner. 2nd ed. Oxford: Clarendon Press, 1989. OED Online Oxford University Press. 26 August, 2006. < http://dictionary.oed.com/cgi/entry/50181179?query_type=word&queryword=play&first=1&max_to_show=10&sort_type=alpha&result_place=1&search_id=dKWR-Ipx15b-4893&hilite=50181179 >

In as much as the language one uses to describe play creates its own set of limits, casting those familiar with a language as "insiders" and those unfamiliar with it as "ousiders," it becomes like play, both limited and limitless. Geogres Bataille draws attention to the complex relationship between language and play in *Literature and Evil*, "literature is a return to childhood [...] but has the childhood that governs it a truth of its own?"[9] The rhetorical question Bataille asks links written language, in the form of literature, to childhood. In doing so, he reminds the reader that literature is both limited and limitless. Narratives are limited in that they have beginnings and endings, they take up definitive amounts of space, and follow pre-determined grammatical rules. But as Bataille keenly implies, every piece of literature is limitless in that, in as much as it is filled with inherent narrative gaps and silences, it becomes a boundless playground. It seems, then, that language and literature become wholly aligned with a symbolic return to the limitless possibilities so often associated with childhood exploration and play. Each reader, akin to a child, becomes an agent, exploring the space of the narrative and making it his own. He/she becomes, together with the author, a sovereign of the text. And, as Bataille suggests, both have truths of their own.

This is a uniquely powerful position for both the writer of the narrative and its reader. In the case of Fernández Cubas's tales, multiple forms of play come together to convey characters' desires to unburden themselves of psychological trauma and despair as well as to gain the recognition of a formidable "other." Thus, in her narratives, play becomes bound to characters' struggles for self-recognition as well as to the development of discursive subjectivity. For Fernández Cubas's female characters, agency is physical, psychological, and profoundly enmeshed in the very telling of stories. Her agents bring themselves

---

9 Georges Bataille, "Introduction" in *Literature and Evil* (Trans. Alastair Hamilton. Marion Boyars Publishers, 2001), x.

into being through physical and literary play, re-creating the roles so often played by women. In doin so, they explode the notion of socio-culturally imposed limits by simultaneously recognizing and rejecting these limits and, in effect, narrating their own invention through language.

"Mi hermana Elba," found in a collection of stories contained within a volume of the same title, is one tale that connects play with psychological trauma and the desire to gain recognition from a formidable "other." In an early critical study of this collection, Catherine Bellver characterizes the four stories contained in *Mi hermana Elba* as sharing a collective concern for the significance and influence of relationships among friends and family members.[10] The title story, "Mi hermana Elba," helps to give rise to Bellver's decisive statement. A bildungsroman, the narrative tells the tale of two sisters whose protective frames are constantly destroyed and rebuilt. Due to parental deception, institutional regulations, and the social constraints of their culture, play becomes a physical manifestation of psychological defense mechanisms. Thus the tale also foregrounds play as a vehicle through which to rupture the limits between innocence and experience and by which to undermine the mythic notions that idealize childhood as a paradise of innocence. Specifically, ludic aspects of the tale cover over memories of trauma caused by the instability of the family unit, physical separation, and death. Moreover, while some critics seem to discount Elba as having a secondary role in the tale—as merely the "abnormal" sister of the un-named narrator and principal protagonist of the story—I argue that each defines herself as an agent of transgressive behavior through play. The sisters' extraordinary movements these characters make between the exterior world of adult logic and the childhood play define them as ultimate agents of feminine transgression.

---

10 Catherine Bellver, "Two New Women Writers from Spain," *Letras Femeninas*. 8, no. 2 (1982), 3-7, 3.

The first person, un-dramatized narrator briefly prefaces "Mi hermana Elba" by telling her reader that the events about which she is to speak were originally contained in a diary she kept as a child, "Aun ahora, a pesar del tiempo transcurrido, no me cuesta trabajo alguno descifrar aquella letra infantil plagada de errores, ni reconstruir los frecuentes espacios en blanco o las hojas burdamente arrancadas por alguna mano inhábil."[11] Begun on the 24th of July in 1954, the diary's entries end some two years later, on the 7th of August in 1956. Other details within the framework of the narrative make clear that these years mark the period of time within which the narrator moves from childhood to adolescence. One generally thinks of childhood as a period of time during which an individual explores reality and his/her own ontology, especially through play. The skills and coping mechanisms experienced and learned through individual and group play aid the child in growth and development. Nonetheless, the reader of Fernández Cubas's story quickly discovers that for the narrator of "Mi hermana Elba," this critical period filled with memories of childhood fantasies and play is equally filled with sadness, trauma and violence: all effects of the destruction of the family as an institution meant to order the production and development of its members and the social body at large. The narrator continues to make this interpretation of the story possible by saying that while she cannot conclusively recall whether she continued her diaries in some other notebook after 1956, she is inclined to think she did not, adding:

> Ignoro también el destino ulterior de varias fotografías, que en algún momento debí arrancar—y de cuya existencia hablan aún ciertos restos de cola casera petrificados por el tiempo—, y el instante o los motivos precisos que me impulsaron a desfigurar, po-

---

11 Cristina Fernández Cubas, "Mi hermana Elba" in *Mi hermana Elba y Los altillos de Brumal* (Barcelona: Tusquets, 1988. 53-81), 53.

siblemente con un cortaplumas, una reproducción del rostro de mi hermana Elba.[12]

The verbs used to set the stage for the story's telling—*arrancar, desfigurar*—coupled with the narrator's first allusion to Elba all poignantly foreground the narrator's desire to wipe her mind clear of the pain associated with memories of Elba. Having already repressed the reasons for doing away with the photos, she still communicates the wish to re-construct a protective frame that will shield her from additional psychological upset and displacement.

The protective frame first introduced in the narrative emerges as a result of the parental desire to shelter the narrator and Elba from needless distress. On the verge of separation and divorce, the parents attempt to shield Elba and her sister from this information by hiding any details about the state of their relationship. Nonetheless, the narrator intuits the existence of this protective frame, declaring that having closely observed her parents during the summer of 1954, "Sabía que un importante acontecimiento estaba a punto de producirse e intuía que, de alguna manera, iba a resultar directamente afectada."[13]

The subtle allusion to the existence of a barrier separating the narrator and her sister from the problems of their parents becomes increasingly tangible as the tale's plot develops. At one point, the narrator expresses that her mother actively promoted the creation of a secure sphere for her children:

> Mi madre, en una ocasión, se apresuró a ocultar ciertos papeles de mi vista. La niñera, menos discreta y más dada a la lamentación y al drama, dejaba caer de vez en cuando algunas alusiones a su incierto futuro económico o a la maldad congénita e irreversible

---
12 Ibid., 53-54.
13 Ibid., 55.

de la mayoría de los seres humanos.¹⁴

She equally points to her father as a man compelled to protect his daughters from the stigma associated with divorce at that time.¹⁵ His behavior not only underscores his desire to safeguard his children, but also to spoil them, "Nunca como en aquella época mi padre se había mostrado tan comunicativo y obsequioso. Durante las comidas nos cubría de besos a Elba y a mí, se interesaba por nuestros progresos en el mar e incluso, nos permitía mordisquear bombones a lo largo del día."¹⁶ Detailing the respective ways in which her parents and nanny act, the narrator demonstrates how the adults implicitly collude to guard the children from the upset they believe separation and divorce will produce. Mother, father, and caregiver become active players, and equal partners, in a game whose goal is to create a fantasy world where the mere possibility of trauma associated with broken marriage does not exist. Adept at this game, they manipulate the environment within which they live to accommodate the narrator and Elba by upholding the family as a stable organized body.

Yet both mother and father eventually succumb to the stark realization that no amount of game playing will serve to better their collective situation. They tacitly acknowledge they cannot continue to uphold the fantasy they have willingly produced. Their only recourse is to tell their daughters the truth and thus abolish the fantasy of the perfect family. Nonetheless, the dissolution of this first protective frame acts as a catalyst that sets into motion the invention of other protective frames, all functioning to cover over the displacement of stabilizing social structures. The narrator describes the way in which

---

14 Ibid.
15 For a thorough appraisal of marriage, divorce, childbearing and rearing from the period of the Spanish Civil War to the Destape, see Luis Alonso Tejada's *La represión en la España de Franco* (Barcelona: L. de Caralt, 1977).
16 Cristina Fernández Cubas, "Elba," 56.

this chain of events occurs:

> Pero, por fortuna, la decisión estaba firmemente tomada y, aunque las palabras "separación" o "divorcio" nunca fueron pronunciadas, muy pronto me enteré de su más inmediata consecuencia. Elba y yo pasaríamos el invierno en un internado. Los prospectos, extraídos de un cajoncito secreto de un canterano junto al que había transcurrido la mayor parte de sus conversacions, vieron entonces por primera vez la luz. Se trataba de un colegio grande y hermoso, situado a pocos kilómetros de la ciudad donde vivíamos habitualmente y rodeado de bosques frondosos y jardines de ensueño.[17]

At first glance, the narrator's delight at hearing she will be goaing to a boarding school may appear unusual, given that the prospect of abandoning the comfort of a familiar environment to attend an unfamiliar school away from home may be viewed as frightening. Still, for the narrator, the boarding school figures as part and parcel of another protective frame. Her parents extract the pamphlets that describe the school from a "secret" drawer, helping to veil the institution in an air of mystery. Rather than discuss the school openly, the parents make only oblique references to it and keep information about it hidden from sight. The narrator further romanticizes her vision of the school by imagining it as big, beautiful, and surrounded by lush forests and gardens. These points work together to characterize it as wonderful. The almost fairy-tale-like depiction of the school as an enchanted land isolated from the preoccupations of daily life—including the parents' imminent divorce—becomes the locus for the construction of another protective frame.

While the school she imagines temporarily represents a safe haven from which to escape her problems, the narrator soon acknowledges

---

17 Ibid., 56-57.

that her fantasy of what she thought the school would be like and the reality she encounters are very different. Thus, though on arrival she scorned her classmate—an obese, greasy-haired girl with empty eyes who refused to make conversation—the narrator soon becomes conscious of the fact that she is no different from this or any of the other girls at the school:

> Me di cuenta muy pronto de que la mayoría de las niñas formaba un grupo cerrado, y de que yo no era para ellas *la* nueva, como mi fantasía se había encargado de imaginar en la semana que precedió a mi ingreso en el internado, sino simplemente *una* nueva, categoría en la que, además de cuatro o cinco compañeras, se incluía a mi propia vecina de mesa.[18]

Not a notable addition to the student population but rather one of many children finding themselves in similar situations, the narrator fades into obscurity. Even the stigma that might otherwise be associated with being the product of an unsuccessful marriage fails to distinguish her from the other girls, "Muchas de mis compañeras se hallaban internadas por circunstancias similares e incluso, en mi misma clase, había dos huérfanas, condición que en un principio envidié, pero a la que terminé por no conceder, como la mayoría, ninguna importancia."[19] In short, she suggests that she experiences her placement in the school as a kind of humane abandonment. Having to face the breakup of her parents' marriage and now coming to the realization that the boarding school can never meet her expectations, the narrator not only recognizes herself as symbolically exiled from the organizational force of the family, but also ironically exiled from truth and knowledge since the kind of questioning characteristic of academic discourse is not only

---

18 Ibid., 59.
19 Ibid., 59-60.

discouraged but also denied in the school, a place where she will be governed by strict rules and regulations.

Indeed, a rigid system of unspoken and unwritten policies limits her verbal expression and physical movement. She first follows these, opting to be moved by the same mind-numbing regulations that move her classmates. Like them, she gets lost in her teacher's lectures, takes meals in the dining hall at stipulated hours, and goes to sleep in the dormitory at the same time as does everyone else. Even play, an activity that should, by definition, express creative energy and independence is structured by the social regulations of the school. The narrator and her sister are at first allowed to play only certain games and only during the few hours of "recreo" granted by the sisters of the school.

Not until Fátima, another child at the school, befriends the narrator does the latter begin to build independent, psychologically protective frames that transgress the strict rules that govern the boarding school. For the narrator and her classmates, Fátima represents transgression incarnate, "Fátima, lo sabíamos todas, entraba y salía de las zonas prohibidas a las demás con la mayor tranquilidad del mundo."[20] Routinely participating in prohibited behaviors, she buries herself in her school desk and—while staring at her teachers with empty eyes—gets lost in fantasy. This behavior is not indicative of a lack of intelligence or laziness but rather reflects a defiant attitude of independence on Fátima's part. She most clearly demonstrates this rebellious spirit when visiting the narrator one night before going on her habitual jaunt through the school's forbidden zones: "Mordisqueaba [Fátima] un trozo de queso e iba vestida aún con la bata negra de cuello de piqué, como un desfío más a aquella rigidez de horarios que parecían destinados a todas nosotras menos a ella."[21] Out of bed after hours, wearing a non-regulation robe, and eating outside the confines of the dining hall, Fátima repre-

---

20 Ibid., 62.
21 Ibid., 65.

sents the essence of transgressive agency absent in other classmates.

It is Fátima's rebelliousness that catalyzes the narrator into following her lead, "[...] me encontré con Fátima recorriendo los largos pasillos de la zona prohibida, contemplando imágenes y cuadros, abriendo y cerrando puertas, subiendo y bajando escaleras cuya existencia, hasta aquel momento, me había sido totalmente desconocida."[22] The first of many prohibited activities in which the two children participate is undeniably playful. They explore one of the school's most secret zones: the private quarters of the novitiates that run the school. This taboo exploration ultimately leads the two girls to share a fantastic experience when, afraid they will be caught out of their rooms after curfew while rummaging through the novitiates' private possessions, they suddenly hear two sisters approaching. Rather than flee from their quarters as one might aspect, Fátima hides there and convinces the narrator to do the same:

> [...] pero, ante mi estupor, no eligió una mampara cualquiera del dormitorio o el interior del armario, como mi imaginación se disputaba nerviosamente, sino que, sin abandonar su expresión de extrema tranquilidad, se acurrucó en una de las esquinas del cuarto y con un gesto rapidísimo, me indicó que me sentara a su lado.[23]

While one of the two novitiates notices some disturbance in the room, a light that had been previously off is now on, both quickly go about their business and leave without seeming to have detected the girls' presence. Moreover, no amount of reasoning aids to logically explain how the two have escaped the sisters' perception. The narrator articulates that she hesitates believing she has truly gone unperceived. Fátima, for her part, only complicates matters for the narrator by in-

---

22 Ibid.
23 Ibid., 68.

sisting that they were and, at the same time, were not in the room, "Estábamos allí pero no estábamos. Y aunque a ti te pudiese parecer que estábamos, no estábamos."[24]

In as much as this event must be interpreted within the norms of the story, it falls under the realm of fantastic categorization: both the narrator and reader hesitate between belief and doubt, fulfilling one of the characteristic required in Todorov's definition of this genre. Nonetheless, the ability of the two girls to hide in the open and remain outside the scope of visual perception also represents a psychologically protective frame. Regardless of whether or not the girls have miraculously avoided being seen, what remains clear is that both, through their rebellious play, succeed in building a boundary between the harsh world symbolized by the boarding school and the private world of their fantasies. They establish a secret world within which they are not only psychologically protected and able to escape the severity of their situation, but also autonomous and free.

Up to this point, I have systematically foregrounded how the narrator's parents and caregiver construct a faulty protective frame for the children, one that ultimately fails to shield them from the pain associated with divorce. I have also established the significance of the fantastic play in which the narrator and Fátima participate. Together with their violation of boarding school regulations—another example of a break within mandated order—the girls' play activity becomes a fundamentally transgressive behavior indicative of rupture. Their violation of rules demonstrates a display of independence not in keeping with the authoritative discourse of the institutions that inform them.

Yet Elba's role in this process, to this point not foregrounded, increases in importance as the notions of play and transgression converge and split in the latter part of the story. This development is, in turn, related to the significance of the evocative "Elba," a distinctive

---

24 Ibid., 70.

name referring to an island located in the Tyrrhenian Sea off the West Coast of Italy and most often recognized as the place where Napoleon Bonaparte was exiled between 1814-1815.[25] Although at first glance these historical and geographic appear insignificant, having little to do with the plot of "Mi hermana Elba," they notably impact the reader informed by theories regarding psychologically protective frames in play. A developmentally disabled child exiled first from her parents' home, and then from her only sibling's side, Elba participates in prohibited activites—actions violating the protective boundary between the real and fantastic realms of play—that serve as traces of trauma experience.

It is no surprise that Fátima, an agent of transgression whose name links her to the marvelous, is the first to observe Elba's talent for finding private play worlds, "Cerca de aquí, en este mismo jardín, hay uno [i.e., un escondite] muy antiguo. El otro día me encontré allí con tu hermana Elba."[26] Fátima's indisputable admiration for little Elba's adept gift catches the narrator's attention and relocates Elba as the story's main performer of barred activity. She moves through the school—symbolic of institutional discourse and rules—to create private worlds where all three girls experience the autonomy and excitement accordingly associated with transgressive play. Significant for Elba, no limits separate these worlds. The narrator notes this dissolution of boundar-

---

25 A portion of the Island of Elba was Spanish owned between 1596-1709. Naples ruled the island until it was ceded to France in 1815. On the day Napoleon returned to France after his exile, the island was given to Tuscany and later, Italy (1860). These constant changes of governance associated with the island may be related to the "Mi hermana Elba" in that they mirror the sisters' experience of separation, isolation, and exile from each other.

26 Cristina Fernández Cubas, "Elba," 71. The name "Fátima" alludes to the city of the same name in Portugal where, in 1917, three shepherd children were said to have been visited by the Virgin Mary, who told them secrets and performed the miracle of making the sun dance in the sky. Fernández Cubas's Fátima may be likened to this religious icon in that she represents for the narrator the ability to harness and demonstrate power through her marvelous activities.

ies when she describes Elba's ability to surprise Fátima and herself at play:

> Más de una vez, mientras mi amiga y yo hojeábamos los gruesos volúmenes de la biblioteca, deteniéndonos ante la imagen de Sansón o pasando ávidamente los grabados referentes a las plagas de Egipto, Elba, a la que acabábamos de ver jugando en el jardín, aparecía de repente con la expresión inequívoca del pecadillo recién cometido.[27]

Perceiving no restriction of movement, Elba's individual activity transcends the limits that separate the play realm from that of exterior reality. Moreover, and as evidenced by the narrator's words, neither Elba's easy movement between these worlds nor her ability to escape the gaze of those outside it can be logically explained.

Yet the ability to transcend the limits that separate the real world expectations of adults and the institutions within which they live from the protected world of childhood play begins to fail when Elba's slow intellectual progress prompts her parents to place her in a special school for the developmentally disabled. Regardless of what the narrator tells in reference to Elba's astonishing talent for finding protective hiding places where the two sisters might take refuge from the world symbolized by their parents and the school, Elba cannot completely protect herself from the accepted norms of those social realities. Thus, just as her parents guardedly introduced the idea of separation and divorce to both children, so now they guardedly introduce the narrator to the idea of Elba's leaving the academic institution. She first hears word of Elba's possible departure from behind closed doors, doors that continue to represent a protective frame built by the parents to shield both children from this troublesome prospect, "Escuchamos detrás

---

27 Cristina Fernández Cubas, "Elba," 72-73.

de la puerta y nos fuimos enterando de que el próximo invierno Elba no iría conmigo al internado. Mi propia madre intentó explicármelo el día en que cumplí doce años: 'Elba', me dijo, 'necesita estudiar en un colegio especial junto a niñas como ella.'[28]" Crushed by this news, she realizes that no amount of protest will change her parents' decision, "Lloré, supliqué, pataleé, hasta que terminé entendiendo que mis posibilidades de éxito en aquel mundo de adultos regido por la inmediatez eran prácticamente nulas."[29] Incapable of performing in the world of adult reason and action represented by parents and teachers, the narrator remembers this as the moment at which she and Elba were literally and figuratively exiled from each other.

From this instant, the childhood games and fantasies of the narrator's youth begin to lose their fanciful significance and the compelling psychological representation of the protective frames becomes even more evident. Exile from Elba coupled with the onset of adolescence—the narrator receives word of Elba's leaving on her twelfth birthday—goads the narrator forth into an unknown world. She vacilates between taking comfort in her memories of the fantastic worlds the three girls created through the construction of protective frames and the distressful understanding that she must continue on alone. This situation is further complicated in that, returning to school the subsequent year without Elba, the narrator finds Fátima disinterested in maintaining a friendship. Noting they have lost their common bond, Elba, the narrator realizes she has been unsurprisingly exiled from Fátima as well, "Fátima, la gran Fátima que todas—y yo con mayor razón—admirábamos, había dejado de pertenecerme."[30] She admits knowing the cause of this exile, "[...] terminaría comprendiendo que a Fátima no le interesaban ya unos juegos que ella, sin duda, consideraba ahora infantiles, y que mi propio aspecto, aún muy aniñado, convertía

---

28 Ibid., 74
29 Ibid.
30 Ibid., 77.

mi presencia en algo molesto y detestable."³¹ An invisible yet real psychological barrier between the realms of childhood and adolescence separates the girls from each other. As one accepts initiation into adult practices and socialization, the other is left behind.

The divisive line that at first separates the narrator from Fátima soon likewise separates her from Elba. Initially crushed by her sister's parting, the narrator slowly banishes Elba's sad image from memory. Though she initially nostalgically visits their past hiding spots and imagines Elba speaking to her from afar, she ultimately stops frequenting their hiding places, since remembering these only causes her to feel pain and shame.

The narrator's attempt to exile Elba from memory reaches its culmination at the beginning of the summer break from school when she returns to her parents' beach home. Reunited with her sister for the first time since their initial separation, Elba shouts the narrator's name and excitedly throws out her arms to touch her. Yet Elba's presence inspires disgust in the narrator. Elba, for her part, becomes aware of her sister's loathing:

> Elba, desde su mundo, parecía intuir que su presencia me resultaba incómoda. No quiso volver a la playa—aquel lugar donde, un par de años antes, yo misma le había enseñado a nadar—, y sus frecuentes torpezas a la hora de las comidas determinaron que en lo sucesivo tomase sus alimentos en la cocina. Tampoco este año iba a compartir el dormitorio conmigo.³²

Banished now from common worlds of play—their childhood home and hiding places at school—the sisters can never again share the same intimate space and will never communicate in the same way.

---

31 Ibid., 76.
32 Ibid., 79.

Though apparently incapable of expressing her feelings due to her developmental disability, it is ironically the younger sister who intuits the elder's discomfort at their reunion.[33]

Elba's fearless transgressions of order end in physical death and more psychological trauma. The narrator introduces the news of Elba's horrific demise reporting that, while playing on the terrace one morning, she lost her equilibrium and fell to her death. Having been accustomed to transgressing the limits between reality and fantasy, Elba died in a way that epitomizes Apter's description of psychological trauma in play. Unable to distinguish the limit of the protective frame shielding her from danger, Elba chooses to go beyond it and tumbles to her death:

> No quise ver el cuerpo ni mis padres me obligaron a ello. Pero, por las conversaciones que fui oyendo a lo largo de la tarde, me enteré de que la sangre corría a borbotones y de que fue mi padre quien primero acudió en su ayuda y cerró para siempre sus ojos.[34]

The image of blood uncontrollably gushing from Elba's body functions as an evocative symbol rich in meaning for both sisters. For Elba, the blood represents a final and ultimate transgression. Though she has experienced separation and exile from family and lost all freedom with regards to her play worlds, her blood still flows forth in excess, without restriction, in death. Her blood is thus representative of the final life force that no one but she can control. For the narrator, Elba's blood doubles as an indicator of her own imminent initation into the adult realm, the blood of menarche.

Describing her sister's funeral, the narrator momentarily covers over the possibility of this interpretation of her sister's blood as she

---

33 This statement is ironic since it is Elba, not the narrator, who has been classified as being limited in her ability to express herself through language.

34 Cristina Fernández Cubas, "Elba," 80.

points to the possible construction of another psychologically protective frame. During the memorial service, images associated with their shared childhood experience flood the narrator's mind in a spontaneous stream of consciousness, "Fátima, Elba, Eliazar, mi obesa compañera de pupitre, Rebeca, la palabra 'escondite' [...]. No oía ya rezos sino un extraño zumbido. Mi madre me dio aire con las tapas de un misal. Me había desmayado."[35] Overtaken by memories of her childhood and the sudden realization that nothing can safeguard her from the finality of Elba's death, the narrator faints. Unable to manage the sheer stress that has culminated in tragedy, fainting allows the narrator a momentary yet necessary psychological and physical respite from a sad reality.

Yet the final sentence of the tale again uncovers the symbolic significance of the blood, "Era el siete de agosto de un verano especialmente caluroso. En esta fecha tengo escritas en mi diario las palabras que siguen: 'Damián me ha besado por primera vez'. Y, más abajo, en tinta roja y gruesas mayúsculas: 'Hoy es el día más feliz de mi vida..'"[36] The reader will recall that the tale begins with an allusion to a specific date, the 24th of July, 1954. The final date, like the first, marks a limited period in the narrator's life. Yet, whereas the first date refers to a period of vacilation and fluctuation between external and private worlds, the second date refers to the moment at which the narrator must begin to construct another protective frame within the limits of the adult world. Left alone and psychologically naked, the narrator no longer focuses on Elba nor on images of her youth, but rather on a new love interest, Damián—Fátima's cousin. In effect, she reacts by abandoning the transgressive play of childhood, refocusing her attention on Damián, and thus temporarily escaping the reality of Elba's death and all of the preceding traumas that have left her psychologically frag-

---

35 Ibid., 81.
36 Ibid.

mented and unstable. I say "temporarily" because it is the inescapable, all-powerful memory of Elba to which she returns again and again.

In the end, while the narrator may have been able to tear up photos of her sister in scrapbooks, defacing her image with a penknife, she can neither eradicate the pain of childhood memories nor of her sister's passing. The play so indicative of transgressive activity, pleasure, and autonomy in youth accordingly thus becomes a subversive tool by which the narrator simultaneously expresses the very real sufferings that have informed her development and made her unable to find serenity from despair. Forced to abandon her safe havens time and again in order to confront jarring realities, the narrator describes how the consistent dissolution of boundaries and the elimination of protective frames lead to fragmentation. Besides serving to create the world, a child's play serves to help her express and work out unconscious conflicts. Deprived of these, the tale's now middle-aged narrator becomes a consummate representative of what occurs to an individual when divested of independent play and creative powers.

The protective frames constructed and destroyed in the story, "Mi hermana Elba" also come to play in "Los altillos de Brumal." This story differentiates itself from "Mi hermana Elba" by having as its focus not the relationship between sisters, but on the tenuous relationship between mother and daughter. Nonetheless, "Los altillos de Brumal" shares many narrative characteristics with "Mi hermana Elba." Aside from mentioning one of the same significant years alluded to in "Mi hermana Elba," 1954, "Los altillos de Brumal" also employs the fantastic mode, and alludes to games and game playing. Furthermore, there is a predominance of female characters and, as in "Mi hermana Elba," "Los altillos de Brumal " employs a first person, female narrator, Adriana.

Most significant, the beginning of "Los altillos de Brumal," much like "Mi hermana Elba," immediately focuses the reader's attention on the first person narrator's past, specifically an illness suffered early in childhood:

> No podría ordenar los principales acontecimientos de mi vida sin hacer antes una breve referencia a la enfermedad que me postró en el lecho en el ya lejano otoño de 1954. Fue exactamente el 2 de octubre, fecha señalada para el inicio de las clases escolares, cuando el médico visitó por primera vez la casa familiar, pronunció un nombre sonoro y misterioso, y yo, en medio de un acceso de fiebre que me hacía proferir frases inconexas, temí llegada la hora de abandonar el mundo.[37]

As in "Mi hermana Elba," the recollection and naming of a specific date marks a critical period in the narrator's life, one that continues to affect her and spurs her writing. The moment marks, for the narrator, a physical and symbolic threshold that separates a past life experience with a new life. Adriana underscores the importance of this liminal moment by articulating that the mere thought of abandoning one world for another at that point frightened her and incited her to spew non-linear and incomprehensible phrases. Yet what inspires the ailing child to continue living is the sonorous, mysterious word pronounced by her doctor. Although she fails to further specify the word he pronounces, I suggest that this word is "Brumal," the place from which she comes and to which Adriana physically and psycholocially returns as she begins to spin her story. The dates that mark the narrator's sickness, then, define a progression of movement between liminal worlds.

The section of the narration that follows this portion of the tale serves as a cursory introduction expressing Adriana's desire to return to a time prior to her illness. Two prominent features of the tale must be analyzed in order to comprehend the significance of the narrator's

---

37 Cristina Fernández Cubas, "Los altillos de Brumal" in *Mi hermana Elba y Los altillos de Brumal*. (Barcelona: Tusquets, 1988. 155-187), 155.

illness and its association to Brumal. The first salient feature to be analyzed is the inverted or mirror image. Mirror images, representative of the narrator's narcissism, consume and dominate Adriana. The second salient feature to be examined is the primacy Adriana assigns to images associated with childhood games and game playing. As in "Mi hermana Elba," these games become linked as much to childhood memory as to the myth of childhood innocence. Play points to transgressive activity associated with her desire to break free from her mother's controlling, narcissistic gaze, a gaze that Adriana has internalized. Learning to turn this gaze back on itself, effectively mirroring and then inverting her mother's destructive visions, Adriana comes to recognize her own autonomy. This action at once liberates her from her mother's shadow and allows her to realize a self that has been psychologically and socially limited in scope.

Coating a flat glass on one side with aluminum or silver produces a mirror. When light falls on an object placed before a mirror, some of the light is reflected, some is absorbed and some is conducted through the object's body. For a mirror to work well, it must absorb and transmit as little light as possible while still reflecting as much light as possible. Images viewed in the mirror are made by waves of light that do not come from where the image seems to be. Rather, the image viewed, an inverse representation of the object reflected, is virtual. Virtual images, then, while generally interpreted as reflecting and reproducing xternal reality, also serve to remind the reader of the mirror's power of inversion. Mirrors shatter and divide the objects they reflect.

This denotative description of a mirror's function facilitates a discussion of what psychoanalysis has called narcissism; and while many analysts have developed theories with regard to the cause and progression of narcissistic behaviors, Heinz Kohut's model is particularly appropriate in the analysis of Fernández Cubas's tale.³⁸ For Kohut, the process of mirror transference signifies a period during which a mother's responses and reactions to her child reflect, echo, show admiration for, and affirm the child's value. Through this mother-child interaction, the infant develops a "grandiose self" that ultimatley allows him or her to experience the normal developmental processes that lead to a capacity for the pursuit of goals, positive self-esteem, and the development of a matrue, cohesive self.³⁹ Thus, contrary to what one might think, the early grandiose fantasies of a child do not contribute to narcissistic pathology but rather are phase-appropriate and adaptive. According to Kohut, under optimal conditions, a child who both merges with and idealizes his caregiver, eventually experiences gradual disappointment. As the child's image of the primary object (also termed the primary caregiver) becomes increasingly realistic, there is a natural withdrawl of the narcissistic idealizing, and ultimately, the child develops the internal psychological structures necessary to be independent.

But what occurs if a child does not see herself reflected in her mother's eyes? What if a mother refuses to value, comfort, and pronounce her acceptance and confidence in her child? According to Kohut, if a child's relationship with its primary care giver—generally the mother—does not include such mirroring, then the child experiences object hunger.⁴⁰ She never acquires the internal psychological structures necessary to develop, her "psyche remains focused on an

---

38 Among those who have discussed the pathology of narcissism are: Sigmund Freud, Melanie Klein, Otto Kernberg, D.W. Winnicott, Michael Balint, R.D. Laing, Jacques Lacan, and Julia Kristeva.

39 Heinz Kohut, *The Search for the Self: Selected Writings of Heinz Kohut: 1950-1978*. Vol I & II (New York: International UP, 1978), 737-770.

40 I have used the subject pronoun "she" in my example of what might happen to a child who does not receive proper mirroring. However both male and female children are equally subject to the effects that stem from such maladaptive situations. Likewise, while I have characterized the primary care giver as the mother in my description of the mirroring that goes on between mother and child, a father may be equally idealized as a child's primary care giver.

archaic object imago, and the personality will later, and throughout life, be intensely dependent on certain objects."[41] Complicating matters, Kohut suggests that a parent's own psychological troubles may significantly contribute to a child's irregular development. In the case of pathological narcissism, if the primary care giver suffers from narcissism, this psychological disturbance may not be palpable to others. Often narcissistic parents give the impression of being very close to their children. However, the closeness they demonstrate generally represents a merger between parent and child. Though these parents seem close to their children, they are unable to respond to their child's phase appropriate needs because they themselves are unable to fulfill their own needs. Thus they increasingly view their children as extentions of themselves, as capable of satisfying self-lack.[42] They look to their children to fulfill the goals and fantasies they have not been able to fulfill.

So it is in "Los altillos de Brumal": lost in inversion, never seeing herself reflected in her mother's eyes, Adriana becomes a prisoner of such faulty reflections. Caught between deceptive mirror images, images that play with her perception of herself and the world in which she lives, she remains dislocated from the very system of social signification that informs her world.

Adriana initially describes her mother as an austere and unhappy woman obsessed with dreams of a better life:

> La recuerdo a menudo silenciosa, enfrascada en oscuros pensamientos que nunca quiso compartir, santiguándose a la menor ocasión, gimiendo sola en su alcoba hasta que las luces del alba terminaran por vencer su persistente incapacidad de conciliar el sueño. Nunca fue demasiado cariñosa conmigo, pero yo sabía que,

---

41 Paul H. Ornstein, "Introduction," *The Search for the Self: Selected Writings of Heinz Kohut: 1950-1978*. Vol I & II (New York: International UP, 1978. 1-106), 57.

42 Heinz Kohut, *The Restoration of the Self* (New York: International UP, 1977), 274.

a su manera, me amaba. Todo en ella era privacidad y secreto.⁴³

This profoundly telling characterization serves as a point of departure to discuss Adriana's mother as a narcissistic, authoritative maternal figure. Anxious, unable to sleep, and absorbed in dark thoughts she is unwilling to share, she habitually recurs to a higher power in the hopes of attaining a better life. She demonstrates belief in a transcendant God by blessing herself over and over again. Yet when Adriana momentarily disrupts this description of her mother to talk about how she saw herself within her mother's world, she implies that her mother's untold desires and prayers were so overwhelming that they overshadowed her. Depicting her mother as less than affectionate yet loving in her own way, Adriana insinuates that her mother's devotion to God and silent sufferings are symptoms of pathological narcissism. The anxiety she demonstrates and the prayers she mutters while blessing herself become emblematic of an ethic of self-sacrifice employed so that she may be symbolically "redeemed" and realize the fantasies she has associated with being a "good object."⁴⁴

Thus, though Adriana depicts her mother as loving in her own way—*a su manera*—this love does not include her mother's approving gaze nor does it include articulated support for Adriana. Since her mother does not fulfill her mirroring needs, Adriana attempts to please her mother. She hints that by performing in ways that might please her—fulfilling her mother's goals and fantasies—she might gain her acceptance and satisfy the lack she feels. Adriana expresses this saying:

---

43 Cristina Fernández Cubas, "Brumal," 158.
44 Such religious idealizations and demonstrations of martyrdom are common in people who suffer from narcissistic personality disorder. Kohut's *The Analysis of the Self: A Systematic Approach to the Psychoanalytic Treatment of Narcissistic Personality Disorders* is especially helpful in describing the link between this pathology and religion.

> Sabía que me quería y, aunque nunca pude cruzar el umbral de su atromentado mundo, intenté en todo momento crorresponderle con mi cariño. La ayudaba en los trabajos de la casa, devanaba madejas, o bordaba, con la major voluntad, una esquina cualquiera de las labores en las que ocupaba su tiempo.[45]

Adriana's reaction to her mother's seeming indifference shows the lengths to which a child will go in order to gain a parent's attention and acceptance. Even when she is clearly not "seen" by her mother, she attempts to do things that will incite a response from her mother or grab her mother's attention:

> Aguanté con paciencia el lento desfilar de las horas, me resguardé en el silencio y, en el recreo, me mantuve al margen, observando juegos, intentando memorizar canciones. Al llegar a casa, mentí.
> —Ha sido estupendo—dije.
> Madre no levantó los ojos del bastidor y siguió bordando con exquisita delicadeza.[46]

Adriana performs an act that implicitly exhibits a desire to be like her mother. Psychologically merged with her mother, she projects and repeats the same gestures that serve to characterize her mother as silent, isolated. Yet given the total indifference with which her mother greets Adriana on her arrival from school—Adriana addresses her mother but receives no observable response—her attempt seems entirely ineffective. That her mother continues working on embroidery rather than acknowledging her daughter's presence suggests an inattention to the child that screams of maternal negligence.

Still, as the narrative progresses, it becomes clear that Adriana's

---

45 Cristina Fernández Cubas, "Brumal," 158-159.
46 Ibid., 157-158.

presence is not wholly unaffirmed. Her mother's reliance on Adriana's existence as an object outside herself becomes acutely palpable as she, time and again, realizes many of the goals that her mother could not attain. It is only on her mother's death, coincidentally occurring on the day of Adriana's graduation from university—a goal her mother insisted she accomplish—that the narrator affirms experiencing an initial break with the powerfully austere image her mother presents, "Acababa de obtener mi Licenciatura, y Madre, como si nada le atase ya a este mundo, se entregó a un dulce sueño del que jamás despertó. Retrasé con excusas el momento de cerrar la caja. Nunca, en vida, su rostro me había parecido tan hermoso."[47] Looking at her dead mother's face, Adriana perceives her as finally at peace. She describes her mother as smiling, looking more beautiful than she had ever looked in life. Perhaps in some sense the smile evidences the mother's approval of Adriana. However, as a narcissistic mother, this admiration is not of Adriana as an autonomous individual, but of Adriana understood as an extention of the mother. She has, after all, attained through Adriana one of the dreams she herself was not able to fulfill.

In many ways, her mother's death liberates Adriana. No longer needing to perform in ways that might make her the object of her mother's omnipotent yet reluctant gaze, the reader assumes Adriana will begin to act in ways she could not before. This understanding is further advanced through Adriana's own admission, "Mientras viví junto a ella, acaté sus caprichos, y Madre, en su simplicidad, confundió mi auténtico amor filial con el triunfo de una voluntad que a ratos yo no comprendía y a ratos admiraba."[48] Adriana links this largely emotive, psychological reaction to past and future performative activies and denotes a break between imposed and independent behaviors. Forsaking the dreams her mother had forced on her—her wish to have

---

47 Ibid., 161.
48 Ibid., 162.

Adriana study medicine, law, or letters—Adriana rebelliously and independently participates in those activities from which she was previously prohibited.

This freedom may be dually associated with the elimination of a sense of debt the narrator feels towards her mother. Abandoning the house of her youth and pledging to make her own way after her mother's death, she affirms: "No me molesté en solicitar una plaza de profesora de escuela, como hicieron muchas de mis compañeras, ni en conseguir un puesto en la edición de alguna enciclopedia. Mis habilidades eran otras y, cancelada la deuda con mi madre, a ellas me entregué con toda mi energía."[49] In my chapter discussing Riera's narratives, the notion of a debt owed to a primordial mother figure pointed to a symbolic lost genealogy of women; a history of women covered over by Western patriarchal traditions. Making this claim, I noted that it is only by reclaiming this lost genealogy that the daughters of this primordial mother might learn to relate to and value each other as subjects. Likewise, Adriana's conscious decision to relinquish any sense of debt to her mother and to devote herself to developing her own creative abilities may be linked with an implicit longing not to liberate herself from this mythic, primordial genealogy, but rather from the influence of a real mother whose narcissistic values and aspirations aligned her with a history that would not have allowed Adriana to function as an independent agent. This disengagement results in Adriana's search to find fulfillment as a culinary expert, cookbook writer, and host of a radio talk show. While such activities and interests ironically align her with traditionally feminine role models, figures her mother would have resolutely rejected, these creative positions allow Adriana to explore the psychologically fragmented world of the false self that she has developed and to ultimately achieve an authentic self.[50]

---

49 Ibid., 161.

50 For definitions and descriptions of the creation of a "false self" in the "used child"—the child who fulfills the desires of a narcissistic parent—see Stephen M.

Thus from Adriana's gesture to liberate herself from her mother's negative influence follows a narrative rupture that distinguishes the preceding somber, nostalgic tone from the subsequent fantastic, whimsical style. While examining a number of prepared food items, the recipes of which fans of her radio talk show have sent for inclusion in a cookbook she is editing, Adriana stumbles across a curious jar of strawberry-flavored preserves. She strains to make out the faded letters on the jar's label and, reading the word "BRUMAL," she tastes the marmalade. This consumption—which may in itself symbolize the way Adriana has shifted her mirroring needs from the visual to the oral—triggers a sudden proustian recuperation of past memory.[51] In effect, though the preceding section of the narrative delineates an austere, largely negative relationship with a mother who failed to mirror and emotionally nourish her daughter due to her own narcissistic pathology, eating the marmalade propels Adriana to remember an early, fanciful time of her youth, "Leí: 'BRUMAL'. Y al instante me sentí muy pequeña, y también muy alta, inmensamente feliz y desesperadamente desgraciada [...]."[52] The thoughts and feelings that flow from Adriana's ensuing stream of conscious narration suggest a profound psychological attachment linking her present experience of herself with past maternal lack. For while she remembers her mother constantly repeating, "*Huimos de la miseria*," in referring to their escape from Brumal, it is to this exotically appealing yet seemingly impoverished place that Adriana wishes to return.[53] This return to Brumal is representative of the

---

Johnson's *Humanizing the Narcissistic Style* (New York: W.W. Norton, 1987).

51 It is not all too uncommon for one, having once been deprived of visual mirroring, to satisfy object hunger by other means. Adolescent and adult on-set eating disorders, as well as alcohol and drug absue have been linked to narcissistic personality disorder. A range of narcissistic psychosomatic disorders have been delineated by Richard D. Chessick in his *Psychology of the Self and the Treatment of Narcissism* (Northvale, NJ: Aronson, 1985)

52 Cristina Fernández Cubas, "Brumal" 165.

53 Ibid., 157.

desire to return to a nurturing place, a place where she might finally experience the positive mirroring she needed as a child and by symbolically "reborn."

The conflicting images presented of Brumal as both an impoverished and marvelous place grow confusing when Adriana, inspired by the marmalade, decides to make a trip to this place. She arrives at the town's outskirts only to find that hardly anyone can tell her anything about it. Inhabitants of the area remain silent or simply shrug in reply to her inquiries. When she meets one old man willing to talk about Brumal, the only information he can positively assert is that the town can be found at some distance from the sea. On finally reaching Brumal, Adriana becomes increasingly disconcerted since the only other person she sees in the town, a little old man sitting alone on a bench in the town's desolate plaza, sits silently smoking a cigarette. Discouraged with her findings and the conditions of the town, Adriana sits next to the lold man, lights up a cigarette and thinks, "nunca debí regresar a aquel lugar odioso."[54]

Nonetheless, the austerity within which Adriana inscribes Brumal ruptures when a ball suddenly rolls across the ground before her. This moment serves as a narrative break separating the sterility of the previous scenes from the realm of subsequent ludic scenes, "Un balón de juguete rodó hasta mis pies. Lo alcé y miré en mi entorno, pero ningún niño vino a recogerlo."[55] Both narrator and reader hesitate at this detail since Adriana has previously specified that she sees no children in Brumal, and since no one—save the little old man—appears to inhabit the town. The unexpected and inexplicable appearance of the ball, a consummate icon representative of play, not only indicates a psychological return to childhood, but also the unconscious desire to confront the trauma of having never experienced mirroring as a child.

---

54 Ibid., 171.
55 Ibid., 171-172.

This interpretation of the ball, emerging from knowledge of Jungian archetypes and symbols, suggests that circular motifs and spheres are directly associated with perfection of form and wholeness in being.[56] Indeed, it is on seeing the ball roll infront of her that she decides to take decisive action: she gets up from the bench, walks across Brumal's plaza to the town's church.

Adriana's passage from the plaza to the church culminates not in a religious experience as might be expected, but in her entrance into multiple private spaces that serve as protective frames associated with excessive consumption, mirror (inverted) images and, ultimately, the recovery of self. Entering the seemingly empty church, she approaches the main alter and finds a book, presumably a bible, inscribed with the names of Brumal's parishioners, including her father's name. Adriana senses someone watching her, "No pude responder. La silueta acababa de ponerse en pie y se dirigía hacia mí a grandes zancadas. —Soy el párroco." Leaving together after this brief meeting, the priest invites Adriana to his house, an untidy, disorganized place, for what she thinks will be some friendly conversation and drinks, "Pensé que necesitaba beber algo. Pero ya el cura, adivinando mis deseos, se me había adelantado. Sirvió dos copitas de aguardiente de fresa. Apuré la mía de un sorbo."[57] While the priest's offer of drink may be viewed as a hospitable gesture meant to welcome Adriana into the community, the significance of alcohol lends symbolic depth to the narrative. Cirlot clarifies in his *Dictionary of Symbols* that "alcohol," deriving from the words, "aqua vitae" (fire-water), is a symbol "of the *coincidentia oppositorum*, the conjunction of opposites, where two principles, one of them active, the other passive, come together in a fluid and shifting, creative/destruc-

---

56 Mario Jacoby, *Individuation and Narcissism: The Psychology of the Self in Jung and Kohut* (Trans. Myron Gubitz and Françoise O'Kane. New York: Routledge, 1985),143.

57 Cristina Fernández Cubas, "Brumal," 174.

tive relationship."⁵⁸ This imagery is even more patent in the Fernández Cubas's tale since the drink the priest and Adriana share, *aguardiente*, literally translates as "water-fire" (agua ardiente). In as much as this symbolism communicates the conjunction of opposites, Adriana's consumption of alcohol, like her consumption of marmalade, represents the inversion of images. Wanting of maternal nurturance and having had to suppress her own needs for as long as her mother imposed her own desires on her, Adriana's alcoholic consumption communicates a figurative desire not only to recuperate the past, but also to make up for the lack she suffered at the hands of a narcissistic mother, one who would not accept her daughter's independence but treated her as an extension of herself. Her ensuing discussion of childhood memories underscores this possible interpretation:

> El párroco se apresuró a rellenarme la copa. El antiguo desconcierto se había convertido en euforia. Creí llegado el momento de agradecerle su hospitalidad y empecé a hablar. Hablé durante largo rato: horas quizá. Hablé de mi padre, recordé la tía Rebeca e intenté recuperar los rostros de las amigas del desaparecido colegio.⁵⁹

Adriana consumes the brandy, literally internalizing the conjunction of opposites that it symbolizes. As she does this, she is psychologically transported to another time, her childhood, where she re-experiences memories of those who surrounded her in her youth.

Still under the influence of the brandy, Adriana agrees to visit the priest's "altillo," after he tells her that it is there that she will find what originally compelled her to travel to Brumal, strawberry-flavored marmalade, "'No puede marcharse ahora sin ver antes lo que le interesa. Mermelada de *fresa* [...]'—y subrayó la última palabra con una

---

58 Juan Eduardo Cirlot, *A Dictionary of Symbols* (Trans. Jack Sage. New York: Dorset P, 1991), 8.
59 Cristina Fernández Cubas, "Brumal," 175.

sonrisa."⁶⁰ Yet rather than find marmalade in the attic, she finds something quite different:

> Era una estancia espaciosa y, al contrario de todo lo que había contemplado hasta entonces, extremadamente ordenada y limpia. Un infiernillo de alcohol ocupaba una mesa central rodeado de ollas, tarros y marmitas. Las paredes estaban cubiertas de anaqueles. En algunos había libros. En la mayoría, pomos minúsculos, vasijas de barro, tinajillas mohosas sin inscripciones ni leyendas.⁶¹

In contrast to the rest of the house, Adriana finds the attic organized and clean. The pots, pans, casserole dishes and jars she observes, like the alcohol, may again indicate an underlying symbolic desire to produce (cook) and consume (eat) in order to compensate for the object hunger she suffered as a child.

Yet apart from the fact that the priest apparently lies to Adriana—telling her she will find strawberry marmalade—in order to coax her into exploring the attic, what most strikes the reader is the way this passage dialogues with Gaston Bachelard's *The Poetics of Space*.⁶² According to Bachelard, many people revisit the house of their youth in dreams because of the house's maternal characteristics. He suggests that the enclosed spaces of houses, like the mother's body, inscribe themselves on the individual.⁶³ Moreover, Bachelard proposes that houses are popular images in dreams and that, in them, one often drifts "into the *intoxication of inverting* [emphasis mine], daydreams and reality."⁶⁴ Adriana's description of the attic thus precisely repeats

---

60 Ibid., 176.
61 Ibid., 177.
62 Gaston Bachelard treats the psycho-symbolic representations of the house in *The Poetics of Space* (Trans. Maria Jolas. Boston: Beacon, 1994).
63 Gaston Bachelard, *Poetics*, 8.
64 Ibid., 34.

Bachelard's proposition in that the attic, filled with objects used to cook and associated with the strawberry-flavored marmalade, may be figuratively connected to the maternal body, nurturance, and the fulfillment of mirroring need. In effect, the protective frame of Brumal's *altillo* provides Adriana a place where she not only comes to grips with the loss and lack of nurturance she experienced as a child, but where she also might have the opportunity to invert those memories, and thus begin to unmask her "real self."

Nowhere is this thematic inversion of memory more apparent than in a scene where Adriana, still in the protective frame of the attic, vividly remembers herself as a child in Brumal. She recalls playing with other children: bathing in the plaza's fountain, wallowing in the cracked, muddy earth of the town and later walking over that same earth with bare feet:

> Otnas Sen reiv se yo-h
> Sotreum sol ed a-íd
> Y yo de pronto conocía la respuesta. Sin ningún esfuerzo podía replicar:
> Sabmut sal neib arre-ic
> Ort ned nedeuq es e-uq
> No necesitaba implorar ¿raguj siajed em? ¿raguj siajed em? [...] porque formaba parte de sus juegos. Me estaban esperando y me llamaban: Anairda[...]. Anairda[...] '¡Sí!', grité. "¡Estoy aquí!" Y me apoyé en el alféizar de la ventana.[65]

The lyrics she remembers her friends singing during this time are anagrams that call to mind Lewis Carroll's *Through The Looking Glass*. They particularly mimic a scene in Carroll's narrative where Alice, shortly arrived in the Looking-glass house, attempts to read a book

---

[65] Cristina Fernández Cubas, "Brumal," 178-179.

she finds lying on a table. While turning the book's pages she exclaims that she cannot read it, "—for it's all in a language I don't know."[66] Alice soon realizes that the book is a "Looking-glass book," and that if she simply holds it up to a mirror, the words will read from left to right and she will be able to understand it. Yet when Alice does this, the words she reads remain unintelligible. These words, the verses of "Jabberwocky," are largely meant to be playfully inventive, not determined or interpretable in any fixed manner. Yet in Fernández Cubas's Brumal, the anagrammed words the children sing ("hoy es Viernes Santo/ día de los Muertos") and the similarly anagrammed words with which Adriana replies ("cierra bien las Tumbas, que se queden dentro") convey a chilling reality on multiple levels. First, in referring to Good Friday, the day marking the crucifixion, they thematically foreground death and coincidentally remind the reader that Adriana's mother is now dead. Second, Adriana's final statement ("¿me dejais jugar? ¿me dejais jugar?") reminds the reader of her memories of being marginalized in play. In a very concrete way, she remembers what it was like to have to stand on the margins of play.

Yet on another level, the protective frame of the attic combined with the church, the figure of the priest, symbols of satisfying lack through consumption (the marmalade and alchohol), and finally the image of Adriana watching other children at play, suggest what Kohut refers to as a "self-state dream" experience. These types of dreams try to link nonverbal tensions of traumatic states with verbalizable dream-imagery.[67] Adriana's trip to the impoverished yet magical land of Brumal thus seems to culminate in the manifestation of a latent desire to protect herself from her narcisstic mother's power by merging with an archaic idealized parent imago—God. That is, in mentioning the girls singing about Good Friday and in wanting to join the group in play

---

66 Lewis Carroll, *Through The Looking Glass* (New York: Random House, 1965), 95.

67 Heinz Kohut, *Restoration*, 109.

implies a desire to be absorbed and figuratively reborn. In a metaphorical sense, the merger fantasy can be understood as partially stemming from Adriana's idealization of her real father, a man she never really knew. Since her father died early in her childhood—a fact she mentions only in passing—one might suggest that Adriana felt not only deprived of mirroring from her mother, but totally deprived of a father. By creating this fantasy, she thus overcompensates for these losses.

What makes the self-state dream interpretation of Adriana's experience in Brumal possible is that the reader never finds out whether Adriana's trip ever really took place, as she subsequently declares, "Pero todo había sido efímera ilusión."[68] The ball that rolls before her, the inverted images that capture the reader's attention and Adriana's memories of being excluded from childhood play, like Carroll's nonsense poem, remain not wholly decipherable. Like Alice who exclaims, "Somehow it ["Jabberwocky"] seems to fill my head with ideas—only I don't exactly know what they are!" the reader wonders exactly how to make sense of Fernández Cubas's story[69]. The only thing one can be sure of is the playfully transgressive agency of the narrator, for as Adriana retrospectively affirms on her return home:

> Nadie sabía de dónde venía ni adónde pensaba dirigirme, y las escasas frases que logré balbucear fueron tachadas de desvaríos y alucinaciones. Existía una única evidencia. Mi garganta rezumaba aguardiente, y ese simple detalle, a los ojos de aquellos médicos, explicaba sobradamente lo inexplicable.[70]

Adriana's ultimate act of defiance, which closely follows her assertion that excessive consumption of alcohol may have played a part in her ludic, fantastic experience of Brumal and the attic is closely preced-

---

68 Cristina Fernández Cubas, "Brumal," 179.
69 Lewis Carroll, *Looking Glass*, 96.
70 Cristina Fernández Cubas, "Brumal," 181.

ed by her decision to make a final break with the memory of a destructive mother. Though no longer amongst the living, Adriana's mother's gaze continues to fall on her, not only in dreams, but also during her waking hours. From a portrait hanging on one of the narrator's apartment walls, her mother's eyes seem to follow Adriana: "Pero sus ojos me perseguían a lo largo y ancho de la casa, me taladraban la espalda cuando yo intentaba ignorarlos, me conminaban a permanecer inmóvil sobre las frías baldosas, obediente a lejanas máximas y consejos."[71] The symbolically notable verb "perseguir," which not only means, "to pursue" but also "to persecute," significantly shapes the interpretation of the meeting of these gazes. The spectral mother's eyes do not simply threaten Adriana to remain immobile, figuratively under her control, but also punish her for her insolence in gazing back. Yet rather than bow to her mother's status, Adriana splits with her by simply inverting and turning her mother's gaze on itself. Looking at the painting, she verbally censures her mother—"'¡Estúpida!', grité"—and then erupts with laughter. No longer willing to live according to her mother's negative image, Adriana defiantly lays her mother's memory to rest, "Por eso te miraba por última vez, venciendo la aversión que me provocaban tus desabridos ojos verdes, y, con un carbón encendido, marcaba sobre tu rostro tres cruces negras. Ahora, por fin, Madre, estás muerta y enterrada."[72]

Following this, Adriana renounces her given name, and renames herself once and for all Anairda—the anagram of Adriana—the name she remembers calling herself as a child in Brumal. This change in name, another playful rupture of language, along with the narrator's final return to the protective frame of Brumal, represent a penetration of the figurative mirror image that she has had to confront and combat in real life as well as in dreams:

---

71 Ibid., 185-186.
72 Ibid., 187.

> Porque Adriana dejaba de existir aquí, en este preciso instante, mientras una feliz Anairda bajaba presurosa las escaleras, se dirigía a la estación, pronunciaba por última vez el nombre de la odiosa localidad de mar, montaba en el tren y, recostada en su butaca, indiferente a los demás viajeros del vagón, se entregaba a dulces sueños recordando que, al mediodía, es ya de noche en Brumal.[73]

Bounding down the stairs on her way to the train station, Anairda, taking Adriana's place, demonstrates a reversal in existential thought. She emphasizes this change by talking about herself in the third person. Through this syntactic split she distances herself from her(self) and underscores a feeling of being reborn. The third-person narrative voice that speaks as and for Anairda affirms that she will not perform as an extension of her mother and that she will not feel ashamed for not fulfilling her mother's narcissistic needs. Acting on this impulse, she heads to a train station where she will begin another journey to Brumal. Anairda/Adriana literally and figuratively surrenders herself to this land: a place of painful yet liberating mirror images and play. The narrator thus transgresses the indissoluble specular plane separating reality from fantasy (separating object from reflected object), metaphorically buring herself in the psychologically protective frame of Brumal, only to be figuratively reborn.

In the end, perhaps Adriana's most transgressive act is showing how "acting like a woman"— finding fulfillment in cooking and having a penchant for other stereotypically "feminine" activities—is ultimately for her more authentic than trying to play a role for which she is badly suited. Adriana communicates as much while remembering her mother:

---

73 Ibid.

De poco te sirvió eliminar un sutil personaje de las historias de hadas y prodigios que me contabas de pequeña, porque ese personaje maldito estaba en mí, en tu querida y adorada Adriana, arrancada vilmente de su mundo, obligada a compartir tu mediocridad, privada de una de las caras de la vida a la que tenía acceso por derecho propio. La cara más sabrosa, la incomparable.[74]

She now clearly suggests that her mother rejected her because she was too maternal and too feminine. Adriana was, in other words, paradoxically what her mother could not be for her daughter. Yet by boldly confronting the trauma she suffered as the child of a narcissistic mother and declaring how she feels, Adriana simultaneously subverts the conventional feminist view that a woman must "act like a man" to be valued in contemporary Western society. For, while she may have half-heartedly attempted to please her mother by doing precisely this in her youth, Adriana shows the reader that this did not and could not make her authentically happy. Her statement notably echoes Kohut's observation regarding the healthy development of children in *The Search for the Self*. According to him, parents' admiration and affirmation of both male and female offspring provides them with the security and idealizability they need to grow. Parents must "love a little girl as a little girl, in her sweetness, in her future bearing of children, in whatever potentials of her femininity she displays" just as they must unconditionally mirror and accept a boy as the boy he is to encourage individuation.[75] That Adriana goes back to Brumal in an attempt to rupture the limits of tradition underscores that she recognizes the value of self-authenticity and femininity as categories unique to the individual.

In "Mundo," from the collection of stories *Con Agatha en Estam-*

---

74 Ibid., 186.
75 Heinz Kohut, *Search*, 777.

bul, the narrator employs both protective frames and mirror images, combining narrative characteristics found in "Mi hermana Elba" and "Los altillos de Brumal." Like "Mi hermana Elba" and "Los altillos de Brumal," the first person narrator of "Mundo," Carolina, is a woman looking back on her youth and adulthood. As in "Los altillos de Brumal," where a priest facilitates Adriana's/Anairda's journey, the religious life takes on a certain significance in "Mundo," since Carolina becomes a member of a religious order and lives in a convent, a place traditionally associated with severity and restriction. Likewise, the convent has long been associated with feminine passivity since it represents surrender to the rules and regulations of religious life. This is not to say that one should dismiss Carolina as a less playful figure than the previously described protagonists. We have already witnessed the religious boarding school as a locus of transgressive activities in "Mi hermana Elba." What's more, if "Mi hermana Elba" and "Los altillos de Brumal" serve as points of departure for a discussion of the importance of childhood play in the development of feminine subjectivity, "Mundo" serves as a point of departure for a discussion of the way in which Fernández Cubas de-stabilizes familial terms in her stories, re-writing what it means to be a feminine agent. For her, it appears that play between women in close relationship with each other—mothers, daughters and sisters—assists in the re-writing and re-negotiation of these gendered categories.

Although unclear at the story's onset, Carolina enters the convent as a form of punishment. Having been the cause of her mother's death in childbirth, her alcoholic father forces Carolina to surrender herself to the sisters' supervision and to enter the religious order on the grounds that she has been involved in a sexual relationship with one of his hired hands. Though she plainly denies having had such a relationship, Carolina's father leaves her no alternative:

> Mi padre había apalabrado hasta el último detalle. [El chofer]

[m]e conduciría a mi destino, acarrearía el equipaje a través del jardín hasta el portón de madera y entonces, podía volver al coche y regresar al pueblo. Y aunque al principio el chófer protestó—se necesitaba por lo menos dos hombres para mover la pesada carga—el tintineo de unas monedas primero y un expectante silencio después—el momento, imagino, en que mi padres tras rebuscar en sus bolsillos daba al fin con uno de esos billetes que por las noches gustaba de contar, doblar, desdoblar o mirar el trasluz—terminaron por disipar sus reticencias.[76]

The narrator's account of her father's plan indicates that, for him, Carolina is nothing more than a commodity to be bought, sold, or traded. She has no identity of her own and is not consulted with regards to her destiny precisely due to this lack of self. Despite the fact that she herself is treated as a commodity, she brings only two material items with her on this life-changing journey: a chest engraved with regressive images (a sailor with his back to a ship that in turn holds an image of a sailor with his back to a ship) and her mother's wedding dress. As we shall see, these items draw attention both to an intimate relationship between the visual image and language as well as to the ability of these to re-create mother/sister substitutes, surrogates that Carolina must have if she is to become an autonomous female agent in her own right.

Carolina's entrance into the convent literally and metaphorically signifies a passage to a protective frame, an inner world where she will be free to act independently. Though this declaration might seem to fly in the face of reason—convents prominently figure as symbols of religious austerity and asceticism—for Carolina, the convent's space marks the limits of a new found playground. The way Carolina de-

---

76 Cristina Fernández Cubas, "Mundo" in *Con Agatha en Estambul* (Barcelona: Tusquets, 1994. 11-72), 13.

scribes her arrival to the convent makes this interpretation possible. On being dropped off by the chauffeur her father hired to transport her there, she recalls:

> Pero no tuve tiempo de preguntarme nada. De admirarme de que las verjas herrumbrosas pudieran hablar o de atribuir al calor una ilusión de los sentidos. Enseguida la despedida que me espetaba la cancela se mezcló con el saludo que una voz, desde lo alto, se empeñaba en repetir, y al que yo contesté con una frase aprendida.[77]

The rusty, iron-gate marks the boundary that separates the base, secular world from the peaceful, spiritual world of the convent. The gate literally and metaphorically stands as a threshold between worlds. As Cirlot points out, a threshold oftentimes represents "transition and transcendence" as well as "the reconciliation and the separation of the two worlds of the profane and the sacred."[78] If Carolina begins her convent life with only words she has learned from others on the outside, the convent designates a space wherein she will learn to uniquely express herself as she builds relationships with other women, women to whom she not so coincidentally refers to as "mothers" and "sisters." Carolina accentuates this symbolic interpretation when she responds to the abbess, madre Angélica who, in turn, refers to Carolina as her "hija." When the abbess inquires as to how Carolina has managed to pack so lightly, she tells madre Angélica, "'Afuera' [...] 'he dejado el mundo.'"[79] This declaration strikes a chord with the abbess since she assumes Carolina's reference to a "mundo" alludes to the material world, a demonstration of the adolescent's desire to relinquish her attachments to the secular world as she surrenders to the spiritually grounded rules of the convent.

---

[77] Ibid., 15-16.
[78] Juan Eduardo Cirlot, *Dictionary*, 341.
[79] Cristina Fernández Cubas, "Mundo," 16.

Carolina's word choice, nonetheless, carries ludic significance. While it is true that the term "mundo" refers to the commonplace world, it also refers to the "mundo," or wooden chest, she carries with her to the convent. Madre Angélica quickly recognizes this word play, "'Hacía tanto tiempo que no escuchaba esa palabra, que por un momento pensé [...]'. Y se puso a reír. 'Nunca hubiera creído que los jóvenes de hoy usaran aún ese término.'"[80] The word play initiates the reader into an unusual playing field filled with similarly playful characters. Like madre Angélica, the sisters with whom Carolina comes into contact do not naively take words at face value. Reading the wor(l)d is complex, not only for Carolina, but for all of the convent's inhabitants. Carolina and the sisters constantly find themselves at odds with the wor(l)d. They recognize the indeterminate nature of language. Yet these women ultimately use language to their benefit. Through language, they transcend the categories of "mother" and "sister," defying convention and becoming women of their own making.

Nowhere is this inventive process more evident than in Carolina's relationship and dealings with madre Perú. This nun, who mysteriously arrives at the convent from the other side of the word, shares Carolina's interest in language. If Carolina often draws attention to her personal fascination through distinctive word choices (using the term "mundo" for the more common "baúl," for example), madre Perú's draws attention to language through her "pumpkin narratives," stories she carves on gourds from the convent garden:

> Y aunque yo no sabía del todo de qué se trataba—el arte extraño se llamaba 'burilar', me lo había dicho ella con su letra redonda—, sí sospechaba que no nos lo quería enseñar hasta que estuviera terminado, y que era ésa una forma de mostrarnos, ya que las palabras no le acompañaban, lo que era capaz de hacer. Y si en su país aquellos,

---

80 Ibid., 18.

fuera lo que fuera, se vendía, a lo mejor—y ahora en los ojos de la abadesa se encendió una pequeña chispa—, aquí podía ocurrir lo mismo.[81]

Though she has yet to see any of the stories the South American nun carves into her gourds, Carolina recognizes that madre Perú's continued welcome is contingent on her ability to contribute to the religious community's welfare. Carolina directly relates madre Perú's value as a member of the convent to her ability to provide the sisters with some viable means of income. Since madre Perú does not know how to embroider, like the other nuns, and since she cannot speak or hear, she must demonstrate some other talent to earn her keep and remain under the sisters' care. Once Carolina convinces madre Angélica that madre Perú might be able to do so, the abbess grants her the opportunity to stay and demonstrate her talent.

It is no coincidence that Carolina wishes to support madre Perú in her effort to remain at the convent. Just as Carolina is "traded" to the convent by her father and must earn her keep by yielding to the vows she takes, so too must madre Perú. As we shall see, however, the two share more common ground in that each finds her own agency and worth through language. For both, written and spoken words represent the creative production of self. Through their respective narratives, these women become able to define "sisterhood" and "motherhood" for themselves in multiple ways.

Nowhere is this ability more patent than in the telling and re-telling of the story of the convent's cats. According to Carolina, who overhears the story from other sisters, the problem began one day when a half-starved litter of kittens, hidden and carefully wrapped inside a basket, appeared in the convent's orchard. Thinking that the basket contained an offering from a devout member of the outside community, the nun

---

[81] Ibid., 45.

who worked in the orchard picked it up. According to the version of the story Carolina tells, the nun may have rescued the kittens because she saw them as a blessing, or she may have grown too attached to part with them, "Y como si aquello fuera una bendición, un signo del más allá destinado sólo a ella—o porque temía, quizá, que el cuidado de unos gatos no estuviera contemplado en la rigurosa regla—los bautizó en secreto, les dio un nombre, y desde entonces pasó a considerarlos como a unos hijos."[82] Compelled to be a "mother," to provide for these defenseless creatures, this sister fed the kittens from her own rations and became weaker as the kittens' appetites increased. The other sisters, who knew nothing of the cat-loving sister's self-sacrifice, viewed her declining health as indicative of "acedía," sourness, a common ailment among the sisters. This sickness, however, comes to be regarded as of secondary importance when the cats, forced by hunger, overrun the convent's kitchen to look for food, "Y mientras la monja enferma, postrada en la cama, seguía gritando en sueños el nombre de sus hijos y de la celda surgía un hedor insufrible, ellos, los hijos, no tardaron en registrar la llamada de su protectora y en acudir en torpel a los pies de su lecho."[83] The cats, finding the food their protector had hidden away for them, encounter the nun in a state of decomposition.

The tale becomes more gruesome as Carolina tells how additional litters found their way to the convent. While no one recalls how the sisters relieved themselves from caring for the first litter, Carolina reports that the convent's neighbors assumed that the sisters knew how to care for the cats; which increased the number of stray cats left at the convent. This in turn left the convent overrun with the animals:

Y en es transferencia desdichada de responsabilidades surgió de pronto la voz de una postulante. Madre Pequeña, la más joven de

---

82 Ibid., 31.
83 Ibid., 32.

la comunidad, casi una niña. Ella sabía cómo actuar, en su pueblo lo había visto muchas veces. A los gatos se les podía escaldar, envenenar o ahogar de una forma limpia, incruenta.[84]

If at once one sister acted out of maternal kindness to nurture and keep the cats, the sisters now become asassins, performing horrific and habitual "bloodless" acts by which to keep order within the convent. In itself, this description of events perverts the categories of "mother" and "sister." Rather than align maternal and sisterly relations with creation, productivity, collective sustenance and a sacred regard for life, these women align maternity and sisterhood with a feminine agency embracing bloody violence, death and destruction.

Madre Perú's pictorial re-telling of the same tale further subverts the agency assigned to these familial categories. Serving as the interpreter of madre Perú's pumpkin narratives, Carolina describes the visual images as follows, "Allí estaban los gatos, el bautismo, la madre cuidando de sus hijos, alimentándolos a escondidas; la enfermedad, su postración en el lecho. Y luego, el alboroto, el motín. La pobre monja cocinera caída en el suelo con los pies en alto [...]. Y aquí todas nos pusimos a reír."[85] Quite literally re-inscribing the tale told to her by Carolina onto the gourd, madre Perú further pushes the envelope with regards to definitions of "motherhood" and "sisterhood." Rather than inspire sadness or serious reflection with regards to the cat-loving nun's passing and madre Pequeña's cat-killing, the carvings evoke horror and the laughter of abjection. By "abjection," I refer to Kristeva's understanding of abjection as a psychic dis-ease and anxiety over those aspects of the self of which the individual cannot be rid, for example, blood, urine, feces, nails, and the corpse. Laughter is an extreme response to psychic worry. When the women see the prostrate body of

---

84   Ibid., 33.
85   Ibid., 46.

the dying sister, they are overtaken by horror. Their confrontation with this image of death reminds them of their own mortality.

What's more, just as the body reminds the women of the finality of their own lives, it reminds them that the boundaries that determine identity are frighteningly permeable. That is, their reaction to the body signals their own monstrous natures and draws attention to the innate desire to seek recognition by creating an identity of one's choosing in relation to the abject. Thus, when the women laugh in response to these pictures, their laughter signals the acknowlegment of a disturbance in identity as well as a recognition and desire to transcend whatever limits have existed with relation to the self. Indeed, it is no coincidence that the sisters begin to speak, disobeying their vows of silence, as madre Perú becomes more prolific in producing her carved narratives. They respond to her narratives by articulating their own experiences in relation to her texts, carving out, as it were, their own identities as sisters and mothers within the context of the convent.

Madre Perú's depiction of the cat story obliges the reader to consider the intricate relationship between the visual images of the gourd, the story being told, and how these work together to inform the women's roles within the tale. Perhaps one way of responding to this complex web is by suggesting that the emphasized visual and textual images ultimately subvert feminine agency as aligned with maternal passivity and celebrated idealization. Such agency is part and parcel of many legends that would have women perform according to narrow social scripts of permitted sexual behavior. Yet, as we have seen, these women will not be passively inserted into such legends:

> Y eso era exactamente lo que había ocurrido aquí. Ninguna de nosotras había conocido a la madre prohijadora de gatos ni era capaz tampoco, sin acudir a los archivos, de fijar con exactitud las fechas en que sucedieron los hechos citados. Con lo cual madre Perú no había hecho otra cosa que narrar una leyenda (la historia de las

primeras camadas de gatos era ya una leyenda).⁸⁶

Carolina points out that the story, part of an oral history, is nothing more than a "leyenda." The events told therein cannot be traced to a precise origin or date. One may assume, moreover, that those who hear the story in the future will continue to re-tell and, perhaps, embellish it.

Carolina's decision to stop defending madre Perú coincides with madre Angélica's realization that the South American nun's alibi regarding her transfer to the convent fail to substantiate information she has received in letters from a network of convents. As madre Perú's story unfolds, Carolina learns that the nun is not deaf or mute but the witness of a serious crime, "Porque ¿cuál había sido su delito, pobre madre Perú? Presenciar un crimen, un asesinato. Y huir. Verse obligada a escapar, correr de un lado a otro, refugiarse en conventos hasta que los verdaderos culpables la olvidaran. Alli estaba todo explicado."⁸⁷ If Carolina must enter the protective frame of the convent in order to foster her own individuation and identity as a female agent, madre Perú enters the convent in order to dissolve any sense of self and agency. The two thus become inverse images of each other. Nowhere is this inversion more evident than when Carolina narrates her final confrontation with madre Perú. The conflict between the two women occurs when, in attempting to save madre Perú from being denounced by the sisters or taken by the police, Carolina goes into her cell without first making her presence known. Carolina finds madre Perú gazing into a mirror, entranced in her own reflection. When she finally becomes aware of Carolina's presence, madre Perú grabs her rosary from around her neck:

---

86 Ibid., 48-49.
87 Ibid., 62.

"Mírate ya. Vieja revieja", gruñó aún. Y entonces por primera vez en mi vida, grité en silencio. Porque, aunque cerrase enseguida los ojos, aunque apretara ls párpados para no ver, hubo una fracción de segundo, apenas un instante, en que el azogue me devolvió un rostro arrugado, sorprendido, aterrado. Y aunque todavía no puedo explicarme cómo ocurrió, sí sé que de inmediato lo reconocí. Allí estaba ella. Su rostro olvidado. Allí estaba –¡otra vez! ¡Madre Pequeña![88]

The reader may interpret madre Perú's declaration and Carolina's reaction in several ways. On a first reading, the event may be interpreted as fantastic since Carolina reacts with hesitation. She cannot understand how the mirror could reflect madre Pequeña's image rather than her own. A second reading, however, recalls the image of the body on madre Perú's gourd. Unlike the sisters who respond to the image of the prostrate nun with laughter, Carolina responds with a silent scream. This scream represents another kind of limit to her agency as it has thus far been defined. If Carolina has become a narrator of tales, finding her own subjectivity by literally giving voice to madre Perú's narratives and articulating the stories of the convent's sisters, this scream conveys an unwillingness to passively continue telling their tales without interjecting her own. She embraces the abject—the image of her aged self, itself an image associated with mortality. With this, she submits to annihilating whatever self has existed to create her own identity as a sister, to write and re-write her own identity.

As Ruth Burke recalls in *The Games of Poetics: Ludic Criticism and Postmodern Fiction*, one of many purposes of mirror games—games of reflexivity—is the subversion of mimesis.[89] Through mirror play, an author may implicitly or explicitly question the autonomy of his/her

---

88 Ibid., 63-64.
89 Ruth Burke, *The Games of Poetics: Ludic Criticism and Postmodern Fiction* (New York: Peter Lang, 1994), 49.

narrative and comment on its existence as a work of art. In this case, the mirror image serves as a metaphor for ruptures in the visual and linguistic construction of self. Just as madre Perú's pumpkin narratives reveal a very real void between one's vision of the world and one's constructed, linguistic representation of the world, so too is their a void between Carolina's self-reflective envisioning and any linguistic construction of self that has previously existed. As the self-proclaimed youngest member of the convent, she feels threatened when new novitiates enter, "¿Eran acaso niñas? Volvíamos a los tiempos en que en los conventos (y lo había leído en los libros de la abadesa) se aceptaban niñas, se las instruía, aprendían a bordar, a escribir, educaban su voz en el coro de la iglesia, y luego salían al *siglo* y contraían matrimonio?"[90] Carolina's silent scream now represents the excess that goes beyond the temporal limits she has constructed for herself in language. The reflection she sees in madre Perú's mirror cannot be contained by language; her reflection transgresses the confines of narrative. It is precisely for this reason that I emphasize the word "siglo"—another pun—above. For, while the term "siglo" means "century," it is also a synonym for "world." Despite the fact Carolina may think of herself as a young person, it seems evident that time stopped for her when she stepped over the threshold separating the external world from the convent. And while new novitiates may have the freedom to stay or leave the convent as they please, Carolina seems to have missed out on this freedom.

As we have already seen, Fernández Cubas's narratives often draw attention to feminine agency as linked to tellings and re-tellings of stories. Such re-tellings are necessarily valuable in the re-negotiation of the terms "mother," "sister," and "daughter" in her works. Two of Fernández Cubas's more recent works, the novel *El columpio* (1995) and the hybrid narrative-drama *Hermanas de sangre* (1998) serve as powerful capstones to this reading of Fernández Cubas's writings. In

---

90 Cristina Fernández Cubas, "Mundo," 49.

both, the space normally occupied by the father as the head of a family or the male social gaze, is disrupted by playful, yet extremely aggressive female protagonists. In the case of El columpio, significant symbolic elements from the fairy-tale genre, along with allusions to play and play objects, help the un-named narrator not only recovers an unknown family history, but also salvages a particular history, that lived by her mother, Eloísa. As the narrator does this, so she too re-defines the relationship between mother and daughter. Hermanas de sangre, for its part, foregrounds theatre as a genre celebrating ritual and spectacle. In this work, Fernández Cubas'ss presents her audience with a number of female characters who take center stage to physically demonstrate the ways in which women claim narrative authority within a family's history. What is most clear is that, in both works, the author presents generations of women—mothers, daughters and sisters—as volatile agents who explode family dynamics via ever-shifting gender and genre roles.

A death precedes the re-telling of the family story in *El columpio*. The nameless twenty-five year old first person narrator begins her tale by telling the reader of a strong desire to travel from her native France to a small Spanish town nestled in the Pyrenees mountains, the place her mother, Eloísa, abandoned years earlier. There, she hopes to relive her mother's edenic childhood experiences and get to know the characters who populated her mother's stories, namely, her brothers, Lucas and Tomás, and cousin, Bebo. Collectively known as "the uncles," these men serve as the principle leads in Eloísa's family.

Though the narrator sends word telling of Eloísa's demise and of her own decision to travel by train to make their acquaintance, the men never receive this news. The narrator realizes this when no one comes to greet her at the train station. Increasingly aware that her uncles are removed from the town and all the trappings of town life, she notes that "la Casa de la Torre"—the uncles' home—is remote, located at a physical distance from the town center. The house and its inhabitants are temporally removed from town life: they resist collecting mail with any regularity (like the mail sent by Eloísa's daughter), refuse telephone service, and have not redecorated the house since before Eloísa abandoned it.

Once the narrator finally meets her uncles, they welcome her with open arms, toasting her with champagne. During her stay, the narrator not only becomes more familiar with her extended family but also with her mother and the roles she played within the family. Of most interest, she finds out that Eloísa had a great talent for playing with the diabolo, a toy made up of a wooden spool juggled, tossed, whirled, and balanced between two sticks connected by a long string. So adroit was Eloísa with the diabolo that it was purported that she had not only killed a rabid dog with it, but that she had attacked Bebo, leaving him with a scarred neck.

Though one might wonder why Eloísa would have attacked her cousin so viciously with the diabolo, we find the uncles collectively appear less and less hospitable towards their niece, suggesting the existence of a family dynamic that has never been welcoming of feminine agency. They ultimately shut her out of their lives when Tomás, in concert with Lucas and Bebo, packs her bags early and takes her to the train station, surprising her with a return ticket to Paris. The narrator refuses to return to Paris on principle, saying Tomás has forgotten to pack important items she wished to bring with her: Eloísa's letters to them, letters they had left unopened and unread in a secret drawer in her mother's room. Later that evening, Tomás brings her food and wine and explains, "Estamos acostumbrados a vivir solos y, como es natural, a lo largo de tantos años hemos generado una serie de hábitos. Algunos eneludibles. Hoy, por ejemplo, es viernes. Y el viernes, para nosotros, es un día sagrado, el día de la semana dedicado a despachar asuntos de familia."[91] The narrator, though nodding as if to show understanding,

---

91 Cristina Fernández Cubas, *Columpio* (Barcelona: Tusquets, 1995), 109.

not only suddenly realizes that she is not considered part of the family, but grows suspicious of Tomás, who will not leave her until she drinks the wine he has brought. She drinks the wine and promptly purges the drug-laced concoction once he has left. She escapes the unwelcoming house, pausing briefly to have one last look. As she spies into the dining room, she sees her uncles sitting around the dim light of the dining room table, speaking in each others' voices and mimicking the voice of none other than Eloísa.

The novela reaches its fantastic climax when the narrator, having taken flight on a rainy night, is stricken by an object. She screams in terror as she realizes that she has been stricken by her own mother returned from the dead as a child. Calling for her mother to stop the abuse, she finds a diabolo wrapped around her neck. The two characters share a moment in an indefinable zone outside time and space. Later, on her way back to Paris, the narrator realizes that her mother's "attack" was, in fact, not an attack but rather an attempt to save the narrator from the House of the Tower as well as its inhabitants, "Y les gustara o no a mis tres tíos, de poco había servido la gruesa llave con la que todos los viernes se encerraban a solas con sus fantasias. Yo había visto a mi madre. Y ella, desde su sueño, me había salvado la vida."[92] The spectral Eloísa returns from beyond the grave to keep her daughter from being re-cast in her roles within the family. Though the narrator does not specifically mention the roles Eloísa performed in this passage, she alludes to the saving merit of her mother's violent assault. This act of aggression ultimately represents a sacrificial movement meant to rescue the daughter from the uncles' "gruesa llave," the key that not only symbolizes a systematic pattern of exclusion that barred Eloísa from participating in the family's business, but that also symbolizes her decision to live freely, abandoning that system to live as an exile outside it.

---

92 Ibid., 136.

It is not coincidental that Eloísa's family lives in the House of the Tower. When the narrator first describes the house, she frames it within the context of the fairy tale genre as she recalls idyllic vignettes her mother told her about growing up in the house.

> Una casa grande rematada por un torreón. Allí, en el último ventanuco, debía de hallarse el desván, el cuarto de los juguetes, el arcón de los tesoros. Imaginé a mi madre probándose sombreros, disfrazándose, interpretando los papeles que Bebo, en las tardes de septiembre, escribía para los cuatro. Iban a ser actores, los mejores actores del mundo.[93]

At first glance, the House of the Tower appears to provide a bucolic refuge for the children in as much as it is a place where the three can safely create and imagine other worlds. A play room, with its toys and treasure chest filled with costumes, becomes the stage on which Bebo, the children's leader, will write scripts. There, the four play dress up and perform as they practice to become actors.

Despite the idyllic characterization of the house as sanctuary where the children may play, thereby facilitating their physical, emotional and psychological growth, the House of the Tower perpetuates a common motif of popular fairy tales wherein towers serve as phallic symbols, not only representing male authority within the family structure, but also quintessentially representing how that authority is intimately linked to power and the economic well-being of the family.[94] First implying this by saying she feels as if she grows smaller—

---

[93] Ibid., 20.

[94] In countless fairy tales, most notably the Grimms' "Rapunzel," princess's like the one in Fernández Cubas' story are essentially locked up in towers, large phallic structures that communicate an imbalance of power wherein one figurehead of authority imposes his/her will on another. Cognitive Psychologist George Lakoff more recently discussed this imagery in relation to the tragedy of September 11th,

symbolically less powerful—as she approaches the looming edifice, the narrator continues to support this interpretation when she recalls a story told to her by Eloísa:

> Una vez yo era una princesa cristiana y ellos, tus tíos, unos terribles sarracenos que me tenían presa. Me habían encerrado en lo alto de la torre y querían hacerme renegar de mi fe. Por un momento llegué a asustarme de verdad. Pero entonces Bebo, sin avisar a mis hermanos, cambió el argumento de la obra. Les envió a guardar las puertas de la mazmorra, se quitó los ropajes de moro, se puso una cruz y, allí mismo, en el desván, cuando nadie nos veía, me dio un beso.[95]

The story the narrator recounts repeats a common fairy tale plot wherein a strong male protagonist, in this case Bebo, the script writer, rescues a meek princess, Eloísa, who has been locked up in a tower.[96] In his role as Saracen turned Christian, Bebo schemes to outsmart his

---

2001. When the World Trade Center towers, symbols of phallic authority, collapsed, terrorists reinforced the idea of loss of power in our collective imaginations.

95   Cristina Fernández Cubas, *Columpio*, 21.

96   Eloísa recalls the fairy tale of Rapunzel in which a wicked witch catches a father steeling rampion from her garden to satisfy his pregnant wife's cravings. To punish him, she threatens to do the couple harm unless he agrees to surrender their unborn child to her. The witch, now an adoptive mother, cares for the child until, at the age of 12, she locks the girl up in a tower from which there is virtually no escape, just a small window. The witch does this to quash her adoptive daughter's growing sexual maturity and keep her from sexual predators. Nonetheless, a young Prince passing by hears the maiden singing and convinces her to let him visit by climbing up her long hair. The first visit leads to many more as the two eventually become lovers and agree to marry. When the witch finds out that the Maiden is pregnant, she sends her far from home. Later, when the witch, claiming to be the Maiden, convinces the Prince to climb up to the tower, he learns that she has banished her and, in distress, throws himself from tower's window, losing his eyesight. Years later, when the Maiden and Prince happen to meet again, she throws herself on him weeping, and her tears restore his eyesight. The two then make their way back to his kingdom where they lived happily ever after.

cousin-infidels. He re-writes the script to his advantage, enabling him to physically overcome the Christian princess with a kiss, forcibly conquering her and the territory represented by her body. As the primary script writer and figurehead among the children, Bebo fulfills his obligation as a male authority within the family dynamic.

Later the reader realizes that Bebo not only controls the scripts from which the family members read, but also attempts to control visual images of the family, "El reparto de papeles entre los tíos empezaba a parecerme claro. Bebo, el artista, el inventor."[97] He is their creator, an artistic director who manages and informs each one of the family members' performances. The narrator sustains this interpretation of Bebo, making countless allusions to the theatrical nature of the brothers. She says she gets the feeling that Lucas wears make-up and is "posiblemente el peor actor del mundo sobre un escenario" while, Tomás "en el estricto reparto de funciones...no controlaba su propia fuerza, tenía todas la[s] cartas para cargar con las culpas."[98] The narrator even sees herself becoming an actress among these actors, influenced and manipulated by them, "Yo me limitaba a sonreír, sin saber muy bien si en ese gran teatro se me había asignado un papel de comparsa, o si, simplemente, yo formaba parte de aquel mundo hecho de espectadores invisibles que ahora...debían de jalear su actuación, en una ovación cerrada, emocionada, intensa."[99]

Most revealing, however, is the visual image Bebo creates of Eloísa:

> Sobre la consola pendía un cuadro que en la penumbra había pasado por lo alto. Tampoco la débil luz de las arañas ayudaba ahora gran cosa, pero sí pude reconocer a mi madre de niña, a los doce años, vestida con un traje vaporoso muy parecido al de las fo-

---

97 Cristina Fernández Cubas, *Columpio,* 41.
98 Ibid., 45.
99 Ibid., 39-40.

tografías. Tenía una expresión entre angelical y enfurruñada, estaba mal sentada, se diría que mal sentada a propósito, como si más que un cuadro aquello fuera una instancia tomada sin su consentimiento, o como si el autor la hubiera querido precisamente así. Con un mohín de disgusto, de desafío. Una niña a quien acababan de romperle un juguete. Pero el juguete estaba ahí. En el suelo.[100]

Although not a photograph, the narrator likens the portrait to a photograph, a moment captured in time through film. I would suggest that the portrait marks Eloísa's relationship to her past and therefore to an implied future of her choosing. If the gaze of a male author(ity), in this case, Bebo, largely constructs the girl as a social category within the family, then Eloísa may be viewed as a subject trapped in good-girl scripts. Indeed, if we look beyond the central image of the portrait, Eloísa, to her chosen object of affection, the diabolo, we find a powerful icon that tangibly communicates a rejection of Bebo's authority and the system he represents. Yet in his portrait, Bebo removes the diabolo from Eloísa's hands, placing it, along with its string, on the floor before her. As long as the diabolo remains there, Eloísa cannot play. Although all the uncles concur that, "Eloísa sin su diábolo no es Eloísa,"[101] the strategic placement of the diabolo makes it difficult, if not impossible, for Eloísa to act independently. Not only does he force her to play the role of a meek princess held hostage in a tower by enemy infidels in a drama of his making, but, in this portrait, he forces her to visually represent an image of femininity that she repudiates. We vividly see this rejection in Eloísa's uncomfortable stance and sulking grimace. They draw attention to her painful entrapment.

Yet again and again throughout the novel, we are reminded that the narrator's re-telling of this family history is not primarily guided by

---

100 Ibid., 31.
101 Ibid., 56.

Bebo, but by the narrator's memories of her mother. Thus the narrator constantly re-frames Eloísa outside the context of the portrait painted by her cousin. As she re-frames her mother in different positions, we, together with the narrator, discover gaps and silences that create open space for a revision of social roles and positions. Not surprising, while we find that Bebo disarms Eloísa in his painting, assuring that she remain halted and at a distance from the diabolo, the narrator repeatedly re-frames her mother in motion with the toy. In turn, Eloísa's constant acting and reacting serve as a metaphor for the change that occurs with every re-telling this female agent's story.

A significant moment during which the narrator re-frames Eloísa as a key figure within the family drama occurs when the four characters, Lucas, Tomás, Bebo and the narrator, sit down to eat dinner on the second night of the narrator's arrival. The narrator asks where Eloísa had acquired her first diabolo. While Bebo replies that he does not know where or when she found her first diabolo, he says, "Tenía muchos. Algunos se los había construido yo mismo."[102] If Bebo serves as a script writer who gives his actors props and costumes, then it is not surprisingly he who often arms Eloísa with the tool by which she comes to blatantly disobey his directions. He reaffirms this by displaying a neck scar he received when, he confesses, Eloísa attacked him for having once kissed her. Within the context of the novel up to this point, we find the original family story—in which a valiant Saracen turned Christian convert saves a princess from infidels—is significantly revised by the female narrator to include the princess' outright refusal to surrender and submit to a male authority. Eloísa strikes her so-called rescuer with the diabolo to free herself from him.

Just as the narrator revises the family story to include her mother's skillful use of the diabolo as a weapon of defense, she equally associates it with her mother's reliance on another common childhood play

---

102 Ibid., 70.

object, the swing. The swing set in the garden, from which the novel's title derives, is one of the many toy objects with which all the children play. In one notable passage, the narrator remembers her mother associating the swing with her relationship to Bebo:

> Bebo y yo queríamos casarnos de mayores. El primo me decía que era muy sencillo; bastaba con pedir permiso al Papa. Pero mis hermanos se molestaban muchísimo. Antes de hablar con el Papa se les tenía que pedir consentimiento a ellos. Entonces yo me columpiaba con rabia, como si estuviera enfadada, y decía que era inútil, porque si seguían así discutiendo tontamente, cruzaría los Pirineos, me casaría con un francés y no volverían a verme.[103]

While several elements of the passage merit attention, an especially problematic phrase catches the reader's attention, "queríamos casarnos." With these words, Eloísa appears to confess complicity, a mutual desire and interest in marriage. Yet the narrator's memory of her mothers's story implies a possible reframing of this desire. While swinging, she refers to her mother's acting as if angry. But one wonders, at what or whom is Eloísa angry? At the uncles for their scatterbrained ideas? At Bebo for wanting to marry her? At a system that requires a male suitor to obtain the permission of male authorities (the permission of Lucas and Tomás as well as that of the Pope) over female authority (Eloísa's own desire) to marry? Because she labels the uncles' plans useless and threatens to leave the valley to marry a Frenchmen, I suggest that the narrator's re-telling of Eloísa's story reveals proud defiance. It shows a blatant unwillingness to follow a script written for and by men. As long as Eloísa keeps swinging, she remains free to oppose Bebo's dialogue, free to fulfill her own destiny, inserting herself only into those dramas she sees fit. In direct opposition to Bebo's portrait of

---

103 Ibid., 16.

Eloísa, the visual metaphor provided by the narrator captures Eloísa's individual agency and transgression within the family system.

It is no coincidence that Fernández Cubas chooses the diabolo and swing as objects representative of feminine agency. Both the diabolo and the swing repeat a back and forth movement along an axle. While she lived in the House of the Tower, Eloísa participated in a family drama and, at times reluctantly, performed those roles she was expected to perform (princess, possible marriage partner). Moreover, it seems that it is for her daughter that she maintains a semblance of bucolic perfection when discussing her childhood in the valley and the roles she played while there. Yet once Eloísa has died and the narrator is free to return to the valley, we see that the chimera her mother created to cover over painful memories cannot be maintained. The narrator vividly foreshadows this at the novel's beginning: "Todos los caminos conducían al mismo lugar, a los mismos personajes. Y, cuando no ocurría así se aferraba al recurso de aquel sueño imposible, pretendiendo tal vez que, al implicarme, yo la escucharía con mayor entrega."[104] Referring to the stories Eloísa would tell her as a child, the narrator uncovers that family history as nothing more than a fiction. The family members are "personajes," and to make the family stories more appealing, her mother would involve the narrator in them, giving her, too, a role to play.

Nowhere is the narrator's own role in the family drama more evident than at the fantastic climax where the narrator, having departed the uncles' house without their knowledge, comes upon her mother, fulfilling a dream Eloísa told the narrator she had had as a child:

> Pero enseguida nos encontramos frente a frente, en el centro mismo del jardín. Muy pronto me di cuenta de que su aspecto angelical era desmentido por una mirada fuerte, impropia de una niña,

---

104 Ibid.

y que lo que en un principio me había parecido una expresión de enfado no era más que una sonris desafiante, engreída. Agitaba en la mano una de aquellas cuerdas sobre las que ejercía el más dominio.[105]

Just as Eloísa's angry swinging in response to Bebo's marriage proposal represents self-determination, here a determined gaze represents a challenge to the system. The spectral Eloísa's fantastic appearance in the garden, together with the subsequent attack she makes with the diabolo, function as part of a violent re-casting of family roles. Though the assault on the narrator may at first glance appear an all out attack on daughterhood, it may also be interpreted as giving the narrator definitive permission to behave inappropriately. According to the narrator, the child Eloísa never told anyone in the family about the uncanny fantasy of meeting her daughter in the garden. She could not do so because it would be, "impropio de una niña."[106] However, according to the narrator's descriptions of Eloísa thus far, such behavior was not rare for her. The narrator's re-telling of her family's story consistently revises the notion of "proper" and "improper" female behavior. For Eloísa, acting "improperly" means achieving freedom of movement, first through play and the play objects afforded to her, then through physical movement beyond the House of the Tower. Self-exile to France and a subsequent marriage to a Frenchman suggest not only a physical distancing from the inertia of the valley and the House of the Tower, but also possible changes in political and social allegiances. She will not stand for the stagnancy represented by her brother's house.

Impropriety furthermore becomes aligned with motherless daughterhood. Time and again, the narrator notes that Eloísa never mentioned her own mother in any of the stories she told her, "Pero

---

105 Ibid., 123.
106 Ibid., 10.

en el mundo sin prohibiciones ni castigos que tantas veces evocara mi madre, los adultos habían sido eliminados, expulsados de escena, ignorados. Sin embargo, ahora me daba cuenta, alquien tenía que permitir aquella libertad salvaje."[107] While the narrator conjectures that it was Eloísa's own mother who first gave her a diabolo while the two played together in the Tower—"¿No podría ser que un día cualquiera, en el torreón, descubriera un diábolo, y su propia madre, recordando su infancia, se decidiera a enseñárselo?"—this conjecture is never confirmed or denied.[108] Nonetheless, one might suggest that Eloísa, a woman who could not openly discuss her mother's influence in her life, attacks her daughter with the diabolo not to do her harm, but ironically to save the narrator, just as her own mother had saved her by showing her how to play with the diabolo years before. Having introduced this toy to her daughter, she encouraged Eloísa to wield power and defy a system that readily assigns prohibitively passive scripts to women. Perhaps the greatest lesson the narrator's mother teaches her is to always move forward and to live free from the prohibitions of such scripts, "Ahora era yo quien tenía la certeza de haber estado durante aquellos días balanceándome en un columpio, suspendida en el aire, ingrávida sobre un inmenso abismo. Hacia atrás, hacia adelante... De nuevo hacia atrás, sujeta al mismo vaivén que a ella, de niña, le impulsaba milagrosamente hacia delante."[109] The aggressive assault has a transformative, positive effect; it is a saving action meant to keep her moving forward.

Permission to transgress fairy tale roles further gives both mother and daughter permission to reject economic status as a mark of power. While her uncles proudly call themselves "rentistas" and live by the understanding that "el mundo era un gran teatro y el dinero, ese dios menor, pero dios al cabo, les permitía diseñar el escenario a

---

[107] Ibid., 96.
[108] Ibid., 70.
[109] Ibid., 134.

su único, absoluto e indiscubible albedrío," mother and daughter do not. Although the uncles attempt to give the narrator Eloísa's share of the family inheritance by giving her a check, she refuses it. While the uncles view capital as a way of inventing their own world, she views it as part of the trappings of the House of the Tower and the dynamics by which those who dwell in it live. The freedom the narrator feels at ripping up the check indicates a triumph against that system. Once she destroys it, she feels free to remember the same words her mother spoke to her as a child, "Un día, fíjate qué tontería, soñé contigo."[110] These words reify that the bond between generations of women, here mother and daughter—serves as a capital able to create new worlds, capable of salvaging women's narrative authority within family histories. This mother, like her own, would not have her daughter made incapable of movement, locked up in the Tower by the "gruesa llave" of male authority.

Just as Eloísa's death serves as an impetus for the re-telling of a family story and the re-casting of female roles in El columpio, Hermanas de sangre foregrounds the death of Clara, one in a group of girls attending a boarding school, as the basis for another re-telling of a family history. Unlike *El columpio*, which focuses on the mother-daughter dyad, the girls in *Hermanas de sangre* are not biologically related but become blood sisters, thereby solidifying their relationship to each other as members of a symbolic family. If the former novel emphasizes female agents' use of violent play to assume control within the narrative of a family drama, *Hermanas de sangre* emphasizes play as part of a ritual sacrifice that pits sister against sister. As the work unfolds, the reader/viewer becomes increasingly aware of the play metaphor as a mechanism by which the female agents and blood sisters become the makers of their own history and culture. If, as René Girard argues, all cultural myths and religions are based on a founding murder, then

---

110 Ibid.

the violent death of one sister, Clara, at the hands of her blood sisters serves as the very murder on which this re-telling of a history is based. What is most provocative about Fernández Cubas's play, however, is that unlike male counterparts, whose intense desires compel them to vie for objects in order to gain attention and be recognized in the community, the female murderers seem to remain invisible. Though the perpetrators wish for the murder to carry weight so that Clara's sacrifice has meaning, that sacrifice seems visible only to the sisters, remaining unseen or lost in a rhetoric of forgetting by outside members of the community. If the sisters' killing is to have meaning, if the reader is to salvage Clara, such meaning can be found only in a radical reinterpretation of feminine violence, one that views violence between sisters from a perspective of difference.

The drama composed of three parts—"El misterio de los reservados," "Acto primero," and "Acto segundo"—begins with a section in which the author discusses her own experience of receiving a mysterious message to attend a school reunion. "El misterio de los reservados" thus uncannily prefigures the action of the drama, wherein seven classmates attend a reunion in a banquet hall. Declaring that banquet halls both fascinate and terrify her, the author affirms, "Los reservados son casas de todos en terrenos de nadie. También, a menudo, auténticas encerronas."[111] It is no surprise that Fernández Cubas describes the locus of the event in this way. She sets the stage for the commemoration of a sacrifice in an enclosed space, an environment not unfamiliar to her readers. In its limitedness, the banquet hall suggests a spot that has been cut off from progress, modernity and enlightenment, all characteristics associated with Gothic narratives, superstition, and ultimately the murderous. Drawing from Eve Kosofsky Sedgwick, Kathleen Glenn notes Gothic aspects in several of Fernández Cubas's earlier

---

[111] Cristina Fernández Cubas, *Hermanas de sangre* (Barcelona: Tusquets, 1998), 13.

works, including those taking place in boarding schools and convents. Glenn asserts that the spaces within which the author situates the action of her narratives foreground a "concern with boundaries, boundaries between self and other, inside and outside, center and periphery, the subjective and objective, dream and reality or dream state and wakefulness, life and death."[112]

Hermanas de sangre repeats these Gothic features. Yet the liminal space of the banquet hall not only calls to mind all that is encompassed in this Gothic reading but also gestation and possible transformation. By characterizing the hall as a place where individuals mark ritual functions—"un lugar despersonalizado, inhóspito, más adecuado para 'Bodas, Comuniones y Bautizos'"—the author immediately positions the hall and the events that take place there as contained within Girard's sacrificial logic.[113] Indeed, in that the rites mentioned are those of initiation, the author wittingly or unwittingly situates Clara's sacrifice within the realm of rituals having to do not with the perpetuation of a status quo but with the acquisition of a new status, a particularly helpful reading if the audience is to understand Hermanas de sangre as challenging the ways in which violence between rivals has been previously understood.[114] The drama's setting thus becomes a metaphor of the human psyche. It is at once a tomb of physical and spiritual death as well as a womb of transformative rebirth.

Attending the reunion, the narrator introduces and describes seven women: Marga, Julia, Alicia, Lali, Toña, Monste and Luisa. Of the seven, the most important is Marga, the dynamic presenter of a television program called, "La verdad al desnudo" (the Naked Truth),

---

112 Kathleen Glenn, "Gothic Indecipherability and Doubling in the Fiction of Cristina Fernández Cubas" *Monographic Review/Revista monográfica*. 8 (1992): 125-141, 125.

113 Cristina Fernández Cubas, *Hermanas*, 12.

114 René Girard, *Violence and the Sacred* (Baltimore: Johns Hopkins UP, 1972), 280-81.

who sports trendy clothing and always appears to be acting as if being taped on film. Marga's characterization is central to the work in that, as the drama develops, we realize that it is she who has reunited the women to view two black and white home videos filmed some thirty-four years earlier at an end of term school party. The first of the two videos begins with a scene of the private road leading to the boarding school the girls attended. Two large dogs, ferociously jump and bark behind a wire mesh gate. Later, as images of the school gardens fade, we see an open air theatre where the seven girls, dressed as tarantulas, dance and sing. During the performance, two of the members of the ensemble fall. This causes another to laugh and fall out of character. Nonetheless, one of the seven, Clara, saves the day by taking center stage, improvising a monologue, and bowing. As the camera pans back, we see the girls' family members, teachers and tables set with afternoon snacks and juices. One of the school's caretakers, Cosme serves as the function's waiter. The camera vacillates and then re-focuses on the girls' legs, their socks and shoes. We suddenly see a shot of Clara, smiling with an open mouth and a camera-shy Marga hiding her face from the camera.

Bitter sadness and shock follow for the unsuspecting viewer as, one by one, the women not only remember Clara's dying soon after the film was shot but also acknowledge their involvement in her demise. Marga provokes their confession after they watch a copy of the original video that has been cleaned up and remastered thanks to "máquinas milagrosas, material impecable última generación [...]."[115] In the copy, we see Clara's failed attempts to breathe between gasps as the camera pans out to show a few of the girls kicking her in the belly while the others watch. In subsequent scenes, the women not only come to terms with their status as collective assassins but also with their status as blood sisters, as bound to each other not only by their fellowship

---

115 Cristina Fernández Cubas, *Hermanas,* 57.

in a girls' club, the Tarántulas, but also by virtue of their complicity in this violent act.

The role of sisterhood within the group becomes increasingly evident since, for these women, coming together to attend a reunion suggests that their bond to each other, though forged long ago, is not only strong, but also uniquely comparable to that which one might have with a family member. Since a child derives some of her identity and sense of self from the people to which she is exposed, children in boarding schools frequently look to peers as primary agents of socialization. Physically removed from the biological family unit—mothers, fathers, and siblings—the boarding school itself and the girls who populate it substitute as potent sources from which to cultivate a sense of family and communal belonging. Lali plainly describes this phenomenon as a fundamental reason for which she attends the reunion, "Las internas formábamos una familia. Éramos como hermanas. Mucho más que hermanas [my emphasis]. Durante años hemos compartido dormitorio, comedor, juegos…. Si he venido aquí es porque me moría de ganas de veros."[116] Time and again the women refer to the school and those within it as a family, an influential locus where formative developmental experiences and processes take place.

Though Lali foregrounds the primacy of shared bedroom and dining areas, a particular word she uses in her description of the group —juegos, games—further implicates play as equally interconnected to their roles as sisters. Just as the games the girls played as children were highly codified, so are the temporal (class grade and age) and spatial contexts (the school buildings and grounds) they shared. In turn, through these contexts, the girls participated in a series of rigidly structured activities and events rooted in social hierarchies, contests and rivalries. Exemplifying both the ritual and carnival quality of the reunion, the women remember the school's annual end of term party

---

116 Ibid., 60.

as celebratory. Attended by caregivers, teachers and nuns as well as students and their family members, the event marked the successful completion of the year. The first film Marga projects at the reunion demonstrates this festive air. In it, we view the idyllic garden setting, an assortment of foods and beverages to be consumed and enjoyed, and the girls dressed not only in their customary school uniforms, but also making special appearances in unique tarantula costumes as they dance to entertain their audience.

While the importance of this gathering at the conclusion of the year could be defined as a banal mandate of the institution, it is much more than this. From the seasonal aspect of the party to the consumption of banquet foods and beverages; from the donning of unique costumes to the performance of a choreographed dance, each of these elements correspond to René Girard's description of the cathartic function of ritual sacrifice. According to his *Violence and the Sacred,* violence proliferates within a community when social distinctions among individuals or groups become confused or are contested. When an established social hierarchy is challenged through rivalries, jealousies, quarrels and acts of dissent, community infighting escalates into reciprocal acts of vengeance and retribution. The only way to restrain aggression, says Girard, is through the collective and climactic sanctioning of blood sacrifice. The blood sacrifice is a unanimous yet limited act of violence vented upon that representative of the community who is deemed responsible for the eruption of internal discord.[117]

Initiated into the "Tarantulas" and dressed as spiders, the girls projected in the second film embody the carnival spirit as described by Girard. Their membership in the exclusive group defines them as a subset within the larger school community. For the Tarantulas, this means that each member agrees to adhere to bylaws and statutes as written in the club's constitution. Though Toña declares, "todos los niños, a

---

[117] René Girard, *Violence*, 94.

determinada edad, fundan un club," as if to dismiss the group as being like those created by countless other children, she adds "el nuestro, a ratos, parece una religión. Ritos, palabras mágicas, 'honor', 'amistad.' Normas y más normas."[118] In saying this, she affirms that, no matter what the original intention of the group, it became fundamentally inscribed in and informed by the language of religious rites and norms. Reflecting on the group as it existed, the women make this explicitly clear:

> ALICIA: (pasando las jojas): Normas: "Honor", "Amistad", "Solidaridad"...(Corrigiéndose.) 'So-li-ra-li-dad." Y una disposición final: "El miembro del club que se atreva a saltarse una de estas normas y no desmuestre arrepentimiento será considerado un traidor y castigado con..." (Se detiene.)
> MARGA: ¿La muerte?
> ALICIA: Falta un trozo.
> (Lali, sorprendida, mira la última hoja.)
> MARGA: Como prueba de inocencia [...].[119]

It appears members of the secret club retained the right to mortally punish any member who transgressed rules.

The name "Tarantulas" further draws attention to members' orthodoxy with reference to the sisterhood's bylaws. For Girard, the loss of distinction between humankind and animal is always linked to violence.[120] By dressing as tarantulas and performing at the end of year banquet, the girls undergo a physical, emotional and psychical transformation. No longer girls, they become members of the animal world. As tarantulas, the largest of the spider breeds, the girls become capable of aggressively stalking prey and thrusting venomous fangs

---

118 Cristina Fernández Cubas, *Hermanas*, 76.
119 Ibid., 62.
120 René Girard, *Violence*, 128.

into their victims to destroy them. In other words, members not only pledge allegiance to the regulations of the group, but to the behaviors expected of tarantulas as members of the animal world. Alicia implies how their own bloody actions are aligned with those committed by animals, suggesting that animals will go to any lengths to ensure their own survival:

> Los animales son de una coherencia envidiable. Desde el primer día saben lo que tienen que hacer. Sobrevivir. Y en esa dirección encaminan su conducta. Las larvas, por ejemplo. Las orugas, los gusanos de seda del colegio... Entonces no nos preguntábamos nada, pero ¡cómo tragan!, ¡qué voracidad! Toda su vida de larva está en function de su futuro. Invierten, digamos, para cuando se conviertan en mariposas. (Excusándose.) Pongo el ejemplo más conocido.[121]

Just as larvae voraciously devour in order to grow strong, survive and continue the cycle that leads to their ultimate metamorphosis into butterflies, she implies that all animals take part in such cycles to ensure survival.

Though one might at first wonder why the group preys on Clara, if we associate cyclical violence with the framework of the survival mechanism—a repetition of violence that ultimately restores order—then we may also observe the killing as providing a necessary outlet for mass anguish. The sisters wish to oust Clara because, according to them, she has betrayed them, causing them grief and distress. Toña accuses her of plagiarizing a story from a book in the school library in order to fraudulently win the school's prize for best writer. Alicia, for her part, insinuates Clara's involvement in sabotaging the worms she worked with in the school's laboratory. Finally, Julia admits that the

---

[121] Cristina Fernández Cubas, *Hermanas* 118.

girls united against Clara because, having "saved" the Tarantulas by becoming the star of their end of term production, Clara had gone too far, broken too many rules, "Clara nos había fallado y quisimos darle un escarmiento. En el lugar donde tantas veces nos reuníamos para jugar, para hablar de nuestras cosas. En nuestro escondite."[122] In other words, she did not function within the highly regulated system accepted within the sisterhood, but acted as a radical agent who would work to ensure her own survival rather than preoccupy herself with the communal survival of the sisterhood.

Returning to the importance of the play metaphor, it is not inconsequential that the girls choose a playing field and shared hiding place as the ground on which to assassinate their friend. The women consistently refer to Clara's behavior in terms of fair and unfair play.[123] The transformation of the playing field into an area of sacrifice thus describes what Girard calls, "a repetition of the original, spontaneous 'lynching.'"[124] Girard's use of the word "lynching" in the description of the ritual action is essential in that the women repeatedly refer to Clara's death as a lynching. Marga tells the women that there were "unas horas de diferencia entre el linchamiento y la muerte," and Toña admits, "fuimos nosotras. La linchamos."[125] The drama of the mob working in unison to restore order through lynching reestablishes "around the figure of the surrogate victim, that sentiment of social accord that had been destroyed in the onslaught of reciprocal violence."[126] Thus, the event on which the women "found" an enduring sisterhood commemorates

---

122 Ibid., 76.

123 Toña most emphatically uses this metaphor. She points out that Clara "hizo trampa y jugó sucio" (77) when she dishonestly won the school's writing award by plagiarizing a story she had read in the school's library. Toña also implies that Clara suffers from arrogance and pride, two defects of character, when she "saves" the Tarantula's dance.

124 René Girard, *Violence*, 95.

125 Cristina Fernández Cubas, Hermanas, 77.

126 René Girard, *Violence*, 95.

a spilling of blood that eternally binds each to the others.

But what makes Hermanas de sangre most original as well as disturbing is that Clara's death and the manner in which the blood sisterhood is founded exemplify the ways in which women often appear to remain invisible participants in processes linked to the evolution of culture, processes like those described by Girard. Even Girard, in his interpretation of the Maenads in the Bacchae, states, "We may therefore wonder whether the preponderance of women does not constitute a secondary mythological displacement [my emphasis], an effort to exonerate from the accusation of violence, not mankind as a whole, but adult males, who have the greatest need to forget their role in the crisis because, in fact, they must have been largely responsible for it."[127] He later suggests, "We can therefore postulate a mythological substitution of women for men in regard to violence."[128] In other words, women's agency remains not an inherent or necessary part of the sacrificial logic, but symbolic, representative of some deviant "illness" or the result of a displacement wherein "woman" as a sexual category temporarily abandons her "marginal status" to adopt agency—here, in the form of violence—often ascribed to men.

One has only to examine the ways in which the women describe the conditions to which they returned the next school year. Julia, for example, explains, "Al volver al colegio me encontré con la historia del accidente. Esos benditos perros que me liberaban de toda la culpa. Terminé por convencerme de que lo que habíamos hecho no tenía nada que ver con lo que había pasado."[129] For her, their violent history has been displaced by another "historia," that of the vicious dogs who monstrously attacked Clara. Alicia and Toña likewise suggest that the school administrators responded to the tragedy by physically changing the look and chain of command at the school. Thus, when the girls

---

127 Ibid., 139.
128 Ibid.
129 Cristina Fernández Cubas, *Hermanas* 74.

return, they find that some of the school's property has been sold, a new pavilion has been constructed, and the girls have a new head mistress. Finally, Marga reminds her peers that there was no yearbook that year. As Julia keenly notes, wittingly or unwittingly, all those involved conspired to keep the tragedy under wraps, "Borraron todo un año del calendario."[130] Although, at first glance, the boarding school system and all it represents protects them from having to pay the price for their crime and from labeling them as killers, the women recognize their own brutality for what it is: a blood sacrifice that is part and parcel of cultural evolution.

On several levels, an underlying male social gaze disavows the potential threat posed by female agency and covers over women's fundamental experience of violence. Perhaps most obvious, two males—Marga's brother and father—record the event on film. Yet neither "see" the violence captured therein nor do they make the girls' violence visible to their public. It is only when Marga, a woman with knowledge about how the lens narrates, comes to control and manipulate the images that we see the "naked truth." Laura Mulvey's "Visual Pleasure and Narrative Cinema" (1975) assists our understanding of how this truth comes into existence:

> It is said that analyzing pleasure, or beauty, destroys it. That is the intention of this article. The satisfaction and reinforcement of the ego that represents the high point of film history hitherto must be attacked. Not in favor of a reconstructed new pleasure, which cannot exist in the abstract, nor of intellectualized unpleasure, but to make way for a total negation of ease and plenitude of the narrative fiction film. The alternative is the thrill that comes from leaving the past behind without rejecting it, transcending outworn or oppressive forms, or daring to break with normal pleasurable

---

130 Ibid., 75.

expectations in order to conceive a new language of desire.[131]

Mulvey's article is particularly illuminating, since Fernández Cubas's stage drama includes film. For Mulvey, visual pleasure is bound up with the structure of the look and the localization of male authority. The girls in the first video are not captured on film to be analyzed but simply to be gazed upon. They are constructed as objects of sexual, and dare I say social, satisfaction. They give pleasure in that they reinforce and represent conventional patriarchal ideology which generally posits the female as the object of the male gaze. Their status as adolescents further posits them as attractive objects of male desire. As passive objects, these girls are principally seen as performing in accordance to the laws of male desire. They conform to a narrative "ease" and "plentitude" that censors their words and actions, thus protecting them from transgressing accepted social-sexual laws of behavior.

Yet Marga, speaking from outside the margins of the principally male-structured society, responds to the layers of secrecy that otherwise envelope the sisterhood within a code of silence. Drawing attention to her ability to speak from outside this structure, she asserts, "En mi profesión, he aprendido un montón de cosas. Entre ellas el valor de la palabra, del tono y sobre todo, del silencio."[132] She is not simply an actor following an ideological script; rather as Paul Smith might argue, she is an agent who "reads from them in order to insert him/herself into them—or not."[133] There is a conscientious break with cultural script, and it is this conscientious break that allows for a radical reinterpretation of the violence of Fernández Cubas's sisterhood.

---

[131] Laura Mulvey, "Visual Pleasure and Narrative Cinema" in *Art After Modernism: Rethinking Representation*, eds. Ann Snitow, Christine Stansell, and Sharon Thompson. New York: New Museum of Contemporary Art, 1984. 361-73),

[132] Cristina Fernández Cubas, *Hermanas*, 67.

[133] Paul Julian Smith, *Discerning the Subject* (Minneapolis: U of Minnesota P, 1988), xxxiv–xxxv.

The subject position from which Marga speaks transgresses the visual paradigm and distances itself from patriarchal ideology. Although the women mimic male counterparts who engage in ritual violence as described by Girard, these female agents ultimately break from seeking recognition through ritualized acts of physical violence to seek it through the written and spoken word as well as through silence.

If the women's sacrifice appears largely visible only to the sisters (remaining unseen or lost in a discourse of forgetting by members of the community), ruptures in the play suggest a more positive reading through which the reader may, in fact, find meaning in Clara's death. First and foremost, several characters, especially Montse, refer to the second film as a "montage." This term refers to the editing processes that create narrative continuities, discontinuities and juxtapositions in the structure of the film. Marga's editing skills show the women to be other than what her brother and father would have them be. The girls in the second film are reconstructed not as passive objects, but as active subjects. Montse alludes to this phenomenon when she states, "A partir de las piernas se pueden reconstruir los cuerpos de sus propietarias."[134] Marga's filmic version of the events that transpired challenge the point of view captured by both her father and brother. If these masculine points of view would keep the girls' violence locked away, Marga's narrative lens seeks to shed light on it. The volatile bodies the audience sees in her film give weight not only to the sacrifice but to those who physically participate in it.

Fernández Cubas foregrounds the value and significance of the written word in the drama's epilogue. Here, the author comes forth as a witness to tell her readers about her own experience of writing and of telling this story of violence:

No eran nadie y, al tiempo, eran. Cualquiera las hubiera recono-

---

134 Cristina Fernández Cubas, *Hermanas*, 63.

cido de inmediato. 'Antiguas compañeras de colegio que se reúnen una noche.' Una abstracción. Pero ¡qué abstracción más empecinada! Dejé todo lo que entonces estaba haciendo y me dediqué a escucharlas. O, mejor, fueron ellas quienes no me dejaron otra opción. Reclamaban para sí el derecho a presentarse, a moverse libremente, a hablar.[135]

She claims that it is not she, the author who writes, but rather her characters who act through her to powerfully seize control of the writing. The play itself thus becomes a place of rupture wherein these women articulate, without guilt or shame, what is forbidden, or even unacknowledged in the male symbolic. Indeed, though Girard himself refers to Euripides's *Bacchae* as a classic tragedy about two male rivals wherein women take up "the most violent masculine activities, hunting and warfare," he also argues that the play is about the "destruction of distinctions as the god sweeps away all the barriers that usually divide mortals: wealth, age, sex and so on."[136] I would thus suggest that Fernández Cubas's *Hermanas de sangre* is about liberating women's violence from a space off-stage. If in *Hermanas de sangre* there is a destruction of boundaries, it is in the casting of women as principal writers, actors and directors who perform on stage and screen to do away with the limits of cultural scripts.

Not surprisingly, the character most physically absent within the play, Clara, is also the character most present. She symbolically rises from death to reappropriate a locus of power. Clara, in her absence, acquires more presence than her sisters, who have found themselves defined by her until their reunion. Once elevated from the collectivity of the group to the status of the divine, her murder commemorates the way in which the women's experience of violence is extricated from its

---

[135] Ibid., 17.
[136] René Girard, *Violence*, 126.

previous invisibility. Clara's murder brings about a new order, one that not only foregrounds the myth of Dionysus as read by Girard, but of Athena and Arachne, another Greek tale of rivalry between women. At the end the play's second act, Lali suggests the women reunite each June 21, the day on which Clara was murdered, "Todos los veintiuno de junio. Pasaremos la película. [...] Y brindaremos. Una vez al año."[137] Toasting and wine drinking call to mind the role of Dionysus not only as god of wine but also as a liberator.[138] Although the women's act of remembrance will not give life to Clara, it will continue to give life to the blood-sisters. Nowhere is this more apparent than in the following exchange of dialogue:

> JULIA (al sentirse descubierta): Una superstición [...] Siento como si a partir de esta noche, me fuera a cambiar la vida.
> ALICIA: (para sí misma): No sólo la tuya, Julia. No sólo la tuya.
> JULIA: Y creo que Clara ha sido muy generosa con nosotras. Todas unidas contra ella y ahora...
> Alicia (gravemente): Y ahora ella no va a permitir que nos separemos nunca.[139]

Emphasizing the permanence of the sisterhood, the women suggest that Clara's sacrifice leads to greater possibilities for all of them. In replacing male rivalries with female rivalries, as well as male divinity with female divinity, Fernández Cubas sets up the possibility for her reader to consider women as subjects of culture since religion—

---

137 Cristina Fernández Cubas, *Hermanas*, 132.

138 It is worthwhile noting that Romans identified the Greek god Dionysus with both the gods Liber, god of fertility and growth, and Bacchus, who was more properly the god of wine. As such, Dionysus represented creativity as well as liberation.

139 Cristina Fernández Cubas, *Hermanas*, 139.

and ritual sacrifice as part and parcel of religious practice—is a discussion central to the processes of cultural evolution. Clara thus not only remains part of the collective sisterhood but is transformed into a creative mother-sister, one who gives life as she sheds blood for her fellows.[140] As tarantulas, they will continue to come together to artfully spin and weave their webs, telling and retelling their stories to an audience that will not see them made invisible.[141]

Hermanas de sangre showcases female agents who consistently recast and revise the roles played by women as they tell and retell a story of violence within sisterhood. As Marga helps her blood sisters to confess the truth of their killing, making a murder that was largely invisible to the community patent, she draws attention to the power of the stage and screen as well as the graphic space of the text to gain public authority. Through the process of telling and retelling their tale, reminiscent of Freud's "talking cure," these women explode the ways in which females have been understood to function in the sacrificial logic of culture. Through her protagonists' performances, Fernández Cubas encourages her audience to reconsider the ways in which women narrate and reflect on their own histories of sacrifice. In doing this, we

---

140 Irigaray's reading of Girard has been especially influential in this writing in that she champions the debt owed to the mother for the sacrifice of birth. Irigaray argues that in Christianity, the body and blood ritually consumed are the body and blood of women. She opposes the value of sacrifice with fertility. Since the sisters in Fernández Cubas's play come to acknowledge Clara's sacrifice and vow to keep Clara's memory, they symbolically elevate her to the status of a deity. She thus becomes not only a sister, but a maternal symbol representing the debt owed to woman.

141 Bulfinch recounts the Greek myth wherein Arachne offends Athena, patron goddess of weaving, when she claims to be equal, if not superior, to the deity. Slighted by her insolence in a public contest, Athena destroys both a tapestry Arachne has woven and her loom. Arachne runs away in shame and hangs herself. Athena later takes pity on Arachne and brings her back to life as a spider, condemning her and all of her descendants to forever hang from webs and be weavers. Along with highlighting the symbolic value of seeing Fernández Cubas's sisters as weavers of a complex tale, the Greek legend highlights rivalry between women who vie for the recognition and acknowledgement of a group.

ourselves take part in a dynamic dialogue meant to expose individual anxieties with regard to violence and uncover the wounds we have inflicted so that they, too, may heal.

Perhaps an interesting manner to end this chapter on Fernández Cubas's treatment of women's re-negotiation and re-writing of feminine agency through familial roles is by taking a closer look at "Ausencia," from the collection of stories *Con Agatha en Estambul*. In this tale, the narrator employs sleuthful play, mirror images, and protective frames, combining characteristics of narrative elements found in "Mi hermana Elba," "Los altillos de Brumal" and "Mundo" to underscore the evolving role of women's identity outside the family dynamic. Like the narrators of "Mi hermana Elba," "Los altillos de Brumal" and "Mundo," Elena, the main protagonist and narrator of "Ausencia," draws attention to ludic characteristics that become symptomatic of a desire to flee from the life she has created. Unlike these stories, however, Elena's tale de-emphasizes childhood. Elena's divinations regarding mirror images, past memories, and protective frames ultimately reveal the middle-aged narrator's discontent with adult life and a deep-seated wish to "absent" herself from the world in which she lives, a world from which she appears unable to escape. This final characteristic aligns Elena with those agents of transgressive activity found in Fernández Cubas's other narratives since all of them express, through their playfulness, an uncontrollable desire to subvert paradigms of femininity and embody an excess of spirit that will free them from those cultural constructs that would otherwise restrict their actions.

Elena Vila Gastón, the second person narrator of "Ausencia," begins to tell her tale by describing the café where she sits, the people she sees and by noting the time, ten minutes after eleven in the morning. Suddenly becoming cognizant of her amnesic state, Elena asks herself, "¿Qué hago yo aquí?"[142] The deceptively simple question becomes epis-

---

142 Cristina Fernández Cubas, "Ausencia," 153.

temological as she continues, "Pero un sudor frío te hace notar que la pregunta es absurda, encubridora, falsa. Porque lo que menos importa en este momento es recordar lo que estás haciendo allí, sino algo mucho más sencillo. Saber quién eres tú."[143] As the tale unfolds, the only fact of which the narrator remains certain is her sex, "Tú eres una mujer. De eso estás segura."[144] This detail is significant in that Elena knows her sex before looking in a mirror or seeing her image reflected in windowglass. Because of this, for Elena, sex and gender do not coincide as observable constructs to be physically embodied but are separate and perceivable categories functioning beyond the visual framework. As Janet Pérez notes, Elena must discover all other information about herself.[145] She must ascertain her name, address, age, marital-status, likes and dislikes, profession and even her native language. Although the details she finds out should delight the narrator—Elena eventually discovers she lives in a penthouse and that she has a influential job as a magazine editor, the job she alludes to having dreamed of as a child—they do not. Rather, as she becomes re-familiarized with who she is, the person she has apparently constructed herself to be, the narrator begins to feel empty. She describes this sensation as "una insatisfacción perenne, un desasosiego absurdo con los que has estado conviviendo durante años y años."[146] Ending the tale with a trip to her office and thinking about how difficult it has been to "awake" from the numbing aphasia she has suffered, she comments, "tu vida ha sido siempre gris, marrón, violácea, y que el día que ahora empieza no es sino otro día más. Un día como tantos. Un día exactamente igual que otros tantos."[147] In the end, it seems her sleuthing, interest in making

---

143 Ibid.

144 Ibid., 153.

145 Janet Pérez, "Cristina Fernández Cubas: Narrative Unreliability and the Flight from Clarity, or, the Quest for Knowledge in the Fog," *Hispanófila* 122 (January 1998): 29-39, 35.

146 Cristina Fernández Cubas, "Ausencia," 166.

147 Ibid., 170.

up stories regarding her past identity, and attempts at living the life of Elena Vila Gastón—a woman the amnesic Elena does not know—lead to the recuperation of a self the narrator does not want to know.

At the start Elena approaches her amnesic state without trepidation, greeting the absence of memory, and with it any notion of identity, in a playful, whimsical manner. She communicates this attitude through her ingenious detective-like work. On first realizing she does not know who she is, Elena picks up the woman's handbag she sees lying beside her and, after deciding it must be hers since the color of the leather matches her shoes, begins to go through it, "Hurgas en el bolso y das con un neceser en el que se apiñan lápices de labios, colorete, un cigarillo deshecho [...]. 'Soy desordenada,' te dices."[148] Likewise, she not only discovers her name by reading it on the credit cards she finds in her purse, but also successfully calculates her age by comparing the date of birth given on a gym membership card to the latest date printed on one of the daily newspapers lying nearby her at the café. The game-like quality of Elena's sleuthing, the way she examines identity cards to systematically and logically deduce what and who she is, becomes concrete as she states, "'Ausencia,' te dices, 'Eso es lo que me está ocurriendo. Sufro una ausencia.' Y por un buen rato sigues con el *juego*" [my emphasis]. [149] The game-like methods Elena utilizes to begin uncovering who she is lead to a thematic emphasis on mirror images, the duplicitous nature of which underscore the psychological doubling by division of the narrator.[150] First contemplating her image in a mirror bearing the brand name of a French cognac, she thinks, "El rostro no te resulta ajeno, tampoco familiar. Es un rostro que te mira asombrado, confuso, pero también un rostro obediente, dispuesto a parpadear, a

---

148 Ibid., 154.
149 Ibid., 156.
150 Robert Rogers Rogers, *A Psychoanalytic Study of the Double in Literature* (Detroit: Wayne State UP, 1970).

fruncir el ceño, a dejarse acariciar la mejilla."[151] This cursory observation shows Elena as bravely confronting herself as an "other" within the amnesiac state. Rather than inspire fear, the act of contemplating the reflection in the mirror inspires her to realize that the corporal self can be played with, manipulated. Moreover, she becomes familiar with the pliability of the reflected image she sees, noting that it is at once obedient and capricious: she makes herself frown with as much ease as she winks. Apprehending this, Elena exhibits an awareness regarding the performative, theatrical character of the body she inhabits. She implies that the relationship between the objectified image viewed in the mirror and the aphasiac self may be distant, unfamiliar. The alien appearance of the exterior self remains separate from the interior, emotional self.

Leaving the café, the narrator continues to playfully reconstruct the image she has of herself by trying to imagine what she might have been like prior to entering the fugue state. Somewhat reminiscent of Adriana in "Los altillos de Brumal," she enters a church. Although Elena doubts that the priest will listen to her while she speaks, she enters one of the confessionals thinking, "Pero necesitas hablar, escuchar tu voz, y a falta de una lista de pecados más acorde con tu edad, los inventas. Has cometido adulterio. Una, dos, hasta quince veces. Has atracado un banco. Has robado en una tienda la gabardina forrada de seda."[152] A word the narrator uses in her confession, "inventas," is telling. Admitting a need to speak and listen to her own voice, Elena fabricates sins in order to make a history for herself, to give herself a context and motivation in her present amnesic state. The prominence she places on her voice as a basis for creating this image of herself further suggests a need to re-create a multi-sensory, multifaceted self not limited by the visual scope.

---

151 Cristina Fernández Cubas, "Ausencia" in *Con Agatha en Estambul* (Barcelona: Tusquets, 1994. 151-170), 153-154.
152 Ibid., 161.

The importance attached to re-creating herself as a multisensory being becomes more evident as the narrative progresses:

> Te has quedado sorprendida de que te guste la gimnasia y también con la extraña sensación de que a este nombre que aparece por tercera vez, Elena Vila Gastón, le falta algo. "Helena", piensas, "sí, me gustaría mucho más llamarme Helena." Y entonces recuerdas—pero no te detienes a meditar si "recordar" es el término adecuado—un juego, un entretenimiento, una habilidad antigua. De pequeña solías ver las palabras, los nombres, las frases. Las palabras tenían color. Unas brillaban más que otras, algunas, muy pocas, aparecían adornadas con ribetes, con orlas. Elena era de un color claro, luminoso. Pero Helena brillaba todavía más y tenía ribetes.[153]

Elena's response to the memory she has of her imagined self, renaming herself Helena, runs the gamut of perception. Beyond the attention she places on the voice as a unique and individual attribute capable of recreating the self, she demonstrates an acute fascination with the ability of language to be perceived in color. The particular word she remembers at that moment of the narrative, Helena, further lends significance to this re-imagining of the self in that the names Elena/Helena are homonyms in Spanish. The difference between the two must be graphically perceived.[154] Yet in the mind of the narrator, the name Helena seems appreciably clearer and brigher than her own. Ultimately thinking of herself as Helena rather than Elena, she displays agency symbolically renaming herself, abandoning her given name for another much like Adriana/Anairda of "Los altillos de Brumal." This gesture demonstrates autonomy and a desire to exceed the limitations

---

153 Ibid., 156.

154 The synesthetic Elena not only visually perceives the addition of the letter "H" to her name, but also associates this transformation with certain, more vivid colors.

imposed on her by those who would have named her:

> Café es marrón, Amalia, rojo, Alfonso, gris-plomo, mesa, entre beige y Amarillo. Intentas recordarte a ti, de pequeña, pero sólo alcanzas a ver la palabra "pequeña", muy al fondo, en colores desvaídos y letras borrosas. Repites Amalia, Alfonso… Y, por un instante, crees que estos nombres significan algo.[155]

That Elena acknowledges the effect naming has had on her without fully disclosing the identities of those who named her, presumably her parents, is telling. At an earlier point in the tale the narrator declares she does not recognize the names "Amalia" or "Alfonso." Elena simply muses over these names and, as she does here, associates their names with the sensation of having felt small, figuratively unimportant as a child.

Yet the vague memories of these names, like her playful detective work and interpretation of mirror images, eventually help her to accept the ugly fact that she is not happy with who she has become, whatever that may be. While Elena is able to interpret her past life as an "other" for the greater part of the tale, it becomes increasingly evident that the benefits of pathologic memory loss are fleeting. Amnesia may make the past temporarily inaccessible to her conscious state, but it cannot totally exempt her from refamiliarizing herself with the past, and it cannot keep her from confronting the psychological split represented by the mirror images she sees.

The process of re-familiarization and acknowledgment becomes evident as, having found her address on another identity card, she decides to journey home to find out more about what kind of life she has lived: "En tu tarjeta de socia de un club se indica que vives en el ático. Piensas: 'Me gusta vivir en un ático'. El espejo del ascensor te

---

[155] Cristina Fernández Cubas, "Ausencia" 156.

devuelve esa cara con la que ya te has famliarizado y que ocultas ahora tras unas oportunas gafas oscuras que encuentras en el bolso."[156] Although Elena first meets her reflection in the elevator's mirror with ease, demonstrating familiarity with it, a trace of discomfort may be read in that she hides under cover of sunglasses, suggesting a desire to retain anonymity from the outside world.

Once she comes to the door of the penthouse and walks over its threshold, the narrator more fully confronts the Elena with whom she has split. As she walks into the apartment she declares, "Eres Elena Vila Gastón. Sabes dónde se encuentran los quesos, el azúcar, la mermelada. No dudas al abrir los cajones de los cubiertos, de los manteles, de los trapos."[157] The door to the apartment literally and metaphorically stands as a threshold between mental states. As Cirlot points out, a threshold oftentimes represents "transition and transcendence" as well as "the reconciliation and the separation of the two worlds of the profane and the sacred."[158] In Elena's case, the apartment's threshold thus not only serves as a physical point of entry to a past life, but also as a point of entry to the psychological condition she has up to this point eluded.

Yet unlike "Mi hermana Elba" or "Los altillos de Brumal" and "Mundo" whose protagonists pass through such thresholds to metaphorically enter increasingly ludic protective frames, spaces wherein they might confront psychological traumas, Elena passes over this threshold to become increasingly disturbed by what she finds. Quite literally, she passes over the threshold to recognize her own mental state of fragmentation and discovers that the person whose image and memories she now recuperates are not those of the person she wishes to be:

---

156 Ibid., 163.
157 Ibid., 164.
158 Juan Eduardo Cirlot, *Dictionary*, 341.

> Desde hace un buen rato—desde el mismo momento, quizás, en que te desprendiste de la gabardina, sin darte cuenta, como si estuvieras en tu casa, como quien, después de un día agitado, regresa al fin a su casa—, es tu propia mente la que se empeña en disfrazar de descubrimiento lo que ya sabes, lo que vas reconociendo poco a poco. Porque hay algo hermoso en este reencuentro, algo a lo que te gustaría aferrarte, suspender en el tiempo, prolongar. Pero también está el recuerdo de un malestar que ahora se entrecruza con tu felicidad, y que de forma inconsciente arrinconas, retrasas, temes.[159]

Elena communicates the complexity of the situation by articulating the liminality of the aphasiac experience. At once the subject and object of her own detached discourse, she again observes herself as an "other," as one who has split and disguised herself so that she might be rediscovered. That Elena experiences this rediscovery as frightful rather than wonderful or surprising, however, suggests that the penthouse to which she returns and which, one might assume, should function as a protective frame, actually represents all that which has imprisoned her and which continues to limit her growth. As long as she remained outside the walls of her home, having escaped her life through memory loss, she could elude the environment that had informed and shaped her. However, in having ventured back to this place, nothing, including her amnesic "ausencia," can keep her from remembering the sobering details that make her present life unappealing.

Elena ultimately abandons the game-like methodology she originally used to rediscover herself when she realizes that she has become someone she cannot stand, someone not only limited by her name—a name she clearly dislikes—but also by her lifestyle and life choices. She most patently displays this discontent when she goes to her office and

---

[159] Cristina Fernández Cubas, "Ausencia," 165-66.

admits she detests working as a magazine editor, "La mesa de trabajo está llena de proyectos, dibujos, esbozos. Coges un papel cualquiera y escribes 'Ausencia' con letra picuda, ligeramente inclinada hacia la derecha. Con ayuda de un rotulador la rodeas de un aura. Nunca te desprenderás del papel, lo llevarás en la cartera allí a donde vayas."[160] The revealing declaration literally and figuratively conveys dissatisfaction. By writing down the word "ausencia" Elena makes concrete the distance she senses to exist between the self she imagined herself to be in the amnesic state and the self she rediscovers. Through this passage Elena expresses she will not be able to return to the playful, albeit momentary, state of bliss the fugue state afforded. Affirming, "Nunca te desprenderás del papel, lo llevarás en la cartera a donde vayas," she not only emphasizes her inability to undo herself from the piece of paper bearing the word "ausencia," but also emphasizes the stark realization that she is unable to escape from the identity she has created.[161] Interestingly, the complex word play communicating this apparent impossibility underscores that the word "papel" refers not only to the piece of paper on which she writes the word "ausencia," but also to the countless identity cards Elena keeps in her wallet. As the narrator ironically notes, she cannot distance herself from them. These items (*papeles*, papers) provide her with a *papel* (a role, identity). Still, the multiple ways in which this final reference to the word "ausencia" can be understood leaves the tale open for interpretation with regards to feminine agency the roles women play within families. For while taken at face value, Elena's statements demonstrate the difficult realization that she may never elude the way in which she has constructed herself, the very fact that she is cognizant of this detail and communicates this through word play suggests some degree of hope. In a sense, even for the doubtful Elena, escape from past roles is not only possible, put within reach;

---

160   Ibid., 167.
161   Ibid.

within the grasp of the piece of paper on which she writes the word "ausencia."

Clearly, Fernández Cubas's female characters engage in play in order to cover over traumatic abandonment, loss, and despair. At the same time, their psychological retreats to memories of childhood, dreams, and fantasies become thematically indicative of ruptures in the cultural framework that informs her protagonists. The narrators of these writings break through liminal worlds, penetrating the barriers imposed by written language and the self-same institutions that inform that language to deconstruct the notion of feminine agency through reference to familial roles. I further suggest that play, always linked to subjective autonomy, requires a powerful degree of self-assuredness such that those involved do not fear how their activities will be judged by outside interpreters. As such, the protagonists' very willingness to live in worlds of play ultimately demonstrates their affinity toward self-exposure. They share a willingness to reveal and deconstruct themselves as unique individuals beyond any gendered category, any familial category that might otherwise limit their behavior. This tendency may be ultimately attributed to their wish to understand and violate the very social and cultural institutions that have traditionally served to produce sexual categories in individuals, both males and females. Each female agent's activities, thus, become representative of a quest to bring herself into being within a cultural fabric that has more often than not dictated women's social scripts.

4
Erotica or Monstrous Subtexts in Mercedes Abad's *Ligeros libertinajes sabáticos* and *Sangre*

MERCEDES ABAD'S IMPACT ON Spanish contemporary literature has been, to say the least, explosive. Winning the Sonrisa Vertical Prize in 1986 at the age of 25 with her first collection of short stories, *Ligeros libertinajes sabáticos*, Abad immediately gained the attention of the Spanish print media. She followed this early success with *Felicidades conyugales* (1986), another collection of erotic short stories. More recently, she has written *Soplando al viento* (1995) and *Amigos y fantasmas* (2004), volumes containing stories that, unlike her earliest work, can hardly be called pornographic.[1] Not wholly dedicated to the short story genre, Abad published *Sólo dime dónde lo hacemos* (1991), a series of essays, in which she entertains and develops the topic of alternative spaces for making love, while continuing to compose articles and tales for newspapers such as *El País* and anthologies, such as *Veintinueve dry martinis* (1999). In *Sangre* (2000), one of the author's more recent works, Abad leaves behind short fic-

---

[1] While the individual tales of *Soplando el viento* cannot be categorized as erotic or pornographic, many, like "La bisabuela está loca," "El placer de callar," "El placer de escuchar," "Gabriel Bender, love me tender," and "Adán y Eva," underscore narrative elements that align them with transgression as I have defined it. For example, they refer to physical and linguistic games similar to those employed by Fernández Cubas, and use irony and paradox, as in many of the stories of *Ligeros libertinajes sabáticos*, to disrupt conventions of discourse.

tion to tackle the novel.

A discussion of the Sonrisa Vertical and of the image recognized as synonymous with this literary prize is in order before examining Abad's contribution to Spanish contemporary literature. The inherent nature of the award associated with eroticism and pornography leads me to consider the underlying culturally transgressive implications of the author's work.

From 1979 to 2004, renowned Spanish film director Luis García Berlanga headed a committee of jurors who selected and presented the Sonrisa Vertical, or Vertical Smile. Jury members bestowed the prize to the author who had submitted the manuscript judged most erotic. Those selected as jurors came from the literary community. Distinguished authors such as Camilo José Cela, Juan Marsé, Juan García Hortelano, and Jaime Gil de Biedma as well as former winners of the prize—such as Almudena Grandes, who won in 1989 for *Las edades de Lulú*—lent their names and prowess to the award.[2] The prestigious Tusquets Editorial, which published works awarded the Sonrisa Vertical, produced each winning text in the same distinctive style. Each work was printed in paperback with a glossy, pink cover, a color that might easily be associated with the sex industry. The image printed on each work and linked to the Sonrisa Vertical, the figure of a young female child, further connects these narratives to transgressive sexual acts and pornography. At first glance the reader who looks at the figure traced in black sees nothing more than a girl of five or six years of age. From the back cover, her pouty lips attract the reader, and her eyes induce wonder. They entice the reader to ponder: what could this child be thinking? A second glance at the image reveals the primacy of the white triangle that overlays her mouth. The inside cover of any one of the works shows an enlargement of this section of the image, empha-

---

2 Many past judges have themselves been associated with transgressive activities. Most notably, Camilo José Cela, ironically a censor during Franco's Spain, authored *La familia de Pascual Duarte* and *La enciclopedia de erotismo*.

sizing that the child's facial lips have been transformed into a "vertical smile," vaginal lips.

As well as being synonymous with the literary prize, the child's figure underscores the subversive nature of Abad's literary works, especially *Ligeros libertinajes sabáticos*. This image, like the collection, transcends the category of the pornographic in that its value is steeped in an aesthetic subtext that paradoxically rejects pornography as solely entertaining the sexual fantasies of a (primarily) male audience. Like the duplicitous image of the child, Abad's stories should not be read as transparent, linear narratives but as highly charged, multidimensional tales infused with the potential to transform male and female sexual roles as they have been previously defined. In her writings, diverse agents transgress the boundaries traditionally placed on both men and women in sexual relationships.

In this chapter, I particularly draw attention to the manner in which Abad's narrative agents create attractive "carnivalesque" spaces wherein transformations of gendered categories can occur. In the first section of this chapter, which strictly focuses on short stories from *Ligeros libertinajes sabáticos*, I emphasize feminist re-readings of Sigmund Freud's writings as well as Mikhail Bakhtin's theories of the grotesque body to analyze the ways in which enticing sexual activities performed by both male and female agents demonstrate irreverent resistance towards masculine authority and the capitalist consumerism that drives it. Like Riera and Fernández Cubas before her, far from maintain or idealize categories that align femininity with submission to male agency and power, Abad's female agents critique, reverse and subvert the cultural economics that produce these categories. Abad's descriptions of reverence, or repudiation, of the body culminate in the novel *Sangre*. Permeating with allusions and symbols specifically tied to vampirism, *Sangre* points to the mother-daughter dyad as a culturally transformative condition. Vampires, monstrous creatures that feed from others' blood, become associated with the feminine maternal body as both the locus of cultural origin as well as a site where a struggle for individual recognition occurs. For Abad, the maternal monstrous ultimately signifies a liberating category. In effect, as long as her agents remain monstrous, they can resist classification and social expectation, and thereby keep the body open to cultural re-interpretation.

We may begin discussing the maternal monstrous in Abad's writings by looking at "Pascualino y los globos," a short story that humorously satirizes the normative male-female binary of sexual relationships. Far from perfectly satisfying the model of male agency described in previous chapters, Pascualino Fígaro la Pera, the first-person dramatized narrator, serves as a model of male passivity. At his surprise fifty-seventh birthday party Pascualino experiences the urge to break free from his responsibilities as a bank president, husband and father of two grown children. He abruptly tells his wife, Albertine, "Por cierto querida, he presentado mi dimisión en el banco y he rechazado toda indemnización económica. A partir de ahora eres una mujer separada y pobre, además de idiota perdida. Lindo, ¿eh?."[3] Once breaking from his conscribed role within the family, Pascualino seeks out what he most desires, a woman whose massive flesh will consume him, "lo que yo deseaba era un amasijo monumental de carnes blandas para hundirme en él y olvidar todo lo demás."[4] The narrator encounters his object of desire when he meets Daniela, a woman he refers to as a "globo," a human balloon. She appears to passively comply with Pascualino's fantasy, engulfing him with her enormous body and inciting Pascualino to narrate the circumstances of his own erotic death by asphyxiation. Believing to be near death, he records this testimony of his life to share with readers, itself an act of sexual exhibitionism.

At first glance, Pascualino's words and behaviors align him with traditional male agency. A man who simultaneously renounces his

---

[3] Mercedes Abad, "Pascualino y los globos" in *Ligeros libertinajes sabáticos* (Barcelona: Tusquets, 1986), 52.

[4] Ibid., 53.

wife to find a mistress surely performs as a "man's man," an aggressive actor who makes his will known and acts on virile impulse. However, a thorough consideration of the tale not only lays bare Pascualino's passive nature, but also uncovers a link between what are revealed to be homoerotic fantasies and the role of the monstrous mother within them. For Pascualino, Daniela becomes a surrogate mother with whom he can make his dream of returning to the maternal womb a reality. Her flesh, especially her vaginal lips, comes to symbolize the generative nature of sexual activity. Her sex organs give voice to a transformation in the sexual order.

As suggested in the first chapter, one of the cornerstones of Western civilization according to Freud is the successful resolution of the Oedipus complex. Through this psychoanalytic process, a child separates from his (or her) primordial love object, the mother, to enter into the world of patriarchal authority. Yet as Madelon Sprengnether has observed, Freud was never able to assimilate the preoedipal mother—the mother known to the child before his/her entrance into the symbolic—with the Oedipal mother because doing so would threaten "to subvert the triangular Oedipal structure."[5] Moreover, Sprengnether contends that Freud unwittingly subverts his own model of civil organization by exposing regressive tendencies and urges in his writings.

So it is in the fort/da game Freud describes in *Beyond the Pleasure Principal and Inhibitions, Symptoms and Anxiety*. In the story of this game, Freud quintessentially exposes gaps in the logic of his framework. According to Freud, his grandson invented the "fort/da" game at the age of one and a half, before he was able to utter more than a few short words. The boy would throw small objects away from him and then say "o-o-o-o" with pleasure. The child would also play with a wooden reel attached to a piece of string. Throwing the reel over

---

5 Madelon Spgrengnether, *The Spectral Mother: Freud, Feminism and Psychoanalysis* (Ithaca: Cornell University Press, 1990), 181.

the edge of his bed, he would make it disappear and say "o-o-o-o." Then, as he pulled the wooden reel back to himself, he would say, "da." Freud and the boy's mother understood the child to be saying the German words, "Fort" (gone) and "Da" (there).[6] While Freud indicated that the game represented the efforts of a child to gain authority over the condition of separation from his mother, it dually represented the child's desire for control over the mother's departure as well as his wish for her return. Sprengnether claims that over the course of his career, Freud was never able to integrate the figure of the preoedipal mother into his theory because she was too threatening to his notion of patriarchal authority, posing danger to the social fabric of Western culture. Indeed, Freud linked the desire to return to the maternal womb to the death drive as well as to the repetition compulsion and masochism. Freud notes that, "During the oral stage of the organization of the libido, the act of obtaining erotic mastery over an object coincides with that object's destruction."[7]

In Abad's tale, the author graphically represents Pascualino's figurative return to a maternal womb by having him perform cunnilinguis on Daniela. As he does this, he simultaneously connects his fantasy to the death drive as well as to his infancy:

> He aquí los motivos que me impulsaron a los brazos y al coño de Daniela, a ese cuerpo incontible, incompatible con sujetadores, bragas y fajas, cuerpo expansivo donde los haya, una deliciosa mole en la que hundirse, inhibirse de todo y morir. Oh, Daniela, nunca sabrás cuánto te he buscado y cuánto te amo ahora, mi amor póstumo! ¡Mi última felicidad, tal vez la única![8]

The expansive body to which Pascualino draws attention is sym-

---

6 Sigmund Freud, *Beyond the Pleasure Principle* (New York: Norton, 1961).
7 Ibid., 31.
8 Abad, "Pascualino," 42-43.

bolic of the preoedipal mother. According to Freudian analysis, the son must conquer his early primary identification with the mother as well as his regressive tendencies to surrender to maternal authority and be swallowed up again by the womb. Yet Pascualino demonstrates no desire to do this. Though he acts as an agent, actively moving his lips and mouth to give Daniela pleasure, it is he who is devoured by his object of desire. This symbolism is repeated in that while Pascualino refers to Daniela as flesh to be eaten, he ultimately admits to being reciprocally consumed by her.[9]

Pascualino's return to the preoedipal mother is especially useful in the light of Irigarayan writings that stress the importance of the vaginal lips as positively representing feminine sexuality. If female sexuality has often been located in the clitoris or the vagina, Irigaray positively locates feminine sexuality in the vaginal lips. By pointing to the lips rather than the clitoris or the vagina, Irigaray undermines dominant male notions regarding the very essence of women:

> So woman does not have a sex organ? She has at least two of them, but they are not identifiable as ones. Indeed, she has many more. Her sexuality, always at least double, goes even further, it is plural... Indeed, woman's pleasure does not have to choose between clitoral activity and vaginal passivity, for example. The pleasure of the vaginal caress does not have to be substituted for that of the clitoral caress. They each contribute irreplaceabley, to women's pleasure.[10]

As Grosz emphatically asserts, the image of the lips "is in no way a 'true' or 'accurate' description of women. Its function is not referential but combative: it is an image to contest and counter dominant, phallo-

---

9 Pasualino refers to her as "carne, carne" (54), yet he repeatedly refers to her as swallowing him up, "se me traga poco a poco" (42).
10 Irigaray in Grosz, *Subversiones*, 116.

morphic representation."[11]

In the case of "Pascualino y los globos," I want to suggest that the devouring mother's lips paradoxically liberate Pascualino in several ways. First, as he is consumed by the preoedipal mother, he gets in touch with her. He is not only freed from the rigid restrictions placed on the boy in the Oedipus complex, but also freed to speak from a subject position outside the patriarchal order. He no longer resides within the space of that system. The re-configuration of a relationship with this surrogate mother returns him to a time and place before having gained consciousness of sexual division, before the formation of gender differences. This re-connection with the monstrous mother further enables Pascualino to undergo a kind of "talking cure" wherein the patient, Pascualino, confesses to having repressed regressional tendencies and conceded to living within the confines of patriarchal authority. Freed from this structure by the surrogate mother's lips, he can now speak in excess of the traditional patriarchal family and the conventional male role he learned to play within it.

We see the way in which Pascualino speaks in excess of his previously imposed position as he discusses his childhood and initiation into his family. One of the ways in which he draws attention to this new subject position is by calling himself by his proper name, "La infancia suele ser el punto de inicio de toda frustración digna de llevar este nombre y la mía, es decir, la de Pascualino Fígaro La Pera, no constituyó excepción alguna."[12] This grammatical structure removes him from himself, creating distance between his previous self and the self he is in the process of becoming. The grotesque body as defined by Bakhtin can be associated with Pascualino's reference to himself in the third person as well as to this process of becoming. His connection with Daniela facilitates the creation of a symbiotic relationship

---

[11] Elizabeth Grosz, *Subversions*, 116.
[12] Mercedes Abad, "Pascualino," 43.

through which he produces a new body with which to speak and act. In contrast to Bakhtin, however, who identifies the bowels and phallus as the two areas that "play the leading role in grotesque imagery," I propose that Daniela's vaginal lips take on this leading role.[13]

Pascualino ties his symbolic rebirth to writing, his first love, "Mi primer amor serio, apasionado y profundo fue la literatura."[14] In so doing, he inscribes his own narrative of transformation inside another narrative, one that subverts patriarchy by inscribing it in a rhetoric of compliance. He tells the reader that, early on, his parents deemed his chosen vocation, that of writer, worthless. They demonstrated unwillingness to help him in his literary pursuits by actively taking away their economic support and refusing to assist their "bohemian" son's creative whims, thereby psychologically traumatizing him, "ridiculizaron cruelmente mis pretensiones y se negaron a apoyar económicamente a quien ya imaginaban convertido en un bohemio empedernido."[15] His parents' control is so powerful that he not only gives up his literary dreams to please them, but also takes up banking, a career they consider economically profitable as well as aligned with authority and masculinity. Apathy, inability to deal with even minor confrontations, and lack of management skills all paradoxically bolster his success in the world of finance, "me limitaba a cumplir las órdenes que se me daba sin tomar iniciativa alguna. Pero en el mundo de la banca resultan útiles los peones-pelele, hombres silenciosos, desprovistos de la más nimia sombra de una idea y convenientemente discretos y eficaces en su trabajo."[16] The more Pascualino passively abides by the rules to which his parents conform, the more he gains the admiration of his peers.

These observations undermine definitions of male authority that associate power within patriarchy as active. Though family structures

---

13 Mikhail Bakhtin, *Rabelais* (Bloomington: Indiana UP, 1984), 317.
14 Mercedes Abad, "Pascualino," 43
15 Ibid.
16 Ibid., 46.

have traditionally identified male agents as born figureheads and breadwinners, Pascualino's narrative clearly destabilizes this model. While he submits to his parents' wishes, becoming a banker instead of a writer, it is the system itself that reifies and perpetuates this social pattern. In other words, even before Pascualino submits to his parents, we find that the patriarchal system has already identified him as male and therefore already defined him as an agent within culture.

If Pascualino links his quashed desire to write to his surrender to a patriarchal order, he later links his love for literature to a strong desire to escape his imposed subject position as a man within this system. Pascualino attempts to exceed the boundaries of patriarchy even before his union with Daniela by falling in love with Albertine. According to him, she captures his imagination because her name reminds him of Marcel Proust's masterpiece, *A la recherche du temps perdu* (*In Search of Lost Time*), "al oír el nombre de la francesita, recordé el volumen de *La recherche* titulado *Albertina desaparecida*. Y Albertine no volvió a desaparecer de mi vida. Yo la había encontrado y conmigo se quedó."[17] Conflating his romantic conception of the novel's protagonist with this real life Albertine, Pascualino immediately falls in love. This love, however, does not last. He quickly finds out that though the enigmatic Albertine of Proust's novel appears to be a lesbian who rejects the narrator, his own Albertine lacks the "imagination" of her fictional counterpart, "literatura y vida no quisieron confundirse en mi caso, y Albertine, mi mujer hasta esta tarde, no desapareció nunca, pese a su inicial alarde de buen gusto francés."[18]

I associate Pascualino's love for Albertine with his own sexual frustration and inability to perform within the patriarchal system. Following Kaja Silverman, there are "two broad categories of" of homosexuals, "those who can love only men, and those who can love lesbian

---

17 Ibid., 43.
18 Ibid., 48.

women as well as men."[19] In her discussion of *A la recherche*, Silverman stops short of suggesting that males can in fact occupy a "feminine psychic position" because they, like women, cannot deny the reality of their bodies. They remain trapped by anatomy, physically inscribed within patriarchy by virtue of their physical natures. By alluding to Proust's novel, Pascualino wittingly or unwittingly links himself to his male literary counterpart as much as he links his object of desire to Proust's Albertine. Since Proust's influence on Pascualino cannot be denied, his actions suggest his own latent desire to escape not only his role within the patriarchal family (his role as son, husband and father), but to escape his undeniably male body. By marrying Albertine and thereby becoming "one" with her, he hopes to overcome the limits of the body and to displace these limits with those of his female partner. He hopes to take up a feminine subject position by seeing himself in her. Nonetheless, Pascualino does not and cannot occupy this feminine subject position because, as already mentioned, his Albertine is not a lesbian, but a heterosexual woman, a woman already happily inscribed in the very social order that he rejects.

Pascualino's attempts at transcending his male role and the social constructs that define him as male finally explode on his 57th birthday party. At the event, years of bottled-up inhibitions come to the fore as he describes feeling an existential change, "Aquella tarde, y por primera vez en mi vida, sentí que la abulia cedía terreno a un cosquilleo de felicidad en las aletas de la nariz, como si la fórmula química del aire que respiraba hubiera cambiado sustancialmente.[20] Using terminology associated with Bakhtin's carnivalesque to describe the artificial, theatrical nature of the party, Pascualino admits to feeling like an actor coerced to perform in a play he wishes were not his own, "Fingí participar en aquella comedia, pero la alegría ni siquiera me rozaba los

---

19   Kaja Silverman Silverman, *Male Subjectivity at the Margins* (New York: Routledge, 1992), 381.
20   Mercedes Abad, "Pascualino," 51.

dedos de los pies; aquel espectáculo histeroide me enfurecía."[21]

From this re-contextualizion of Pascualino's life emerges a narrative gesture that shows how the protagonist's frustrated desires again become fused with the grotesque. In the corpulent Daniela, Pascualino sees an image of the fecund mother who both nurtures and consumes him:

> Que no recaiga pues la ira sobre ella porque fui yo, soy yo, un hombre más bien raquítico y escuchimizado, quien la perseguí por toda la ciudad hasta conseguir, tras su inicial negativa, que se encatrara conmigo. Por consiguiente, la pobre tiene más alma de hermanita de la caridad que de sádica asesina."[22]

Characterizing himself as a weak yet persistent sexual agent, Pascualino blames himself for, and takes pleasure in, his impending death. He assures the reader that his desire to possess Daniela prevailed over her own ability to fight off his advances. Furthermore, by saying she has the soul of a sister of charity, he aligns Daniela with the sacred maternal that returns him to the primordial comfort and safety of the womb. This interpretation becomes more prominent in the story's final paragraphs. Here Pascualino both reiterates his pleasure at dying in this, his only independent performative gesture in the story, and reminds the reader that his balloon-like partner should not be blamed for his death, "Será preferible que me engulla, que me ahogue y que el golpe de gracia final me sorprenda entre sus nalgas, bajo su coño 'Oh Daniela, mi ángel exterminador, mi asfixiante globo humano!'"[23]

The epithet Pascualino uses to refer to Daniela, "ángel exterminador" is telling in that it alludes not only to the threatening nature

---

[21] Ibid.
[22] Ibid., 42.
[23] Ibid., 55.

of the phallic mother but to the 1962 Luis Buñuel movie of the same name.²⁴ In *El ángel exterminador*, dinner guests arrive twice at an elaborate banquet. They come to a wide doorway, ascend stairs and come to yet another doorway. Just as these guests enter the banquet room, a cook and servants put on their coats and rush out. The party's hostess becomes incensed at their insensitivity since without them, she will have to cancel the after dinner entertainment planned, a carnivalesque act involving a bear and two sheep. While the repeated arrival of the guests at the beginning of the film and references to the entertainment call to mind Buñuel's early involvement in surrealism, the conversations that take place among the guests represent a common sentiment of the Spanish post-Civil war era. Representative of the governing class in Franco's Spain, the guests succeeded at arranging a symbolic feast for themselves by having overpowered the workers during the War. Now, however, they realize that the feast has no end in sight. Figuratively confined within the limits of their middle class values, they grow increasingly bitter at being shut off from the rest of the Western world and become impatient for change. Though none of Buñuel's characters verbally articulate feeling trapped, the film's viewer perceives this through the guests' lack of activity. Throughout the film, they remain seated or standing, hardly moving.

In "Pascualino y los globos," it seems that the real exterminating angel is not Daniela, but Pascualino himself. The epithet "ángel exterminador" refers to Pascualino's recognition that he, like Buñuel's guests, has been unable to move freely within the social system. He has been figuratively trapped by patriarchy as well as the fictions that have informed his testimony. The fact that Pascualino uses the diminutive form of his name to refer to himself time and again—he is consumed "enterito," for example—reinforces this observation. As his name sug-

---

24 Luis Buñuel, *El ángel exterminador* (Producciones Gustavo Atatriste. Mexico City, México D.F., 1962).

gests, Pascualino recognizes himself for what he is: a paschal lamb that has sacrificed his own will to patriarchy and the roles he has been condemned to play within it.

Yet the very act of telling his tale serves as a testament to a change within the system. If he is figuratively reborn, it is through the mouth and lips of the surrogate mother. As Bakhtin suggests, the central image of the gaping jaws and mouth are a vivid representation of the body "as not impenetrable but open."[25] The devouring mother becomes as much part of Pascualino as he becomes part of her through this cannibalistic consumption. The two physical opposites, male and female bodies, become fused. Joined together, they merge contrary elements, undermine the rules of patriarchy, overcome ontological categories and blur gender role distinctions. Using Daniela's lips to tell his story, Pascualino finally transcends the very real limits of his male body to be empowered by her female body.

Much like the principal narrator of "Pascualino y los globos," who explicitly refers to Proust's *A la recherche* to inform his own narration, the narrators of "Malos tiempos para el absurdo o Las delicias de Onán" rely on extratextual literary sources to tell their tale. The title of this story first and foremost alludes to Onan, the Old Testament character of the Bible whose name has become virtually synonymous with masturbation, coitus interruptus and self-gratification.[10] The biblical passage referring to Onan recounts his transgression and punishment by death:

> Then Judah said to Onan, "Go in to your brother's wife, and perform your duty as a brother-in-law to her, and raise up offspring for your brother.
>
> Onan knew that the offspring would not be his; so when he went in to his brother's wife, he wasted his seed on the ground in

---

25 Mikhail Bakhtin, *Rabelais*, 339.

order not to give offspring to his brother.

But what he did was displeasing in the sight of the LORD; so He took his life also.[26]

Most biblical scholars agree that God takes Onan's life as punishment, but many disagree on the exact reason for his punishment. As it is written, the religious text leaves unclear whether Onan's punishment was for, in the first case, having denied his father's wishes or, in the second case, wasting semen by practicing coitus interruptus. Those who argue the former say that Onan's was an act of filial rebellion and, therefore, a rebellion punishable by death. Others, citing Genesis 2:24, indicate that the very fact Onan was married to his brother's wife eliminates this possibility since his main obligation would have been to his wife, not his father. In the latter case, those who argue that God took Onan's life for wasting semen consider coitus interruptus sinful precisely because it promotes the experience of sexual pleasure outside of matrimony, without commitment and without remaining open to the possibility of having children.

Yet the intertextual reference to the ancient biblical story further serves to subvert the messages communicated and upheld by the tale's narrators. Namely, by referring to Onan in the title of her story, Abad blends the high cultural authority associated with biblical exegesis with the popularity of contemporary pornography. By doing this, she merges the seriousness of Christianity and of Christian morality with the festival imagery of Bakthtin's writings on the carnival. In postmodernist terms, this mixing and merging of high and low art creates "border tension."[27] Commenting on the distinctive interweaving of high and low art that often characterizes postmodernism, Hutcheon identifies combinations of high and mass culture, practices and disciplines

---

26 Gen. 38: 8-10.
27 Linda Hutcheon, *Politics of Postmodernism*, 18.

as producing transgressive oppositions in art and literature.²⁸ Rather than viewing the tensions between these as strictly a phenomenon of postmodernism, I suggest that this tension also results from a carnival suspension of hierarchical values. The tale thus becomes a locus of socio-cultural transformation wherein the language of the pornographic becomes indicative of an underlying change within the structure of patriarchy and its language.

The essential "facts" of the story help to contextualize how "Malos tiempos para el absurdo o Las delicias de Onán" performs the border tensions to which I refer and assist me in demonstrating how the narrators manipulate and influence the reader's understanding of the tale:

> Todos recordaron durante mucho tiempo la conmoción que causó aquel acontecimiento, cuyo eco fue ampliado hasta la naúsea por la prensa amarilla. Las opiniones se dividieron rápidamente en dos facciones opuestas. La primera condenaba a Bernabé Lahiguera mientras la segunda intentaba tener en cuenta las absurdas circunstancias en las que se produjo la muerte de Dolores de la Borbolla.²⁹

The principle un-dramatized narrator, a reporter searching for evidence regarding the "truth" of a criminal case, introduces the topic of Dolores de la Borbolla's death. According to the reporter's initial statement, two factions familiar with Dolores' death have interpreted the evidence surrounding the case in very different ways. There are, on the one hand, those who unquestioningly condemn Bernabé Lahiguera for his supposed involvement in his lover's violent death. This faction proposes that Bernabé killed Dolores while raping her, "el veredicto

---

28 Ibid., 18.
29 Mercedes Abad, "Malos tiempos para el absurdo o Las delicias de Onán" in *Ligeros libertinajes sabáticos* (Barcelona: Tusquets, 1986) 11.

del jurado había sido VIOLACIÓN Y ASESINATO: dos almas gemelas."[30] On the other hand, another faction considers the details of the case so absurd and surreal that they consider alternative causes of death. The reporter-narrator's statements suggest that, outside of Bernabé's first person testimony, the only "fact" on which theses factions—and, as such the reader—can rely is the immediate cause of death: the explosion of a champagne bottle in Dolores' vaginal cavity.[31]

Implicit in the reporter-narrator's comments is that, as in the story of Onan, no one questions what has ultimately taken place. In both tales, all factions agree that someone has died, and that the death is somehow linked to prohibited sexual activity and self-pleasure. As Abad's story unfolds, however, the implied author reveals a subtext to the primary, sexual content of the tale. Namely, she reveals that sexual gratification and pleasure are not only aligned with the activities of the body, but are also aligned with language and the power inherent in the narrators' speech acts.

The significance of language as a tool capable of influencing the reader becomes prominent after the reporter-narrator details the ways in which the factions have interpreted Dolores' death. Although she promises to get to the bottom of the case by interviewing Bernabé and presenting the reader his first-hand, unadulterated testimony, the reporter does not keep her promise, but immediately interrupts him and imagines the scene that she believes must have occurred prior to Dolores' untimely end:

> En primer plano, casi primerísimo aparecen dos objetos cuya identificación no ofrece dificultad alguna: se trata de un sexo femenino desnudo de todo artificio ocultador y de un falo en estado evidente de excitación. Ambos dialogan en paz; están solos y parecen en-

---

30 Ibid., 12.
31 Ibid., "Malos tiempos," 11.

tenderse bastante bien por ahora. La violencia debe andar muy lejos de este lugar.³²

Blurring the boundary between spoken language and the language of the body, the narrator conflates the two metonymically: the lovers speak to each other not through words, but through their bodies. The sexual organs "speak" peacefully, understanding one another, and all possible indicators of violence are absent. In her imagination, spoken language and the language of the body are the mutual domain of both men and women. Each derives pleasure in these and each communicates to the other without difficulty.

Yet when Bernabé regains control of the story's narrative reins, interrupting his interviewer just as she had interrupted him, he describes a scene different from the one previously imagined by the reporter:

> Tras el signo de aquiescencia de Dolores, a quien en la intimidad yo solía llamar Lola, me incrusté lentamente en el pastel cilíndrico y me moví tímidamente al principio, como expectante; desconocía por completo aquella sensación. Luego seguí avanzando hasta sentirme totalmente abrazado por el bizcocho. Era un buen lugar para instalarse.³³

Bernabé, who reports from memory the events that transpired on the night Dolores died, admits he made a conscious decision to forgo having sexual relations with Dolores in order to masturbate with a cream-filled sponge-cake. He directs his energies toward the inanimate object, penetrating it and ultimately using it to bring him to climax. Dolores, for her part, reluctantly yields to Bernabé's desires, accepting his use of the dessert as a masturbatory object after attacking him

---

32 Ibid., 14.
33 Ibid.

and throwing him to the ground. In telling the reader this, Bernabé calls to mind the explicit onanistic implications associated with the story's title. He is, in effect, performing the role of Onan, choosing self-gratification over mutual pleasure. He describes this situation as follows, "Mi falo había perdido por completo la serenidad y le gritó a Lola que prefería el bizcocho, que nunca más volvería a follarla, que no la deseaba, que daba un asco inmenso su coño abierto y dilatado, babeante y sin miseterio alguno."[34] Beyond revealing Bernabé's self-driven impulses, this section boldly demonstrates the personification of the penis as an independent agent within the narrative. For Bernabé, the sexual organ is not his to do with as he pleases; rather it has its own wishes and desires, its own agenda. He highlights this agency by saying that it is not he who screams and distances himself from Lola, but the sexual organ that does so. Through this action, Bernabé comes to embody his name, he is in "lahiguera," slang for "in the clouds."

If the last name "Lahiguera" suggests the experience of a sexual pleasure that briefly removes Bernabé from the moment, the sections highlighted above also draw attention to the symbolic significance of the Lola's name. Bernabé begins by saying that he affectionately calls Dolores "Lola," a pet-name that conveys a double meaning. First and foremost, "Lola" reminds the reader of Nabakov's Lolita, whose name is synonymous with perverse seduction. Seen through the interpretive prism of Humbert Humbert's logic, Lola is a tempting Eve who brings about the protagonist's downfall. At the same time, by telling readers that Lola resists his rejection—she actively attacks Bernabé when he chooses the sponge cake over her as a viable sex partner, spitting on him, verbally castigating him and pushing him down—Bernabé draws attention to Dolores' agency and volatility. In the end, her name is not only reflective of the pain (i.e., dolores) she causes herself through the exploding champagne bottle, but is also reflective of the pain she is

---

34 Ibid, 16.

willing to inflict on Bernabé.

While Bernabé testifies to having fallen into a blissful sleep after masturbating with the sponge-cake, "Quedé echado boca abajo y me adormilé un rato, completamente extenuado,"[35] the reporter-narrator interjects her own imagined scenario of what happened next. Thus, rather than accept Bernabé's memory of what happened and Lola's position within that narrative of desire, the reporter-narrator manipulates the situation, saying:

> Dolores, Lola en la intimidad de Bernabé, Lola para los amigos, se hallaba lejos de compartir la opinión de su amante. Su rostro se agarrotaba en una mueca rígida y dolorosa. (Permítaseme aprovechar la pausa que en el relato impone el momentáneo descanso de Bernabé, descanso de guerrero, para aventurar las reacciones, no menos frenéticas, de la otra protagonista de la fiesta.)[36]

The reporter-narrator's statement undermines Bernabé's testimony regarding his lover and her position within the narrative first and foremost in that it parodies his initial discussion of her pet-name. Beyond this, her intrusion comically reverses Bernabé's self-described status as an onanistic hedonist. By characterizing him as a warrior taking a much-deserved break, the reporter-narrator sarcastically pokes fun at Bernabé not only for portraying himself as important and uniquely self-interested.

Using this humorous imagination to disrupt Bernabé's story, the reporter-narrator offers a distinct and refreshing point of view on what could have happened on the night of Dolores' demise. This perspective characterizes Dolores as aggressive and equally self-interested: "Lola miró el reloj: eran ya más de las doce. El nuevo año había topado con

---

35 Ibid., 17.
36 Ibid.

un mal comienzo. Sin polvo, sin risas y sin champagne. ¿Sin champagne? ¿Por qué sin champagne? ¿Quién podía impedirle que bebiera el champagne?"[37] Although Bernabé may have blissfully fallen asleep and left her alone for all intents and purposes, the reporter proposes that it is not the case that Lola spends the rest of her New Year's evening in dejection. At first gratified just thinking about drinking and enjoying the champagne alone, the reporter-narrator ultimately suggests that, once the thought crossed her mind, Lola desired to use it as a masturbatory object, "Su vulva se movió sin recato alguno sobre el cuello de la botella, succionándola parcialmente luego; el sufrimiento quedaba atrás; aquél sucedáneo de la verga del traidor Bernabé funcionaba a la perfección y añadía el estímulo imaginativo de la novedad."[38] If Bernabé initially rejected Lola in his version of the evening's events, now Lola actively rejects Bernabé. Saying the champagne bottle adds new zing to her sex-life—something Bernabé could not do—Lola mimics Bernabé's behavior. Indeed, when he awakes and tries to take the bottle away from her, Lola reacts by rejecting his advances, just as he had previously rejected her, "Me levanté e intenté arrebatarle la botella que sus piernas ceñían con fuerza. Pero mi irrupción en su placer no fue bien recibida."[39]

Interestingly, the reporter-narrator links the final turn of events that culminate in Lola's death to the reading of erotic tales, "Había leído cuentos sobre botellas que se quedan tercamente incrustadas en los sexos de los masturbadores pero eso no la intimidó."[40] According to her, Dolores had read narratives where characters masturbated with bottles and met with untimely deaths. By making a reference to the existence of such stories, "Malos tiempos para el absurdo o Las delicias de Onán" becomes self-reflexive, suggesting the possibility that this

---

37 Ibid., 18.
38 Ibid.
39 Ibid., 19.
40 Ibid., 18.

story, like so many others, will end in death. In fact, the reference most literally and acutely alludes to the biblical Onan who met with death as punishment for such prohibited self-gratification.

Beyond seeing the connection between the self-reflexive allusion and the biblical story, the reference to erotic tales outside "Malos tiempos para el absurdo o Las delicias de Onán" the reader also recognizes it as an act attributable to the implied author. Speaking through the reporter-narrator, the author's second-self communicates something about the nature of erotic texts, how one reads them, and what one expects from them. First, let me say that Lola's death and what (if any) role Bernabé played in her death remains a mystery. For his part, Bernabé proclaims he had no part in it, saying he merely gazed at her doing herself in, "Supe que no aceptaría ningún gesto mío, de modo que me limité a gozarla visualmente."[41]

Other factions remain at a loss as to where they should lay blame:

> Resulta difícil creer que nadie tomara en serio el relato de Bernabé Lahiguera; sin embargo, así fue. Tal vez porque condenar el champagne por homicidio habría sido una medida ciertamente impopular, y el Tribunal Supremo se habría visto obligado a hacer un montón de horas extraordinarias.[42]

According to the reporter-narrator's statement, the jury that condemned Bernabé did not want to attribute Lola's death to a champagne bottle. Since doing so would have been unpopular and would have necessitated the court's prolonged research into the matter, she suggests that the court made the next best decision: they blamed Bernabé.

Nonetheless, underlying Bernabé's testimony, the reporter-narrator's fanciful interjections, and the decision arrived at by the tale's re-

---

[41] Ibid.
[42] Ibid., 20.

maining factions is the fundamental theme of pleasure. Just as Bernabé delights in telling the reader every detail of his masturbatory activities, and just as the reporter-narrator gratifies herself by interrupting his story and interjecting her own fantasies into his discourse, those who read the tale must please themselves by getting to the bottom of the case. In this sense, the reader, who equally desires and projects himself into the text, behaves in much the same way as these other parties. Yet rather than giving the reader what he or she wants—access to an unadulterated pornographic tale with a closed ending—the implied-author frustrates the reader by prohibiting him from finding immediate self-gratification. The reader, like Bernabé and Dolores before him, must please himself by filling the gaps of the text for himself. If he is to be pleased it will by imagining the events of the night as well as the possible scenarios which led to Dolores' demise.

Finally, the self-gratificatory reading of the text leads me conclude that if one of the functions of an implied author is to impose aesthetic and/or moral limits, then the limits imposed in "Malos tiempos para el absurdo o Las delicias de Onán" may paradoxically represent a resolution to the reader's frustration. Through Bernabé and the reporter-narrator's respective narrations, the implied author indicates that the experience of bodily pleasure, like the pleasure experienced through reading about such taboo sexual activities, is culturally significant. Producing a space for the display and resolution of multiple sexual fantasies through border tensions, Abad pushes against cultural boundaries that reject direct depictions of bodily pleasure. More specifically, by giving male and female characters equal authority in the domain of the text to perform as agents—fully sexualized, physical beings—she implies that narrative space is collectively occupied, collectively both male and female and collectively open to the articulation of bodily sexual desires. While such a space may not yet exist outside the text, by creating this space within the narrative, Abad communicates that such a domain may exist someday. Perhaps more important, the tale suggests that this space would not be the exclusive property of either sex, but would be the mutual domain of both.

If the sexual desires exposed in "Pascualino y los globos" and "Malos tiempos para el absurdo o Las delicias de Onán" directly speak to the ability to transcend sexual constructs and limitations through the grotesque body, a body indicative of cultural transformation, then perhaps an examination of Abad's "Ligeros libertinajes sabáticos" may be in order. The title story of Abad's collection emphasizes both the grotesque body as well as banquet imagery to articulate the way in which the two are intimately related to speech and language. Banquets offer their guests the opportunity to connect with their world in an utterly sublime way. In the social milieu proffered by the banquet scene, guests chew, swallow and consume foods, making the world a part of themselves. They devour without being devoured, overcoming the limits of the body. According to Bakhtin, there is a connection between feasts and language. As they take part in the ritual of banquet eating, guests also participate in a wide array of discursive acts. The table becomes a locus of "free and frank truth" where individuals unite to fearlessly express truths without regard for the regulations of the social order.[43] So it is in *Ligeros libertinajes sabáticos*, a tale wherein guests routinely gather to take part in a feast and orgy at the Johnson residence.

Little has been written about the title story from *Ligeros libertinajes sabáticos*. Nonetheless, one critical study serves as a point of departure for discussing the grotesque body and banquet imagery as ways of representing the transformation of gendered categories. In his article on the work James Mandrell notes a macabre tendency towards violence, characterizing this narrative as a

> stultifying objective account of the ritual Saturday night party at the Johnsons, where married couples reveal and indulge in their

---

43 Mikhail Bakhtin, *Rebalais*, 285.

variously unorthodox desires and practices, ranging from lesbianism to the case of Mr. Robertson, who attempts to play billiards with his forty-centimeter-long penis.[44]

Further stating that the stories of this volume derive their meanings from "the continual frustration of sexual fulfillment," Mandrell contends that the "end of *Ligeros libertinajes sabáticos* evokes not our pity but our loathing for the victim of this text, the female narrator, who has tried to deprive us of the pleasure associated with images of erotica, of what we thought we were reading."[45] He believes that the series known as *La Sonrisa Vertical* "confirms the dominant social and cultural tendencies of the West to objectify and control the other."[46]

Despite the fact that Mandrel may have cause to say that women are often the victims of sexual violence in pornographic media and that a characteristically masculine social order still views women as "other," I do not wholly agree with his argument since to do so would be to accept that order and to fail to see some real value in Abad's narratives. Abad's contribution to Spanish letters does not come at the cost of serving a paradigmatic structure that permits the systematic characterization of women as victims and objects. As a woman reading sexually provocative tales written by another woman, I believe that the power of Abad's discourse is found in her ability to use the language of the existing social structure against itself. If as a matter of custom sexually explicit, derogatory language has been used by those who would victimize and objectify women, I believe that Abad uses and manipulates such language to gain control of those who would use it to harm women.

A clue as to how one might alternatively interpret Abad's aggres-

---

44 Mandrell, James, "Mercedes Abad and La Sonrisa Vertical: Erotica and Pornography in Post-Franco Spain" *Letras Peninsulares* 6.2-3 (1993-1994): 277-99, 287.
45 Ibid., 293.
46 Ibid., 293-294.

sive appropriation of pornographic language can be found in an interview conduced in 1992 by Nancy Vosburg. In this interview, the author states that "Ligeros libertinajes sabáticos" is one of the most difficult in the series to understand. She goes on to cite Romanian born playwright, poet, and essayist Eugène Ionesco as a key influence in the story's writing:

> Bueno, yo creo, por ejemplo, que "Ligeros libertinajes sabáticos," el relato que da título a todo el libro, es un poco un homenaje a Ionesco, a *La cantante calva*. Tiene esos toques de absurdo. Yo tenía un poco presente a Ionesco, incluso el hecho de que haya elegido, como Ionesco que escribía en francés *La cantante calva*, sin embargo, los nombres, si no me equivoco, también son anglosajones. Entonces, yo también elijo a los Sres. Johnson, los Sres. Robertson, los Sres. Ferguson, y bueno, era como un guiño, realmente, un guiño literario.[47]

By acknowledging Ionesco's influence, Abad exposes information crucial to the interpretation of the story and the collection as a whole. Drawing attention to Ionesco's *La cantatrice chauve* ([*The Bald Soprano*], Abad makes a bold connection between the language of the absurdist theatre and her own appropriation of pornographic language. Early in his career, Ionesco linked his writing of *The Bald Soprano* to his failed attempts to learn English. He began learning English in 1948 using a language manual called, *L'Anglais sans peine* (*English Made Easy*). The manual used a dialogue method that emphasized everyday conversation among characters with such names as "Mr. and Mrs. Smith" and "Mr. and Mrs. Martin." In order to learn these lessons, Ionesco claims he copied out and read the dialogues between the char-

---

[47] Nancy Vosburg, "Entrevista con Mercedes Abad," *Letras Peninsulares* 6, no. 2-3 (1993-1994): 321-330, 324.

acters. The process of reading and re-writing these conversations had an intriguing affect on the playwright. He was astonished to find that the banal truths articulated by the characters appeared curiously illuminating in the new language. The experience inspired him to write *The Bald Soprano*, which he deemed an "anti-play," or parody of a play, in order to communicate his experience of language to others. Ionesco recounts that the language of the play collapsed as he wrote it. The drama's language lost logic and linear structure until it was entirely devoid of meaning.[48]

Later Ionesco associated the writing of the play with his distaste for French "salon comedy," a popular and common form of entertainment at the time.[49] He considered the bourgeois melodrama on which the salon comedies were based unworthy of an audience. Thus, in his parodic anti-play, he attempted to use stock idioms and cliché narrative situations to demonstrate the emptiness of language and thereby suggest to his audience that language not be thought of as a reliable way to convey meaning. Language became a figurative weapon used against itself to undermine and destroy meaning through parody. In so doing, the playwright demonstrated not only the inherent distance between sign (written word) and significance (meaning), but also how that distance informs the hierarchical socio-cultural structure.

Ionesco's notions regarding language dialogue with Abad's "Ligeros libertinajes sabáticos" in that the language used to tell the story works against itself. Sexual transgressions occur at every turn. It seems impossible to make the claim that "Ligeros libertinajes sabáticos" has a plot, per se. No one narrative act or series of acts serves to catapult the characters into action or to a specific end; and while every action taken by the various characters transgresses sexual norms, none has any real

---

48 Rossette Lamont, *Ionesco's Imperatives: The Politics of Culture* (Ann Arbor: U of Michigan P, 1993), 41-43.

49 Nancy Lane, *Understanding Eugène Ionesco* (Columbia: U of South Carolina P, 1994), 28.

effect on the narrative since no single act performed is linked to any one meaning. One might propose the anonymous third person un-dramatized narrator would prefer the audience believe that the numerable, random sexual performances enacted by the characters help to mark a space of sexual liberation separate from any socio-cultural hierarchy. The banquet setting marks this space as a locus of free speech. Here, Abad uses language to manipulate preconceived notions with regards to gender role construction by destabilizing the way women and men appear to themselves as well as the way they look at each other.

In "Ligeros libertinajes sabáticos," sexual activities habitually take place at the Johnson residence. Pornography is subsumed within the realm of postmodern parody as the Johnson's Saturday evening banquets, which are at the center of the text, become representative of a subtext critiquing the ability of language to communicate the destructive nature of the performances described. The narrator begins developing her critique through a series of repetitive narrative gestures:

> Todos los sábados la señora Johnson organizaba una fiesta deliciosa.
>
> Los amigos del señor y la señora Johnson acudían gustosos a las deliciosas fiestas que la señora Johnson organizaba todos los sábados.
>
> Entre los enemigos del señor y la señora se rumoreaba que las fiestas que la señora Johnson organizaba todos los sábados eran un tanto libertinas.[50]

Recurring words and phrases, such as "deliciosas fiestas" and "todos los sábados," introduced at the beginning of the tale and used throughout the narrative, firmly establish the third-person narrator's direct style. Simple stock phrases delivered monotonously accentuate

---

50 Mercedes Abad, "Ligeros libertinajes sabáticos," 73.

an important characteristic of pornography as a genre. Namely, the author communicates that the effectiveness of pornography as a genre hinges on a primary specular and speculative detachment that allows the reader or viewer to fully observe the actions and reactions of those involved. Abad's unremitting drone establishes a narrative tone that immediately desensitizes the reader to the narrator's very presence in the text. If, as Carol Adams states in *Transforming a Rape Culture*, language has a tendency to mask violence, it also has the "ability to highlight someone's victimization while simultaneously cloaking the agency and actions of the perpetrator of that violence."[51] The hypnotic effect of the narrator's words work precisely to this end: to cover over victimization as well as agency by manipulating language so as to make its power paradoxically invisible.

The directness with which the narrator delivers stock phrases foreshadows the general tedium with which sexual acts are portrayed throughout the story. Just as the narrator nonchalantly discusses the regularity with which get-togethers happen at the Johnson residence, so too she describes the "mildly libertine" activities that occur:

> Los hijos de los señores Johnson consideraban que las fiestas que su madre organizaba todos los sábados eran ligeramente aburridas. Los hijos de los señores Johnson preferían encerrarse en sus habitaciones. Los hijos de los señores Johnson jadeaban y gemían muy fuerte mientras se hallaban en sus habitaciones. Todo el mundo sabía lo que ocurría en las habitaciones de los hijos de los señores Johnson.[52]

The narrator reveals that the Johnson children prefer to retire to

---

[51] Carol Adams, "'I just raped my wife! What are you going to do about it, Pastor?': The Church and Sexual Violence" in *Transforming a Rape Culture* (Minneapolis: Milkweed, 1993. 57-86), 63-64.

[52] Mercedes Abad, "Ligeros," 75.

their bedrooms during their parents' rather boring libertine parties. Mentioning how the children pant and moan while in their rooms, the narrator implies that they take part in masturbation and/or incestuous activities while locked away. And though the reader is told that parents and guests alike know what the children are doing in their rooms, the narrator goes beyond evoking images of masturbation and incest by saying:

> Todos los sábados, después del primer plato, el señor Robertson se disculpaba azoradamente ante el resto de los invitados y se retiraba de la habitación. Pero no abandonaba la casa de los señores Johnson. Todos sabían lo que hacía el señor Robertson. Todos seguían comiendo y bebiendo.[53]

The narrator implies that Sr. Robertson excitedly excuses himself from the get-together to molest the Johnson children, adding pedophilia to the list of taboo activities taking place at the party.

However, the subversive nature of the succession of activities delineated emerges not from what is said of these behaviors, but rather from what remains unsaid, ambiguous, and un-named. Not once does the narrator employ the words "masturbation," "incest" or "pedophilia" in any of the descriptions given. Not once does the narrator's discursive rhythm alter. The methodic droning continues without pause to create a narrative environment wherein the reader is so engulfed by the frenzy of sexual activity that she cannot stop to ask or think about what is happening. This narrative technique not only demonstrates how the language of pornography masks violence, but also how it allows the violence to go unspecified, as if to suggest its unimportance. Incest and child molestation are horrifying coercive acts that provide one individual the ability to control, intimidate and subor-

---

[53] Ibid., 76.

dinate another individual. Yet these acts are presented here without being named, an unsettling and implicit form of denial that disallows the very naming of transgression. Moreover, in telling the reader that the children pant and moan, the narrator seems to characterize them as vocal, perhaps even willing participants. Having implied this reading, the narrator depicts the children as possibly consenting to sex in whatever form. As such, she also insinuates that the participants are equals: autonomous subjects who perform these acts within the context of a mutually satisfying relationship. Yet none of this is stated; all of this remains implicit. Just as one assumes one knows the names for these activities, one assumes the children's moans and groans are signs of pleasure. But are they?

Far from obscuring the limits of pornography, Abad's "Ligeros libertinages sabáticos," attempts to exploit and de-familiarize those limits through language. The Johnson parties become synonymous with the list of pornographic acts that occur there. Moreover, the greatest transgression committed is subsumed within the margins of the text. That is, although pornography is empirically understood as creating relationships of inequality based on power and authority, the narrator demonstrates how even the most direct, unassuming use of language comes to mask this structure.

This final point leads me to answer the following question: if Abad's writings textually liberate sexual taboo, then what in this tale, and in the series of tales examined, remains covered over? I respond that if Ionesco's anti-play, *The Bald Soprano*, uses language to create a production that is pure performance—a series of dialogues delivered directly yet without reason—then perhaps Abad's "Ligeros libertinajes sabáticos," should be viewed paradoxically as an "anti-erotic," "anti-pornographic" narrative. It is a tale that emphasizes pornography in order to acknowledge and critique the lack inherent in the language individuals use to discuss sexual activity. Pornographic discourse in "Ligeros libertinajes sabáticos" ironically communicates the emptiness of words meant to portray sexuality and, particularly, the violence inherent in relationships of inequality.

In effect, the true protagonist of this tale without a plot, without a linear narrative, is language. Abad cleverly uses the language of pornography to avert the reader's gaze from the more engaging, and far more political, discussions that emerge from "reading" what she does not write. She writes sexually charged narratives precisely to critique the way in which pornography has been stylized and marketed. By both mimicking and perverting the dynamics of pornography, Abad triggers her reading public to question how language is manipulated to produce and re-produce "appropriate" and "inappropriate" demonstrations of sexual behaviors for both men and women. Through the concatenation of acts performed, her implied author asserts that what is worse than censoring pornography is denying that the acts depicted often reflect real truths about the nature of sexual relationships.

It may be useful to return to the image synonymous with the Sonrisa Vertical, to the apparently innocent figure of the little girl whose highly suggestive smile, when inverted, becomes emblematic of vaginal lips. The icon's duplicitous nature, like the language used in Abad's narratives, reminds the spectator who looks at it that the borders individuals construct to define the limits of "good" and "bad" sex roles are strikingly similar. The very way in which the image is marketed—her figure is printed on a pink, glossy soft-cover—seems to suggest that even relatively sophisticated literature "sells-out" on some level to serve the base desires of readers. Mandrell comments on this phenomenon when he affirms:

> So in Spain, as elsewhere, even though women are able to publish erotica, and are published in the series known as La Sonrisa Vertical, nothing has changed in the traditional economy of desire or of erotic literature. Sex is still smutty, even vile, women are the feared and denigrated other, which is to say that the business of

society, culture, and literature carries on as usual. La Sonrisa Vertical: at last, women get to smile; as always, men get to have the last laugh.⁵⁴

Still, if one agrees wholly with this interpretive stance, one is left to wonder if Abad's use of pornography serves women in any way.

As I suggest in the introduction to this chapter, I believe that Abad's writings do subversively serve women. Rather than foreground the "last laugh" of which Mandrell speaks, I foreground the import of analyzing the duplicity that lies beneath Abad's narrators' words. Early on in this chapter, I state that implied authors often impose moral limits beyond those seemingly imposed by the narrators who tell their respective tales. Through diverse narrators, Abad achieves distinct and difficult goals. First, as a woman writing these tales, the author serves other women by essentially lifting the taboo placed on women to associate themselves only with good taste and behaviors. She appropriates a male genre, one typically written for and by men, and uses the language of that modality to ironically critique the repressive nature of that language. At the same time that she breaks rules regarding what kind of language women should use in telling their stories, she turns the language of pornography against itself and against those who would use it against women. This movement empowers women to recognize their own sexuality in terms of bodily pleasure. Moreover, it frees them to think about creating other spaces where such bodily pleasures might be experienced. Beyond this, the narratives Abad writes compel other women to think outside the conventions that so automatically align femininity with passivity and disembodiment.

Second, Abad's implied authors, who speak through various narrators, male and female, serve women in that they constantly foreground how language, especially the language of pornography, is not reliable.

---

54 James Mandrel, "Mercedes Abad and La Sonrisa Vertical," 294.

Abad's implied authors succeed in creating a world wherein male protagonists largely show themselves to be grotesque, weak and pitiful. Pascualino Fígaro la Pera, Bernabé, and the guests of Johnsons' party, far from sexually stimulate female readers, often evoke their laughter and disgust. While Abad does not deny the real power of pornography to do violence, as shown in the analysis of "Ligeros libertinajes sabáticos," neither does she allow that power to intimidate her or to have its way. By controlling it—through carnival humor, ironic twists of fate, and duplicity—she exploits the very language of the modality that has so often restricted women.

In breaking the narrative rules that have dehumanized women and restricted women's participation in the writing of pornography, Abad uses the lack inherent in language to her advantage. Using sexual language to excess, she disrupts how pornography works. Those consumers who, as Mandrell suggests, look to Abad's *Ligeros libertinajes sabáticos* to entertain themselves will be denied the encounter they so covet. Infinitely controversial, yet deceptively facile to read, the short stories of this volume not only thumb their nose at sexual traditions and mores, but also at those who would look on those traditions as giving them license to continue to repress women and their participation in talking about sex.

Having focused on the way Abad's narrative agents produce "carnivalesque" cultural spaces that challenge gendered categories of "male" and "female" in culture, I now want to turn to Abad's novel, *Sangre*. Though few such works have been written in Spanish, vampire fiction is not new to the Western canon. From early, less developed literary characterizations of the vampire, such as John Polidoroi's "The Vampyre," to three-dimensional representations, such as Joseph Sheridan Le Fanu's "Carmilla" and Bram Stoker's landmark novel *Dracula*, these gothic creatures of the undead have consistently captured the imagination of the reading public. Although the legend has always been closely intertwined with discussions of highly charged sexual relationships and the dynamics of power, early manifestations of vampires especially constructed women within the legend as either ill-fated victims of (male) vampires or, once transformed, as voracious blood feeders and deadly femme fatales. More contemporary representations of vampires, including popular fiction by Poppy Z. Brite and the makers of the now defunct television series *Buffy the Vampire Slayer* have gone beyond these conventions to configure vampires as sympathetic yet subversive hybrid figures associated with the breaking down of cultural ideals and the social architecture on which these are based.

Abounding with allusions and symbols associated with vampirism, *Sangre* lends itself to reading monsters through the interpretive lens of Bakhtin's writings on the grotesque body as well as Kristeva's writings on the maternal abject. Though we shall see that the title of the novel first and foremost calls attention to blood that exceeds the limits of the body following violence or trauma, it equally alludes to the genealogical and psycho-social link between mother and daughter. For Abad, the blood shared by the mother and daughter points to a locus of cultural alteration. Here, the volatile transgression of corporal limits between mother and daughter produces change. It is no surprise, then, that vampires, monstrous creatures that feed from others' blood, become aligned with the feminine maternal as both a site of origin and transformation.

Sangre focuses on the complex relationship between Victoria and Marina, a mother-daughter duo torn apart by religious beliefs. Victoria, following her father's lead, becomes a devout member of a conservative Christian sect during Franco's dictatorship. As an "espondolaria," she becomes an open and verbal witness to the Bible, reading and interpreting it literally. Not to be discounted, Victoria's conversion can be understood as a direct affront to Roman Catholicism and the Francoism it supported. When Marina rejects her mother's religious faith as her own at the age of 15, Victoria publicly disowns her. Yet mother and daughter are forced to confront their differences when a tragic bus accident appears certain to take Victoria's life. Having lost a significant amount of blood as a result of this horrific accident, only the acceptance of a blood transfusion might save her life. Victoria refuses this medical procedure on religious grounds and quotes biblical verses from Leviticus saying that since the life of every living creature is in its blood, consuming the blood of certain animals in any form, liquid or solid, is prohibited. Marina responds to this refusal with a threat: if Victoria won't accept the blood that might save her, then she will drink her mother's blood upon her death. Marina takes this step when Victoria dies, drinking every last drop of her blood. In doing this, she becomes a vampire:

> Al beberme la sangre, y con ella el alma de mi madre, me había convertido en una singular modalidad de vampira. La única sustancia capaz de aplacar mi espantosa sed era la conciencia de mi madre, sus recuerdos, material de desecho incluido, sus más secretas aspiraciones, los sueños que por algún motivo se había prohibido soñar, ahí es donde tenía que hincar mis vampíricos colmillos si quería mantener con vida mi conciencia.[55]

In a movement evocative of both Bakhtin and Kristeva, Abad draws attention to the body as transgressing its own limits. Disavowing any feeling of personal revulsion as well as social prohibitions associated with blood, Marina ingests this liquid, readily accepting it as part of her own material organism. In performing this act, the two bodies become one. Within this context, the reader views Marina's developing taste for blood as not only informed by a long history of vampire fiction, but also as linked to the transgression of existing psycho-social, political, and potentially feminist discourses. The daughter who is diametrically opposed to her mother in almost every way in life now seeks

---

55 Mercedes Abad, *Sangre* (Barcelona: Tusquets, 2000), 153.

to come to terms with her in death. Read symbolically, drinking her mother's blood may be likened to a ritual ceremony of communion wherein Marina claims entrance to a liminal space. If Victoria once gave life to her, expelling her through the birth canal, Marina now returns her own abjected body to her mother. The two are thus joined again in a symbiotic relationship in which one cannot exist without the other.

Yet this return to the mother is far from felicitous. Following Kristeva, the corpse "seen without God and outside of science, is the utmost of abjection. It is death infecting life. Abject. It is something rejected from which one does not part, from which one does not protect oneself as from an object. Imaginary uncanniness and real threat, it beckons to us and ends up engulfing us."[56] If, on the level of individual psychosexual development, the abject signals the point at which the child separate from his or her mother, a point at which the child starts to comprehend the existence of a physical limit between self and other, Victoria's dead body now poses a danger to Marina's identity. Despite the fact that Victoria's maternal body once helped to create and sustain Marina's being in the world, it now puts that being in jeopardy. This danger boldly manifests itself in maternal instrapsychic musings. Though Marina first professes to drink Victoria's blood to colonize her consciousness and thereby prolong her mother's life, it becomes apparent that this transgression leads to an alteration whereby Marina becomes little more than a prisoner of her mother's voice.

Psychotherapists such as D. W. Winnicott and Melanie Klein suggest that hearing intrapsychic voices can be either destructive or constructive within a clinical context.[57] In the best case-scenario, an individual undergoing therapy can confront negative voices by respond-

---

56 Julia Kristeva, *Powers of Horror* (Trans. Leon S. Roudiez. New York: Columbia University Press, 1982), 4.

57 See especially Donald Winnicott's "Transitional objects and transitional phenomena" and "The location of the cultural experience" both in *Playing and Real-*

ing to them, thereby expressing ideas that may have otherwise been inhibited or prohibited in the original relationship with the parent in childhood. In therapeutic sessions, the client who suffers from such voices has the opportunity to find mirroring in the therapist who substitutes for the "good enough" maternal figure by reflecting the client's own image back to her. Such an experience allows the individual to see her needs as of primary import and leads her to encounter a primary identity.

In Abad's novel, however, no resolution of intrapsychic voices takes place. The traumatic falling-out between mother and daughter that occurred years before not only remains unresolved but escalates. Victoria shows the power of this voice, dually demonstrating the mind control so characteristic of vampires, through a growing ability to manipulate her daughter. She tells Marina that it is her fault that they share one consciousness, and that she will only continue to placate her daughter's need to feed from her memories on the condition that Marina comply with her rules. Victoria makes Marina promise that she will not swear, abuse her by thinking sinful thoughts, indulge in bodily and sexual exhibitions or otherwise contradict her religious beliefs while sharing one consciousness. If the healthy separation of child from mother depends upon adequate nurturing and mirroring, such nurturing and mirroring cannot be found in Victoria, "De ahora en adelante cualquier infracción del decálogo será sancionada con una inmediata rupture de relaciones. Y no hace falta que te recuerde lo que eso significa."[58]

Marina, for her part, acquiesces to Victoria's demands, "No imprecaré, no renegaré, no te provocaré con palabras soeces ni imagines inconvenientes."[59] Because Marina is drawn to the abject, she finds a

---

ity (London: Tavistock, 1971) as well as Melanie Klein's *Love, guilt, and reparation, and other works* (1921-1945) (New York: Free Press, 1984).

58 Mercedes Abad, *Sangre*, 155.
59 Ibid., 154.

certain joy in abjection as well as in being ab-jected from her mother. She communicates this attraction, saying that even before Victoria's accident her mother continually rejected her for not having become an "espondalaria," "Desde que dejaste la Verdad, no has hecho más que hundirte en el lodo."[60] Yet rather than reject or despise this verbal abuse, Marina repeats variations of it, demonstrating her own preoccupation with the grotesque image and all it connotes. Again, although being consumed by the abject may appear paradoxical, Kristeva links abjection with pleasure saying, "One does not know it, one does not desire it, one joys in it. Violently and painfully. A passion."[61]

Nonetheless, one must ask why this attraction takes place and what purpose it serves. In the case of this mother-daughter duo, it appears that immersion in the abject is likewise linked to catharsis. Clearly, the boundaries between self and (m)other are so wildly blurred that some control or mode of exclusion must exist in order to separate the subject(s) away from the void of abjection, in this case, the blood and corpse of the mother. For Kristeva, control is gained through catharsis, the "various means of purifying the abject—the various catharses—make up the history of religions, and end up with that catharsis par excellence called art, both on the far and near side of religion."[62] In *Sangre*, this purification of the abject occurs through a fantastic re-writing of the family story, and through it, the re-writing of the history of Spain as a nation. The mother draws attention to this process in a scene wherein she condemns her daughter to re-live memories from Victoria's childhood. This key moment on which the novel hinges is particularly telling: it is the day on which Victoria personally came into contact with Francisco Franco, the military leader who would come to rule Spain from the beginning of the Spanish Civil War in 1936 until 1975. Victoria wishes to psychically re-live this moment with Marina

---

60 Ibid., 99.
61 Julia Kristeva, *Powers*, 9.
62 Ibid., *Powers*, 17.

because she believes that if she can go back to it, she will be able to confront the Caudillo and re-write not only her own life experience, but the history of Spain, "No sólo entiendes perfectamente lo que me propongo, sino que llevabas ya un buen rato temiendo que confirmara tus sospechas. Y sé que mañana, después de que Franco me toque el flequillo, tú me ayudarás a reescribir la historia."[63]

Victoria's original meeting with Franco dates to the first of October 1936. The scene occurs in the plaza outside the Cathedral in Burgos, where Victoria grew up. Victoria tells Marina that her siblings and cousins were playing kick ball in the plaza when, instead of kicking the ball to one of her cousins, she kicked it towards Francisco Franco, who had just been named head of the Nationalist Movement and Liberation Army. As the ball rolls past him, Franco picks it up, then returns the ball to Victoria and pats her on the head. According to Victoria, Franco then went inside the Cathedral in Burgos, which inconvenienced God's master plan: "Mi teoría es que esa expeditiva visita de Franco a la catedral incomodó a Dios, no sé si por su brevedad o porque ya le tenía ojeriza por otros motivos, vete tú a saber. Que Dios estaba cabreado es algo de lo que no me cabe la menor duda. ¿Cómo explicar, si no, lo que sucedió a continuación?"[64] What happens next, according to Victoria, is that the head of an angel from the Cathedral came crashing down to the ground, barely missing Franco:

> [C]reo que Dios cometió un error de cálculo tan lamentable como lógico. Debió de suponer que un criminal de la calaña de Franco se sentiría lo bastante culpable como para dedicarle a la expiación de sus numerosos pecados un cuarto de hora de rezos por lo menos. Eso explica que la cabeza del ángel cayera con diez fatídicos minutos de retraso, ¿no crees? Dios iba a por Franco, pero falló.[65]

---

63 Mercedes Abad, *Sangre*, 188.
64 Ibid., 186.
65 Ibid., 188.

Gaining access to her mother's consciousness and reliving this moment with and for her mother, Marina not only exemplifies the ability of the vampire to gain entry into the world of her victim, but also the vampire's ability to literally devour entire generations through the victim's blood. What is most interesting, however, is that Marina's need to consume her mother's blood, consciousness and history ultimately lead to a process of purification whereby she subordinates her own desires to those of her mother. In the course of this catharsis, the daughter joins her mother in meeting with Franco, a symbolic paternal figure, who like Victoria, did not function to mirror the needs of his figurative children, the people of Spain.

It is significant that the meeting between the merged Victoria/Marina duo and Franco occurs while the mother is at play with her siblings and cousins in a plaza outside the Cathedral of Burgos. As I argue in my chapter on Fernández Cubas, play is a creative, communicative experience through which individuals create potential spaces where re-conceptualizations of the self as well as re-conceptualizations of others may occur. When the duo relive this moment, they have the opportunity to congratulate Franco on being named the head of the Nationalist Movement and Liberation Army. Dumbfounded by the little girl's clairvoyancy, Franco asks how she knows this, to which the duo responds, "Porque soy muy lista y estoy muy bien informada."[66] Victoria, through Mariana, goes on to tell Franco of the bloodshed of the Spanish Civil War, the horrors of his dictatorship, and even foretells his death at 3:30 in the morning on the 20th of November 1975. By detaining Franco with their fortune-telling, the two are able to delay the General long enough to carry out Victoria's master plan: "De pronto, hubo un golpe sordo de crujir de huesos y el hombre cuya mano teníamos fuertemente asida se desplomó en silencio arrastrán-

---

66 Ibid., 197.

donos en su caída."⁶⁷ The angel that had barely missed hitting Franco in Victoria's original memory of the event now strikes him down. In this way, the ground on which the merged mother-daughter team play not only becomes a locus where the realization of subjective ontology occurs, but a potential space of cultural change. In symbolic terms, the little girl who meets Franco's gaze and gains his recognition, becomes a monstrous daughter who kills a monstrous paternal imago.

This movement draws attention to the purifying nature of catharsis in carnivalesque abjection. As the mother-daughter duo look upon the figurative father, they not only immerse themselves in a history of abjection (war, bloodshed, death), but also in the ritual and sacrificial origins of culture that, in turn, attract onlookers to the abject. Marina emphasizes this process as she recalls watching Franco shed blood before her, "Mientras mirábamos hipnotizadas el charquito, que crecía y se extendía milímetro a milímetro cambiando de forma como una ameba, me dije que por fin había vuelto el teatro a beber de la fuente de sus orígenes rituales y mágicos, cuando lo que perseguía no era transmitir una visión del mundo sino actuar sobre él."⁶⁸ The world to which Marina refers is a topsy-turvy world where a "suspension of all hierarchic distinctions and barriers among men [...] and of the prohibitions of usual life" has taken place.⁶⁹ In this space where festive pleasure (play, freedom) comes together with the grotesque (violence, blood), a family drama provokes a violent, yet cleansing, sacrifice, "En aquella minúscula mortaja, la sangre de Victoriña—sangre de mi sangre—quedó indisociablemente unida a la sangre que todavía brotaba de la cabeza rota y exánime de Francisco Franco. Por primera vez desde que tengo uso de razón, mi madre me dedicó un largo, caluroso y sincero aplauso que apagó el histérico griterío de la multitud."⁷⁰ Two daugh-

---

67 Ibid., 99.
68 Ibid., 200.
69 Mikhail Bakhtin, *Rabelais,* 15.
70 Mercedes Abad, *Sangre,* 200.

ters of Spain unite to rid themselves of their symbolic father, Franco, and thus to incite change not only within their own family, but within the vast macrocosm of the nation.

But, as Marina states in the introductory notes to the novel, and as I have previously suggested, this story has no happy ending. At what cost does this psychological re-writing of an abject history take place? Victoria, as her name suggests, remains victorious. According to Marina, her mother's meeting with Franco, a not good-enough paternal figure, appears to offer some resolution to psychological trauma. Yet if the maternal generally designates a space and a series of functions and processes through which one first gains access to subjective agency and culture, Marina believes that her mother has abandoned this space and these functions. The merged mother and daughter team who momentarily shared a potential space of re-conceptualization on a playground now split forever, "¿Sabe cuál es mi recompensa por haber corregido un mal paso de la Historia? Hablemos claro: ahora que los republicanos han ganado la Guerra, mi familia jamás irá a Barcelona. Mi madre jamás conocerá a mi padre, estoy segura de ello. El azar la llevará por otros derroteros y yo no naceré."[71] In manipulating history to assure Franco's early demise, Victoria rejects ever having to become Marina's mother and reclaims a space outside the maternal. Speaking about this abandonment, Marina says, "[P]ara disfrutar a fondo de ese futuro nuevo que se extiende ante ella, tiene que expulsar antes de su memoria todo vestigio de mí ¿Cómo iba a ser felíz una madre a quien la asediara el recuerdo de su hija imolada."[72]

This re-writing of history, then, not only takes place at the sacrifice of the symbolic father, but at the sacrifice of the daughter's body. And, if Victoria's name calls attention to the triumph over a horrific dictator, Marina's name calls attention to another familiar matter: the place

---

71 Ibid., 206.
72 Ibid., 206.

of the maternal body in history and culture. Reminiscent of Riera's "Te dejo, amor, en prenda el mar," the name "Marina" refers to water, a substance used to purify before and after rites of religious sacrifice. Of course, water is also employed in the baptism of souls in rituals of initiation. Though Marina ironically rejects being initiated into the waters of her mother's religion, her bloody sacrifice now allows countless others who would have been affected by the bloodshed of the Spanish Civil War to go unscathed. What's more, Marina's name refers to the issue of the maternal in culture and history because, as a derivative of María, it is suggestive of the Marian tradition. The monstrous Marina, like her biblical namesake, lacks a mother. In psychological terms, Marian lacks a mother in whom she might find mirroring and through whom a primary identity might be established. Marina, a woman who has never been a mother, thus comes to represent the monstrous female body as a holy place of origin and source of life, one that remains barred from wholly participating in patriarchal history, culture and discourse.

Yet one question remains: Why does Abad choose the vampire to frame the terms of this discussion? I respond by saying that no other image so perfectly functions to symbolize the trauma Marina experiences in confronting her mother's corpse. As has already been said, the vampire is a monster that, according to lore, feeds off the life-blood of a host, often forming a symbiotic relationship with that host. Perhaps most telling, however, the vampire, because it is a damned creature and has no soul, is said to cast no reflection. Just as vampires fail to find recognition in mirror reflections, so too, Marina is doomed to fail in this endeavor. It is no surprise that Abad so closely allies the vampire with maternal abjection in this novel. For while this creature struggles for recognition, this recognition is often denied.

5
Conclusion: Generational Becoming

FEMININE AGENCY AND TRANSGRESSION in the works of Carme Riera, Cristina Fernández Cubas and Mercedes Abad manifests itself in generational and familial terms. In close texual readings, I have attempted to argue that these authors have written an impressive body of literature that suggests female becoming as continuously negotiated. Framed within the context of narrative seduction, play and the pornographic, grotesque body, respectively speaking, these authors shape the scope of feminine agency in post-Franco Spain. For each writer, feminine authority seems to have little to do with the objectives of any feminist political agenda or movement and much more to do with the recognition that categories that have significantly defined women—"mother," "daughter," and "sister"—have become increasingly defamiliarized. What's more, they maintain their popular status as writers, in part, because they resist making public, categorical statements about what is liberatory and what is oppressive while uniquely shedding light on the ways women write their own stories, create their own mythos, and with it, their own locus of power.

For Riera, an epigraph falsely attributed to Sappho in "Te dejo, amor, en prenda el mar" foreshadows the importance of nurturing love between and among women of all generations. Although I begin my chapter on Riera by drawing attention to the need to fully recognize sexual desire outside the general male-female rhetoric of complementarity, my broader objective is far greater. That is, I directly link Sapphic desire in Riera's short story with the recuperation of the feminine maternal as a highly erotic, reproductive space of agency. By tracing a lost genealogy of women in Riera's writings—the erotic, sexualized mother figure—I hope to have demonstrated that, for Riera, feminine agency is not only intimately associated with the body, but to the written word as an extension of the body. Her writings, and perhaps all writings women leave to each other as "tokens" serve to preserve our own histories, and perhaps more importantly, to protect and nurture our own values, morals and views of ourselves over time. What's more, Riera implies that, though women have historically censored themselves to safeguard their own well-being as mothers, daughters, sisters and lovers, women must write as wholly empowered, sexual beings if they are to fully participate as author(ities) outside the family and be recognized as such. Feminine agency, in this sense, is bond up not only with one's ability to wield power within closely knit units made up of different generations (like the traditional family unit), but also to speak outside the limits of these unites for the many women who have been historically deprived of the right to speak and to leave behind their own testimonies.

If for Riera, feminine agency and transgression is linked to writing from the highly reproductive space of the feminine maternal, for Cristina Fernández Cubas, feminine agency and transgression is linked to the creative space of play. As the mothers, daughters and sisters in her narratives participate in play activities, they negotiate and redefine their roles within families, and therefore, within culture. What is most interesting to note, in my opinion, is the violent, frequently traumatic nature of the play in Fernández Cubas works. Far from depict her protagonists as passive objects, Fernández Cubas creates agents who aggressively partipacipate in acts of self-definition and determination. Fields of play—gardens, playgrounds, hiding places and plazas, among other public places where mothers, sisters and daughters congregate and amuse themselves—become battlegrounds on which to wage a war of idenity. Fantasy and competition lead her characters on journies toward self-discovery.

The underlying brutality of play between different generations of women that is so pervasive in Fernández Cubas' narratives is further suggestive regarding the existence of such violence in culture. That is, the violent nature of the play activities in her narratives, especially *Hermanas de sangre* and *El columpio*, intimately links recreation, and most importantly, feminine imagination, to transformations in the social order. As prime movers and participants in this kind of play, the protagonists in Fernández Cubas's narratives allow readers to re-imagine female agency as radically contesting the cultural fabric that has so long viewed femininity as somehow opposed to violence. What's more, the voluntary participation of female characters in such play links feminine agency to revolution. Like the title character in "Mi hermana Elba," the vast majority of her Fernández Cubas's characters decisively teeter on the brink of death. Taking up provocative spaces on the proverbial margins of society, they unreservedly defy categorization to belligerently challenge social conformity.

Mercedes Abad, for her part, shows feminine agency and transgression as linked to the grotesque, carnivelesque body. Abad's bold and triumphant arrival on the Spanish literary scene, thanks in part to her win of the controvertial *Sonrisa Vertical* prize, marked an important moment for generations of Spanish women.[1] Reminiscent of Riera's oeuvre, in Abad's narratives, feminine agency is linked to sexuality and, particularly, to the female body as a space transformation. Yet unlike Riera, who is frequently identified as a writer of erotic tales, Abad's stories have often been labled pornographic. Having transgressed the

---

1 Though Abad was not the first woman to have won the coveted *Sonrisa Vertical*—the first was Susana Constante for *Educación sentimental de la Sta. Sonia* (1979)—her writings particularly dialogue with those of Riera and Fernández Cubas.

aesthetic boundaries of the erotic to pen pornographic tales such as "Malos tiempos para lo absurdo o las delicias de Onán," "Pascualino y los globos" and "Ligeros libertinajes sabáticos," Abad draws attention to the abject negativity of the grotesque body to alter the reader's vision of feminine agency. By drawing attention to the regenerative power of monstrous female bodies, her work becomes emblematic of the cathartic power of the written word. In writing sexually explicit narratives, Abad implicitly responds as a proverbial daughter of previous generations. If Riera suggests that women stop censoring themselves by embracing the erotic maternal body as a space of social change, Abad reacts to this suggestion in her pornographic writings. Specifically, while Abad's narratives may be highly erotic, foregrounding domination and humiliation in sexual relations, rather than focus on women as the primary targets of coercion, Abad defamiliarizes the sexual and cultural attitudes complicit with pornography. As such, she ruptures gender stereotypes, creating a locus for the renegotiation of sexual roles in literature.

This renegotiation finds its culmination in the novel *Sangre*. In as much Fernández Cubas narratives underscore the playful, yet often violent, relationship between mothers, daughters and sisters, Abad's novel closely dialogues with this work. In the characters of Victoria and Marina, Abad points to blood shared between generations of women as a site of cultural alteration. Here, the surpassing of bodily limits between mother and daughter produces change. Through the fantastic and shocking union of the two, Victoria and Marina succeed in chaging the history of Spain by completely eliminating Franco from the country's socio-cultural landscape. This cathartic endeavor, I would suggest, further expresses a common desire among women of this period: the desire to be freed from an abrasive, all powerful masculine figure that would have women remain subservient passive objects of patriarchy.

The body of literature produced by Riera, Fernández Cubas and

Abad thus accuately responds to a deep desire to never return to the days of Franco's Spain and the Sección Femenina. Their narratives speak to a Spain in which female agents freely speak and dialogue without having to consider the requirements of a dictator. Indeed, if traces of that dictatorship remain, they remain only to inspire the voices of women like Riera, Fernández Cubas and Abad who will not remain silent. What's more, the rising popularity of their writings in the marketplace and their continued success as individual authors shows an intense complicity on the part of Spanish citizens to accept the renegotiation of the roles played by women.

Bibliography

Abad, Mercedes. *Amigos y fantasmas*. Barcelona: Tusquets, 2004
——. *Felicidades conyugales*. Barcelona: Tusquets, 1989.
——. *Ligeros libertinajes sabáticos*. Barcelona: Tusquets, 1986.
——. *Sangre*. Barcelona: Tusquets, 2000.
——. *Sólo dime dónde lo hacemos*. Madrid: Temas de Hoy, 1991.
——. *Soplando al viento*. Barcelona: Tusquets, 1995.
——. *Veintinueve dry martinis*. Barcelona: Edhasa, 1999.
Adams, Carol J. "'I just raped my wife! What are you going to do about it, Pastor?': The Church and Sexual Violence." *Transforming a Rape Culture*. Minneapolis: Milkweed, 1993. 57-86.
Allison, David B., Mark S. Roberts and Allen S. Weiss. *Sade and the Narrative of Transgression*. Cambridge: Cambridge U P, 1995.
Apter, Michael J. "A structural-phenomenology of play." *Adult Play: A Reversal Theory Approach*. Ed. Michael J. Apter and John H. Kerr. Amsterdam: Swets & Zeitlinger, 1991.
Bachelard, Gaston. *The Poetics of Space* (1964). Trans. Maria Jolas. Boston: Beacon, 1994.
Bakhtin, Mikhail. *Rabelais and His World*. Bloomington: Indiana UP, 1984.
Barthes, Roland. *A Lover's Discourse: Fragments*. (*Fragments d'un discours amoureux*). Trans. Richard Howard. London: Johnathan Cape, 1979.
——. *Sade, Fourier, Loyola*. Trans. Richard Miller. New York: Hill and Wang, 1976.
Bataille, Georges. *Erotism: Death and Sensuality*. (*L'Erotisme*, 1957). Trans. Mary Dalwood. San Francisco: City Lights, 1986.
Bataille, Georges. *Literature and Evil*. (La Littérature et le mal, 1957). Trans. Alastair Hamilton. Marion Boyars Publishers, 2001.
Beauvoir, Simone de. *The Second Sex*. (*Le Deuxieme Sexe*, 1949). Trans. H.M. Parshley. Vintage: New York, 1989.
Bellver, Catherine. "Two New Women Writers from Spain." *Letras Femeninas*. 1982. 3-7.
Bergmann, Emilie L. "Letters and Diaries as Narrative Strategies in Contemporary Catalan Women's Writing." *Critical Essays On the Literature of Spain and Span-

ish America. Ed. Luis T. González-Del-Valle and Julio Baena. Boulder: Publications of the Society of Spanish and Spanish American Studies, 1991. 19-28.

Bergmann, Emilie and Paul Julian Smith, Eds. *¿Entiendes?: Queer Readings, Hispanic Writings.* Eds. Emilie L. Bergmann and Paul Julian Smith. Durham: Duke UP, 1995.

Booth, Wayne. *The Rhetoric of Fiction.* Chicago: U Chicago P, 1983.

Bretz, Mary Lee. "Cristina Fernández Cubas and the Recuperation of the Semiotic in *Los altillos de Brumal.*" *Anales de la literatura española contemporánea.* 13.3 (1988): 177-88.

Buchwald, Emilie, Pamela R. Fletcher, and Martha Roth, Eds. *Transforming a Rape Culture.* Minneapolis: Milkweed, 1993.

Bunkers, Suzanne L. and Cynthia Huff. "Issues in Studying Women's Diaries: A Theoretical and Critical Introduction." *Inscribing the Daily*: *Critical Essays on Women's Diaries.* Ed. Suzanne L. Bunkers and Cynthia A. Huff. Amherst: U Massachusetts P, 1996.

Buñuel, Luis. El ángel exterminador. México: Producciones Gustavo Atariste, 1962.

Burke, Ruth. *The Games of Poetics: Ludic Criticism and Postmodern Fiction.* New York: Peter Lang, 1994.

Butler, Judith. *Gender Trouble*: *Feminism and the Subversion of Identity.* London: Routledge, 1990.

Carmona, Vicente, et. al. "Conversando con Mercedes Abad, Cristina Fernández Cubas y Soledad Puértolas." *Mester* 20.2 (1991): 157-65.

Carroll, Lewis. *Through the Looking Glass. Lewis Carroll: The Complete Illustrated Works.* New York: Gramercy Books, 1982. 81-176.

Carter, Angela. *Sadeian Women and the Ideology of Pornography.* New York: Harper & Row, 1978.

Chatman, Seymour. *Coming to Terms*: *The Rhetoric of Narrative in Fiction and Film.* Ithaca: Cornell UP, 1990.

Cheney, Liana. *Quattrocento Neoplatonism and Medici Humanism in Botticelli's Mythological Paintings.* New York: UP of America, 1985.

Chessick, Richard D. *Psychology of the Self and the Treatment of Narcissism.* Northvale: Jason Aronson, 1985.

Cirlot, Juan Eduardo. *A Dictionary of Symbols.* Trans. Jack Sage. New York: Dorset P, 1991.

Copjec, Joan. *Read My Desire*: *Lacan Against the Historicists.* Boston: MIT P, 1995.

de Lauretis, Teresa. *Technologies of Gender*: *Essays on Theory, Film, and Fiction.* Bloomington: Indiana UP, 1987.

de Riquer I Permanyer, Borja. "Social Change in a Climate of Political Immobilism." *Spanish Cultural Studies*: *An Introduction*: *The Struggle for Modernity.* Eds. Helen Graham and Jo Labanyi. Oxford UP, 1995. 259-71.

Etxebarría, Lucía. *La Eva futura: Cómo seremos las mujeres del siglo XXI y en qué mundo nos tocará vivir*. Barcelona: Destino, 2000.
Fernández Cubas, Cristina. "Ausencia." *Con Agatha en Estambul*. Barcelona: Tusquets, 1994. 151-170.
———. *El columpio*. Barcelona: Tusquets, 1995.
———. "Hermanas de sangre." Barcelona: Tusquets, 1998.
———. "Los altillos de Brumal." *Mi hermana Elba y Los altillos de Brumal*. Tusquets: Barcelona: 1988. 155-187.
———. "Mundo." *Con Agatha en Estambul*. Barcelona: Tusquets, 1994. 11-72.
———. "Mi hermana Elba." *Mi hermana Elba y Los altillos de Brumal*. Barcelona: Tusquets, 1988. 53-81.
Folkart, Jessica. *Angels on Otherness in Post-Franco Spain: The Fiction of Cristina Fernández Cubas*. Lweisburg: Bucknell UP, 2007.
Foucault, Michel. "A Preface to Transgression." *Language, Counter-Memory, Practice: Selected Essays and Interviews*. Ed and Intro. Donald F. Bouchard. Trans. Donald F. Bouchard and Sherry Simon. Ithaca: Cornell UP, 1980.
Freud, Sigmund. *The Sexual Aberrations. The Basic Writings of Sigmund Freud*. Trans. Abraham Arden Brill. New York: Random House, 1938
———. "The Uncanny." *The Standard Edition of the Complete Psychological Works of Sigmund Freud*. Trans. & Ed. James Strachey and Anna Freud. Vol. 17. London: Hogarth P, 1974. 318-356.
Girard, René. *Violence and the Sacred*. Baltimore: Johns Hopkins UP, 1972.
Glenn, Kathleen. "Conversación con Cristina Fernández Cubas." *Anales de la literatura española contemporánea*. 18.2 (1993): 355-63.
———. "Reading and Writing The Other Side Of The Story in Two Narratives By Carme Riera." *Catalan Review: International Journal of Catalan Culture*. 7.1: 1993. 51-62.
———. "Gothic Indecipherability and Doubling in the Fiction of Cristina Fernández Cubas," *Monographic Review/ Revista Monográfica* 8 (1992): 125-141.
Glenn, Kathleen M., Mirella Servodidio, and Mary S. Vasquez. Eds. *Moveable Margins: The Narrative Art of Carme Riera*. Lewisburg: Bucknell UP, 1999.
———. "Conversation with Carme Riera." *Moveable Margins: The Narrative Art of Carme Riera*. Eds. Kathleen M. Glenn, Mirella Servodidio, and Mary S. Vásquez. Lewisburg: Bucknell UP, 1999. 39-57.
Graham, Helen and Jo Labanyi. *Spanish Cultural Studies: An Introduction: The Struggle for Modernity*. Eds. Helen Graham and Jo Labanyi. Oxford UP, 1995.
Grosz, Elizabeth. *Sexual Subversions: Three French Feminists*. Sydney: Allen & Unwin, 1989.
Henry, Astrid. *Not My Mother's Sister: Generational Conflict and Third-Wave Feminism*. Bloomington: Indiana UP, 2004.

Hooper, John. *The New Spaniards: A Completely New and Revised Edition.* London: Penguin, 1995.

Huizinga, Johan. *Homo Ludens: A Study of the Play Element in Culture.* Boston: Beacon P, 1960.

Hutcheon, Linda. *A Poetics of Postmodernism: History, Theory, Fiction.* New York: Routledge, 1988.

———. *The Politics of Postmodernism.* New York: Routledge, 1989.

Ionesco, Eugène. *The Bald Soprano. Four Plays.* Trans. Donald M. Allen. New York: Grove Press, 1958.

Irigaray, Luce. *Sexes and Genealogies.* Trans. Gillian C. Gill. New York: Columbia UP, 1993.

Jacoby, Mario. *Individuation and Narcissism: The Psychology of the Self in Jung and Kohut.* Trans. Myron Gubitz and Françoise O'Kane. New York: Routledge, 1985.

Jameson, Fredric. *Postmodernism, or, The Cultural Logic of Late Capitalism.* Durham: Duke UP, 1995.

Johnson, Stephen M. *Humanizing the Narcissistic Style.* New York: Norton, 1987.

Kaplan, E. Ann. "Is the Gaze Male?" *Powers of Desire: The Politics of Sexuality.* Ed. Ann Snitow, Christine Stansell, and Sharon Thompson. New York: Monthly Review P, 1983. 309-27.

Kohut, Heinz. *The Analysis of the Self: A Systematic Approach to the Psychoanalytic Treatment of Narcissistic Personality Disorders.* New York: International UP, 1971.

———. *The Restoration of the Self.* New York: International UP, 1977.

———. *The Search for the Self: Selected Writings of Heinz Kohut: 1950-1978.* Vol I & II. New York: International UP, 1978.

Krauss, Rosalind and Jane Livingston. *L'Amour fou: Photography & Surrealism.* New York: Abbeville P, 1985.

Kristeva, Julia. *Powers of Horror : An Essay on Abjection.* Trans. Leon S. Roudiez. New York: Columbia UP, 1982.

Labanyi, Jo. "Censorship or the Fear of Mass Culture." Cultural Control. *Spanish Cultural Studies: An Introduction: The Struggle for Modernity.* Eds. Helen Graham and Jo Labanyi. Oxford UP, 1995. 396-405.

———. "Postmodernism and the Problem of Cultural Identity." Conclusion: Modernity and Cultural Pluralism. *Spanish Cultural Studies: An Introduction: The Struggle for Modernity.* Eds. Helen Graham and Jo Labanyi. Oxford UP, 1995. 396-405.

Lacan, Jacques. "God and the *Jouissance* of The Woman. A Love Letter."*Feminine Sexuality: Jacques Lacan and the école freudienne.* Ed. Juliet Mitchell and Jacqueline Rose. Trans. Jacqueline Rose. New York: Pantheon, 1985.

Lamont, Rosette C. *Ionesco's Imperatives: The Politics of Culture*. Ann Arbor: U of Michigan P, 1993.

Lane, Nancy. *Understanding Eugène Ionesco*. Columbia: U of South Carolina P, 1994.

Mandrell, James. "Mercedes Abad and La Sonrisa Vertical: Erotica and Pornography in Post-Franco Spain." *Letras Peninsulares*. 6(2-3): 277-99. 1993-1994.

McIntosh-Snyder, Jane. *Lesbian Desire in the Lyrics of Sappho*. New York: Columbia UP, 1997.

Mulvey, Laura. "Visual Pleasure and Narrative Cinema." *Art After Modernism: Rethinking Representation*. Ed. Ann Snitow, Christine Stansell, and Sharon Thompson. New York: New Museum of Contemporary Art, 1984. 361-73.

Montero, Rosa. "Political Transition and Cultural Democracy: Coping with the Speed of Change." Democracy and Cultural Change. *Spanish Cultural Studies: An Introduction: The Struggle for Modernity*. Ed. Helen Graham and Jo Labanyi. Oxford UP, 1995. 315-19.

Montero, Rosa. "Political Transition and Cultural Democracy: Coping with the Speed of Change." Democracy and Cultural Change. *Spanish Cultural Studies: An Introduction: The Struggle for Modernity*. Eds. Helen Graham and Jo Labanyi. Oxford UP, 1995. 315-19.

———. "The Silent Revolution: The Social and Cultural Advances of Women in Democratic Spain." Gender and Sexuality. *Spanish Cultural Studies: An Introduction: The Struggle for Modernity*. Eds. Helen Graham and Jo Labanyi. Oxford UP, 1995. 381-85.

Neuborne, Ellen. "Imagine My Surprise." *Listen up: Voices From The Next Feminist Generation*. Ed. Barbara Findlen. Seattle: Seal Press, 1995.

Nichols, Geraldine. *Escribir, espacio propio: Laforet, Matute, Moix, Tusquets, Riera y Roig por sí mismas*. Minneapolis: Institute for the Study of Ideologies and Literature, 1989. 187-227.

Ordóñez, Elizabeth. "Beginning to Speak: Carme Riera's Una primavera para Domenico Guarini." Eds. Paolini, Gilbert. *La Chispa '85: Selected Proceedings*. New Orleans: Tulane UP. 1985. 285-293

———. "Writing 'Her/story': Reinscriptions of Tradition in Texts by Riera, Gomez Ojea, and Ortiz." *Voices of Their Own: Contemporary Spanish Narrative by Women*. Lewisburg: Bucknell UP, 1991. 127-48

Ortega, José. "La dimensión fantástica en los cuentos de Fernández Cubas." *Monographic Review/Revista Monográfica*. 8(1992): 157-63.

Ornstein, Paul H. "Introduction." *The Search for the Self: Selected Writings of Heinz Kohut: 1950-1978*. Vol I & II. New York: International UP, 1978. 1-106.

Oxford English Dictionary. Eds. John Simpson and Edmund Weiner. New York: Oxford UP, 1993-1997.

Perriam, Chris. "Gay and Lesbian Culture." *Gender and Sexuality. Spanish Cultural Studies: An Introduction: The Struggle for Modernity*. Eds. Helen Graham and Jo Labanyi. Oxford UP, 1995. 393-95.

Pérez, Janet. "Cristina Fernández Cubas: Narrative Unreliability and the Flight from Clarity, or, the Quest for Knowledge in the fog." *Hispanófila*, 122 (January 1998): 29-39.

Piozzi, Hester Lynch. *Thraliana: The Diary of Mrs. Hester Lynch Thrale (later Mrs. Piozzi)*. Ed. Katharine C. Balderston. Oxford: Clarendon Press, 1942.

Rees, Elizabeth. *Christian Symbols and Ancient Roots*. Philadelphia: Jesica Kingsley, 1992.

Riera, Carme. *Tiempo de espera*. Barcelona: Lumens, 1998.

———. *Una primavera para Domenico Guarini*. Tr. Luisa Cotoner. Barcelona: Montesinos, 1981.

———. "Y pongo por testigo a las gaviotas." (1977) *Te dejo el mar*. Tr. Luisa Cotoner. Madrid: Espasa Calpe, 1991. 129-139.

———. "Te dejo, amor, en prenda el mar." (1975) *Te dejo el mar*. Tr. Luisa Cotoner. Madrid: Espasa Calpe, 1991. 52-68.

Riera, Carme. "Una ambición sin límites." *Moveable Margins: The Narrative Art of Carme Riera*. Eds. Kathleen M. Glenn, Mirella Servodidio, and Mary S. Vasquez. Lewisburg: Bucknell UP, 1999. 21-29.

Rodríguez, María Pilar. "La seducción de la carta: El amor como principio de desarrollo en dos relatos de Carme Riera." *Vidas Im/Propias: Transformaciones del sujeto femenino en la narrativa española contemporánea*. West Lafayette: Purdue UP, 2000. 110-142.

Rogers, Robert. *A Psychoanalytic Study of the Double in Literature*. Detroit: Wayne State UP, 1970.

Sade, Donatien Alphonse Francois. *The Marquis de Sade: The Complete Justine, Philosophy in the, Bedroom and other writings*. Eds. and Trans. Richard Seaver and Austryn Wainhouse. New York: Grove Press, 1965.

Salinas, Pedro. *La voz a ti debida*. (1933). *Pedro Salinas: Poemas escogidos*. Pro. Jorge Guillén. Ed. Francisco Javier Díez de Revenga. Madrid: Austral, 1997. 119-152.

Servodidio, Mirella. "Doing Good and Feeling Bad: The Interplay of Desire and Discourse in Two Stories by Carme Riera." *Moveable Margins: The Narrative Art of Carme Riera*. Ed. Kathleen Glenn, Mirella Servodidio, Mary S. Vásquez Lewisburg: Bucknell UP, 1999. 65-82.

Silverman, Kaja. *Male Subjectivity at the Margins*. New York: Routledge, 1992.

Smith, Paul. *Discerning the Subject*. Minneapolis: U of Minnesota P, 1988.

Sobejano, Gonzalo. "La novela poemática y sus alrededores." *Insula*. 40.464-65(1985): 1, 26. 1985.

Sprengnether, Madelon. *The Spectral Mother. Freud, Feminism and Psychoanalysis*.

Ithaca: Cornell UP, 1990.
Suleiman, Susan Rubin. *Subversive Intent: Gender, Politics, and the Avant-Garde*. Cambridge: Harvard UP, 1990.
Tejada, Luis Alonso. *La represión en la España de Franco*. Barcelona: Luis de Caralt, 1977.
Todorov, Tzvetan. *The fantastic: A Structural Approach to a Literary Genre*. (*Introduction a la litterature fantastique*) Trans. Richard Howard. Cleveland: P of Case Western Reserve U, 1973.
Tsuchiya, Akiko. "Seduction and Simulation in Carme Riera's *Una primavera per a Domenico Guarini*." *Moveable Margins The Narrative Art of Carme Riera*. Ed. Kathleen Glenn, Mirella Servodidio, Mary S. Vásquez. Lewisburg: Bucknell UP, 1999. 83-103.
Villiers de L'Isle-Adam, Auguste, comte de. *Tomorrow's Eve* (1885). Trans. Robert Martin Adams. Urbana: U of Illinois P, 1982.
Vosburg, Nancy. "Entrevista con Mercedes Abad." *Letras Peninsulares*. 6.2-3 (1993-1994): 321-30.
Webster's Dictionary of English Usage. Springfield: Merriam-Webster, 1993. Wolf, Naomi. *The Beauty Myth*. London: Chatto & Windus, 1990.
Zatlin, Phyllis. "Amnesia, Strangulation, Hallucination and Other Mishaps: The Perils of Being Female in Tales of Cristina Fernández Cubas." *Hispania* 79.1 (1995): 36-44.
Zöllner, Frank. *Botticelli: Images of Love and Spring*. Trans. Fiona Elliott. New York: Prestel, 1998.